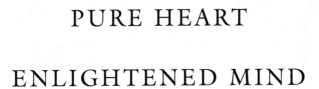

PURE HEART

ENLIGHTENED MIND

The Zen Journal and Letters of
Maura "Soshin" O'Halloran

PURE HEART
ENLIGHTENED MIND

The Zen Journal and Letters of
Maura "Soshin" O'Halloran

by

Maura O'Halloran

Introduction by Ruth O'Halloran
Afterword by Dai-En Bennage
Illustrations by Elizabeth O'Halloran

CHARLES E. TUTTLE COMPANY, INC.
Boston • Rutland, Vermont • Tokyo

Publisher's Note

The material for this book arrived at our offices in November of 1992. Since then we have struggled to determine how best to present these letters and journals of Maura *Soshin* O'Halloran.

Journals are inherently incomplete things, for the most fundamental issues of a life or an experience are understood by the writer and are often unwritten. Because of this, Maura's journals present us with many questions that remain unanswered—why did she want to study Zen, why did she go to Japan, what elements of her Catholic upbringing lead her to Buddhism? We asked Maura's family and the people with whom she studied and, ultimately, the only answers are here in these pages before you. Maura never intended this material to be published. Whatever questions we may have after reading these, her most personal thoughts, are not questions that were most important to Maura. What was important to her was that she become a Zen monk and be able to help other people in some way. This is what mattered to her.

Japanese words are used throughout the text. The first time a Japanese word appears it will be printed in italics with an explanation. It will be romanized thereafter.

We wish to acknowledge the dedication of Ruth O'Halloran in transcribing her daughter's writings be published. She was helped by Kate, Scott and Elizabeth O'Halloran. I wish to thank Tetsugyu Ban, Tessai-san and Shiro Tachibana for welcoming me to Kannonji Temple and transmitting to me their love for Maura-san. I am also grateful to Paul Silverman, Lorette Zirker and Dai-en Bennage for their insight and editorial guidance.

This book is dedicated to Maura *Soshin* O'Halloran.

—Michael Kerber, Editor

Introduction

 In a small Buddhist monastery in northern Japan there stands a statue of a young Irish-American woman who lived there in the early 1980s. During her three years of Zen training in Iwate and Tokyo she was known as Maura-san, or by her monastic name of Soshin-san. She received the transmission of her roshi in 1982 and was killed in a bus accident in Thailand six months later. In 1983, as her mother, I was invited to Japan for the dedication of her Kannon statue, an indication that she had become identified in the minds of local people with the bodhisattva Kannon, the Buddhist saint of compassion.

Her last photo, taken in front of a Bangkok temple just before she boarded a bus which crashed on the road to Chiang Mai, shows a tall, blue-eyed, black-robed young woman of twenty-seven, with a radiant smile. How did this daughter of an American mother and an Irish father, educated at convent schools and Trinity College, Dublin, become not only a Zen monk but a Buddhist saint?

Maura O'Halloran was born on May 24th, 1955, in Boston, Massachusetts, the eldest of six children. Her father, Fionan Finbarr O'Halloran, was a native of County Kerry, Ireland and I, her mother, am a native of Maine. When Maura was four years old we moved to Ireland. Her earliest schooling was at Loretto convents in County Dublin. She briefly attended the same school as Mother Teresa and had hoped to meet her when she went to India after her travels in Thailand. Maura had expressed an intention of doing similar work to Mother Teresa's among the poor of Dublin.

We returned to Boston in 1966, living in suburban Waban while my husband did graduate work in civil engineering at M.I.T. He was killed in a road accident in 1969 and the entire family returned to Dublin in 1970.

In her journal, Maura never mentions the fact of her birth and youth in Boston, but her New England background, and especially her grandmother in Maine, contributed as much to her formation as did her fourteen years in Ireland. Her position as the eldest child, flung into the role of second parent to five younger siblings at her father's sudden death, hastened a maturity that few adolescents experience.

After receiving high honors in her Leaving Certificate from her secondary school in Ireland, she gained early acceptance at Trinity College, Dublin, where she matriculated in 1973. In 1975 she received Ireland's highest scholastic award, the Foundation Scholarship at Trinity College, which provided for all her educational expenses. She continued to do outstanding scholastic work until 1977 when she completed her joint degrees in mathematical economics/statistics and in sociology. As a mathematician and linguist she distinguished herself in school, but as a compassionate and wise human being she early gave promise of a rare spirituality. While in college she did much volunteer social work, especially with drug addicts and the very poor of Dublin. She spent the summer of 1976 at the Rudolph Steiner School in Glengraig, Northern Ireland, where she cared for autistic and retarded children.

Her highly developed sense of the need for social justice sometimes made her impatient with institutional obstacles to human development. This point of view found an outlet in college protests, volunteer social work, union organizing (she antagonized the management of a restaurant in which she worked in Dublin by attempting to organize the staff into a union) and what I can only call a sort of spontaneous poverty. The latter attitude led to such a detachment from material things, especially fashionable clothing, that she often appeared genuinely shabby (years before the current vogue for "shabby chic"). She deliberately limited herself to a very stringent budget.

Over her college vacations she made a series of journeys through Greece, Italy, North Africa, France and the United Kingdom. In the summer of 1977 she returned to the United States and then went to Toronto, Canada, where she worked at several jobs to earn money for cross-continental travel. She drove with friends across Canada, then worked her way down the west coast until she arrived in San Francisco. There she worked at several jobs simultaneously (waitress, hotel desk clerk, telephone operator and research assistant). She also studied photography and Spanish to prepare for a major trip through Latin America.

Describing this trip, she says:

*Starting in April, 1978, I travelled through
Mexico, Central America and most of South America,
remaining in Cuzco, Peru, for almost five months where I
taught English and improved my Spanish. [She also did
volunteer social work in Cuzco.] My lifestyle while
travelling brought me into contact with people from every
social level. I hitch-hiked, walked or travelled second-class,
as did the Indians. People, from local campesinos to
wealthy hacienda owners, continually showed me hospitality, bringing me to their homes and talking for long hours
about their lives, problems, politics and ambitions.*

She ventured as far south as Punta da Arenas and
flew back from Santiago, Chile, arriving in Maine in the
midst of a blizzard on Christmas Day, 1978.

After a visit with her family, who had moved back
to Maine from Ireland earlier in 1978, she went to
Boston where she lived in a studio apartment on
Bromfield Street while working at a Cambridge restaurant to finance her proposed trip to the Orient. In
Boston she became active in the anti-nuclear movement
and continued her study of photography, which culminated in a one-man show of her work in 1979. Her
interest in Japan had been aroused by the enthusiasm of
the family's old friend and solicitor in Ireland, Frank
Sweeney, and by her own long-term interest in meditation. In our Dublin home in the early 1970s one often

came upon her in some corner, sitting in the lotus position, calmly centered within herself, oblivious to phone, TV, and family. She had the ability to focus cheerfully and totally on whatever she did and I have no doubt that this was partly the result of her habit of meditation.

Her last month of living in America was September, 1979, which she spent writing, reading and thinking in her Aunt Anne's lake-side cottage at much loved Wayne, Maine. After a week spent with friends in San Francisco, she flew to Hawaii and then to Tokyo.

Her journals and letters take the narrative from this point. The following are excerpts from the notebooks and journals kept by Maura O'Halloran during the period of her three years' training in Zen at Toshoji Temple in Tokyo and Kannonji Temple in Iwate Prefecture, Japan, 1979–1982. The roshi of these temples is Tetsugyu Ban.

—Ruth O'Halloran

PRELUDE

Dear Family,

Well, the luck of the Irish stayed intact across the international dateline, and I'm doing great. Sure and begorra, let me tell you the tricks.

First off, I arrive in Honolulu at two in the morning and I'm exhausted and bleary-eyed (having, of course, been up with friends in San Francisco most of the night before). So I try to find somewhere to lay my head before trying to track down cousin Ed. I ended up under a palm tree amidst all these bushes, crooking myself in and out of its sinuous roots. Hardly the Hilton, but it does till dawn. Then, stumbling and staggering, I phone a million different numbers only to find that cousin Ed is out at sea. At that stage I'd do anything for a bit of sleep, and that's where my next adventure begins.

When you picture me in Hawaii, do you see me in a bikini on Waikiki Beach, sipping piña coladas? Try envisioning me in a sari, at a Hare Krishna temple, explaining how to make Irish potato bread. That's it. In the airport I got chatting with a girl named Nancy, a recent convert who'd do anything for Krishna, including giving shelter to a poor Irish waif. Well, I ended up there for nearly a week, scrubbing pots and cooking in exchange for my keep. And did I learn a lot about the Krishnas! (To get away, I had to pretend I was leaving for one of their other temples.) They dressed me up in a sari and proceeded to try to convert me. We got up every morning at 3:00 A.M. for service and a Bhagavad Gita lesson. This involved singing, dancing, chanting, and making offerings to the deities—all very pretty, but at three in the morning I was less than enthused. Then we go off to chant our rounds before the sunrise, 16 rounds of 109 beads, each one requiring "Hare Krishna, Hare Krishna, Krishna, Krishna, Hare, Hare, Hare Rama, Hare Rama, Rama, Rama, Hare, Hare." Now let me hear you say that fast, 1,744 times (before breakfast). I developed the knack of curling up in a little niche in the largest banyan tree in Hawaii and grabbing a bit of a snooze.

They start from the premise that the world is a place of misery, is an illusion—maya—a mere unsatisfactory reflection of the real and wonderful world in which Krishna dwells. In order to free themselves from endless reincarnations, they seek to deny themselves any sense of gratification, sublimating all pleasures for the desire to be with Krishna. So if I point out a magnificent sunset sky, I'm told that the colour of Krishna's robe is more glorious. I try to smell a flower but I'm stopped as it hasn't yet been offered to Krishna. There they were in a mini-paradise, Hawaii, and couldn't even enjoy it. The air was positively perfumed and soft and warm. The sun was a huge orb and everywhere grew lush tropical plants, flowers, and fruits. They'll never convince me that I'm in misery.

They must have thought me an awful agent of evil and seduction, judging from the things they corrected me on. One poor guy was caught talking to me. That occasioned two lectures, as the men in saffron aren't allowed to talk to women. I wore my sari too short (I was afraid it would fall off so I rolled it in well). I shouldn't have let the veil fall off my head while I scrubbed the pots. I was told not to smile when talking to the men! That was modified to an intriguing request not to smile "that way." The funniest of all was when we were sitting down in the temple and I was told to cover my feet. Can you imagine my club feet being so provocative as to cause a devotee one uneasy thought?

My sense of humour became strained, though, when they started the line that women were of a lower order than men. Women should be married or they were like lost sheep, unable to fend for themselves. I had a retort or two for that. Yet they were lovely people and kind and good, if a little misguided. And they certainly helped me when I needed it. What was really amusing was dancing out in the streets with them. The reactions were hilarious.

But I got away.

I had been thinking of changing my ticket to Japan and spending time on one of the remoter islands, but when I got to the airport I couldn't be bothered with the hassle. So on I got and a stroke of luck that was, too. When I landed in Tokyo, on an off-chance I tried the number of a friend of a friend from Boston. It was one of those dodgy numbers with a question mark and a smudge. I couldn't believe it when a friendly American voice answered at the other end. She was leaving for the States that afternoon so said I could sleep in her place until Friday when the girl downstairs is leaving and I can have her place until January! Well, I could hardly believe it. If I'd arrived any sooner, there wouldn't have been room at her place. Any later, and I would have missed her.

Her place really is tiny. She shares with another very nice American. It's a doll's house, a two-room affair. The sitting-room furniture gets moved at night for the mattresses to be pulled out. Most Japanese really have no room to entertain. The table is interesting. It's about a foot-and-a-half off the ground but has a quilt attached all around with a heater underneath, so your legs keep cozy. And they really do have those Japanese baths; I'm just over a long, luxurious soak.

Yesterday I went walking around Tokyo for about eight hours. At first I was horrified by what I saw. The day was overcast and grey, the air smoggy and raw. I started in the business district. Seas of people in gray and navy surged around me like so many uniformed army ants. Their faces were expressionless, seemingly choked by their tight, skinny ties. The city, gutted during the war, was modern and bleak; the only relief from the gray was the assault of neon. In my best Japanese accent I could only think "Yuck!" I contemplated a speedy packing and exit.

Then, fortunately, I meandered into neighborhoods where

rigor mortis had not set in and people were smiling. I had fun going
through streets festooned with paper lanterns and streamers, listening,
smelling, and watching. It's funny trying to get anyplace. I sympa-
thize with illiterates because you can't even read street signs. It
becomes a treasure hunt of clues wrestled from waving arms and bro-
ken English. I'm already learning a lot. The girl I'm staying with
has been here a year and a half and is giving me loads of insights.
She's doing anthropological work here and has a ton of books on
Japan and the Japanese that I'm looking forward to delving into. At
the weekend we're going to another town filled with temples and
more traditional buildings. It should be fun. She's great and is cer-
tainly making things a lot more pleasant for me. . . .

Love, Maura

PART I

Arrival

WEDNESDAY, NOVEMBER 18, 1979

I phone Toshoji Temple. Am met at temple by Tessai-san. He guides me through mounds of mandarin oranges, under the paper lanterns, past the vendor plying sweet potatoes. He says, "You came at a good time—tea time." There are four monks like little boys, laughing, innocent, delighted to see me. I meet the master, Go Roshi. When I was told that I could stay there, I felt as if I had come home, very settled and bursting with happiness. There are no other foreigners yet.

THURSDAY

I see Ueno Park and great museum. Rodin's *Thinker* sits there looking at a bed of cabbage. I have a job interview. They want to hire me.

FRIDAY

I go to Roppongi. Disappointing. I go for a second job interview. The eejit blathers for three hours on nothing. He just wants cute young Caucasians—the other three candidates are better qualified than I but I'm offered the job. I turn it down.

SATURDAY

I go to the temple. The master can't speak English. They give me my room, four tatami mats wide. There's a little desk, cushion and mattress. We go upstairs to chant. The statues look pagan. I've no idea what I'm getting into. Dinner is disastrous. We kneel around benches. There is a precise way to do everything, a million bows. Silence. The damn egg roll is so big and greasy that I can't pick it up. I'm behind the others, gobbling, trying to catch up. The voice of the master shatters the silence. "You eat slowly." I don't know if it's a comment or a command. I take it as the latter and relax and am grateful that the one thing he said was so right.

SUNDAY

They told me they didn't begin until six on Sundays but they'd already started when I arrived at six. I didn't know what to do. I knelt in the darkness outside Go Roshi's door. As he comes out he smiles and beckons me into the hall. After breakfast, he asks me if I've completed university and how did I know of the temple. He asks me if I'm willing to shave my head, and to beg [takuhatsu]. I say okay. He jumps up and springs from the room. I thought he'd gone for the razor but he comes back with robes. I model them and everyone laughs with child-like delight. Tomorrow will be my ceremony. I'll get my new name.

I'm late again. I understand nothing, can only watch. I watch as the sun's broad band creeps slowly across the black, glinting on the ivory, catching each monk, one by one. Taro is always at peace. Tenno won't smile. Takeo holds his stomach, tears pricking his eyes.

We do more cleaning. It seems interminable. I sweep outdoors. My bare feet, pink from cold, look wrong peeping from the wooden sandals. I feel wrong behind the whisking bamboo twigs. I cannot understand or be understood.

The afternoon is better. We chat and laugh a bit. They confer for the right word, tell me they are glad I'm here. I love them.

MONDAY

My ceremony. I am named Soshin. I like it. It rhymes with Oisin, a name that has always intrigued me. The others had been given names like 'iron wolf' or 'iron ship,' so I was surprised at how beautiful my name was. It was variously translated as 'great enlightenment,' 'simple mind' or 'warm/open/frank heart.' I'll gladly take any version. I'm to go to Morioka in January to beg. They keep teasing that I'll be famous on T.V. I really enjoyed sawing wood. The monks are not at all sexist. I'm totally "one of the lads" in dress, behavior and treatment. I'd love to be as peaceful and vibrant as Go Roshi. I do wish I could understand him.

TUESDAY

My mind wanders so when I do *zazen [sitting meditation]*. A *gaijin [foreigner]* came, named Frederick. He's been travelling around the world but is still very German. At first I really wanted him to stay but then I realized that I am happier surrounded by only these wonderful Japanese. They are good and pure and simple. Eshin's gentle child's face is so unspoiled, totally without guile. He's loading me with lessons. I hope he tires a bit. Frederick made me glad I wasn't on the outside—there's so much distracting nervousness there.

But I was cold. Bare feet on bare boards. The wind rises between the cracks, and it will get worse. For a little while, trying to be with the cold, I enjoyed it, a nice skin-tensing sensation. Brisk. But, oh my feet!

WEDNESDAY

I finally had a really good meditation. For a few moments my mind stopped its incessant chattering and I was down very deep.

In the morning I felt restless with thoughts of how long I should stay, should I go elsewhere, will I be very old before going back to my own world? In the evening there is meditation and service. I feel very high. We had a banquet afterwards, with sake to drink. I look at these men, laughing, enjoying, knowing. Like the old men in pubs at home, they drink through the grey curls of smoke. They are simple men, kneeling long hours on a cushion, leading spartan lives, but they are no Himalayan hermits. They drink and revel. It would be a good and wonderful thing to grow old like these men.

An ancient man, a great master, comes to pay his respects to Go Roshi. Two women help him hobble up the steps. I gasp in awe and reverence, "He's beautiful." Tetsuro repeats my exclamation and another visiting senior motions for me to follow. We sit, the six of us, in Go Roshi's snug reception room. I feel so privileged. I can't understand a word. The others serve us. I can only watch this man, the power, wisdom and dignity he exudes.

Jiko gives me a drawing of a gold-coloured harp being strummed by a ringleted maiden in an evening gown. "That's you," he says. I'm touched. His name means "sunny." He's always trying out awkward English idioms, like "It's all Greek to me." His face crinkles when he smiles, a Peter Pan. He spends long hours copying chants into *romaji [English characters]* for me.

At the service I feel very high, can't stop smiling. At tea-time the Zen Society gathers and I'm briefly questioned about my intentions.

Jiko tells me I'm to be Go Roshi's jewel. I'm elated. About one mediation a day seems to be a good one.

Today I had my first real *dokusan [interview with Roshi about one's practice]*. (I went before but had no interpreter). Go Roshi gave me the koan of *mu.** Nothingness. Only mu. I become filled with mu.

[*A koan is a challenging bit of narrative that points to ulti-

mate truth. Many koans have been handed down from teachers in early Chinese Zen Buddhist periods, but all masters in all ages find material at hand for teaching.]

The interpreter and Tetsuro call me to their room. They have both attained enlightenment. They question me about my motives and knowledge. All the time my pulse beats "nothingness, nothingness." Poems have come to me between the beats of mu.

Cathy-san was enlightened in three years, one priest in a year. I need not wait for old age, just follow Go Roshi. I have total faith in him. He can see inside me. He has the strength to kill my ego so that I can be free. "Without fail," he says, "you will attain enlightenment." I can scarcely contain myself. "Nothingness, nothingness." It's like a jungle drum beating through my veins, but I must fight for it. I sleep in a frenzy. I keep awakening hearing "Nothingness, nothingness."

SATURDAY

I work to mu. I hate the interruption of talking because slowly through the day and its idle chatter, nothingness slips. I meditate three times. My body. Inside and all around is nothing. No thing. No separation. A geyser in a lake appears to be a separate thing but is the lake. In the morning there is question-time. I ask Go Roshi the meaning of enlightenment. He strikes me. Not hard. When you are hit, you feel pain.

Ice cubes in a glass seem separate, have form. The sun shines; where have they gone? Nothing has been taken away. Their separateness is only form and only apparent, a temporary, illusionary state. Plants have consciousness. If there is reincarnation, our consciousness is different; is that of a plant, for instance and not a man trapped in a plant's shape. Our present body does not continue. Our consciousness according to theory would be different, i.e., that of a plant. Thus there is nothing left of the ice cube. We are all nothingness.

Another Week

I told Takeo-san my answer. He said I was enlightened. Wonderful!

Jiko and I went to the English bookstore. I couldn't contain my joy, looking at the dead people, thinking of nothingness.

I went to dok'san. I was determined not to be tricked into using words. Words give form, apparent substance, to nothingness. Roshi asked me what was mu. I said "nothingness." He hit me. What do I feel? I was about to say pain but due to my resolution to avoid words, I said "nothingness." "Continue," he said. I had reached my answer through logic. He was right. Think only of mu, nothing else. Don't study Japanese or sit in the corridor—only mu.

At the English bookstore, all the conflicting theories of Zen and schools had confused and upset me. I bought a book I already had but then refused to read it. Words. I want to know from inside.

The days went on, full of mu. I avoided the others' company, stopped laughing and only thought of mu. At times it drove me crazy—mu, mu, rattling in my brain, not allowed to think of anything else. I jump up and throw it out, annoyed. Other times I go down, down, down with it, down beneath words where my breath is gentle. Like looking up through the lake and the surface is a sentence and I'm below. Gentle at times. Quiet. A little smile slipping across my face. Sometimes I sit an hour and a half before there's five minutes of calm. At times I'm so happy, other times so vexed with my trivial mind.

SUNDAY EVENING

Takeo suggested how I should breathe. I tried and gradually got more and more excited. Mu rose vibrating up my spine, exploded in my head. Everything was simple. I was laughing. Mu was only mu. I felt ecstatic, couldn't contain my joy. I ran out of the hall, kissed the trees, stood in the garden and was the garden, really was it. All through dinner I beamed. Jiko kept staring. The others had described enlightenment. This was so much stronger. I didn't meditate that night, only lay wrapped snug in bed, listening to the rain.

Dear Family,

*. . . my heart will be with you so think of me at Christmas.
There'll be no plum pudding here. Bean cakes are nice, though.*

*I was settling in nicely to Tokyo life, met a few people and
had loads of work opportunities. But I realized I was only meeting
gaijin and all the foreigners form a little clique with an occasional
Japanese girlfriend or boyfriend. I was speaking no Japanese and
wasn't attracted by the culture, so I've taken a leap into real Japan,
and ancient Japan at that! I'm living at Toshoji temple and get room
and board in exchange for some cleaning every day, and I'm learning
zazen. I'm the only woman and only foreigner studying here.*

*When I arrived at the Togoshi Koen station, I phoned the
temple, and they said someone would come down to meet me. I
stood up straight, expecting to be greeted by some quiet, dignified old
abbot. Next thing, I jump backwards as a bicycle hurtles at me.
Billows of black leap and land at my feet as Tetsuro-san straightens
his glasses, catches his breath, and welcomes me. At the temple, it's
tea-time, and the monks, sitting on the floor, are laughing and
smoking and not looking at all austere. They all try out their high-
school English and laugh even more. They're lovely, like great big
kids, full of fun. I've yet to see one even vaguely vexed. They all*

chipped together and bought a linguaphone set so that they could talk to me better. So I keep getting "Would you like another glass of soda?" or "Take these suitcases to our room, please."

Each day starts at five o'clock. I wash my face by the light of the moon. I have my own room with four tatami mats and my own little outhouse. The food is good. Our staples are rice and seaweed, but the cook is really talented. Monastery life is certainly a change. I've never done so much bowing in my life. There's a very exact protocol, especially during meals, of bowing and joining hands as if in prayer. They must think I'm very polite because now I just bow at every pause. That way I figure I'm covered.

At times I feel like a cow in labour. You see, my koan is mu, and I'm supposed to bellow this (discreetly, where necessary) at every available opportunity. I scared the wits out of the poor cook, who thought the noise was her cat being brutalized.

So I'm happy, healthy, and out of mischief. Imagine, me in bed by nine every night! And cleaning every day. That's not as bad as I feared. I even clean voluntarily. Can you believe that? They have a wonderful cleaning agent here. We use it on floors, sinks, windows, metal, you name it. Elbow grease. That's it. Not even mops. Everything is done with rags and water.

The place is totally non-sexist. I half expected to be pointed towards the kitchen, but I saw wood and move furniture with the best of them. And no condescending "Didn't she do well?" It's just taken for granted. I'm totally "one of the lads," except I'm not bald. Next month we go up to the north of Japan, to Iwate Prefecture, to do begging. That should be an experience, begging in the snow. They say it's very beautiful there. I'm looking forward to seeing some country-side . . .

Love, M.

Christmas Eve: I go to dokusan. "How have you appre-hended mu?" Mu is mu. I'm smiling, happy, not at all ner-vous, still elated. "Continue!" The bell goes ting-a-ding-ding. I'm dismissed.

I felt crushed. He didn't know. Didn't he know? How could he know? But I knew. Damn. It was Christmas Eve. I was cold, and sick of *soji [cleaning]*, afraid that Tenno thought I wasn't doing enough, so from guilt I was working more. Hating the guilt. Thinking of home and family and how long I'd be stuck doing stupid, menial cleaning, and with no enlightenment

Tears prick my eyes. Juro and Eshin, like mother hens, tend me. I sit in Eshin's tiny, dark, freezing hole, wrapped tight in his wool kimono, listening to music. I try to really listen, to stop words. I don't do any soji and wonder what Tenno thinks.

Roshi buys a Christmas cake, the cook buys champagne, and they give me a party. Five monks huddled around wooden benches. When we sing we see our breath. The green plastic holly and frosting tree look odd on the strawberry cream cake. They light the candles. Don't all western cakes have candles? I wait for them to burn down. They toast me and cheer me. Jiko writes out "The Song of Wandering Aengus" on a subway map. It's not Christmas, but it's the Christmas spirit. They gave me a real lift.

Christmas day, like any other day. Even the post office is open. I decide monastery life is not for me. I love life too much to lock myself away. Maybe six months, a good chance to work on myself. It seems my experience of "enlightenment" was as good as Tetsuro's yet Roshi does not accept it. I remember the book says that *Rinzai* and *Soto* [sects of Zen Buddhism] both produce the same effect, so I decide to hell with koans. I'll work on breathing, mental silence, and really being here now. I felt much better. Tetsuro has said several times how hard I work. It's not so, but it relieves my nagging guilt. Zen is very important to me. I think I'll leave by summer but continue to study Zen when I get to Paris.

These men are wonderful. They show me such genuine warmth and love that I'm thriving. At first I took Go Roshi at his word and thought only mu. I wouldn't talk to anyone, dampened myself down. I felt I was going mad. The only variation from day to day was what was on the blue saucer for dinner. Now I'm not so extreme, but maybe it's necessary to go a little crazy to break the ego. Or maybe that's "Zen sickness."

It feels funny to be in my long black robes, darting through the traffic on a sunny bicycle day or waltzing with Jiko in a department store.

Was so still I could feel my heart beat and it was the clock ticking on the wall.

I make it. Making consists of it and me. It and me are one in making.

I tried an experiment to silence my internal chatter, made the running commentary relevant. There is blue, there is smoking, there is sweeping, swish, swish. It made things much richer.

Roshi gave me more clothes. He said my heart was pure. I gave everyone little New Year presents. After dinner, in English, Roshi spoke into the silence. "Very good present, thank you." He bows deeply. I laugh deeply.

New Year's Eve party: These little monks know how to have fun. Here am I, my friends all monks—it seems strange. I sang "Auld Lang Syne." It's the first time I've sung alone in public and not cared. Little by little I'm gaining understanding, though my meditations have been very shallow.

I want to be a Zen master.

PART II

Takuhatsu
(begging)
1980

Funny about my age. Go Roshi's son thought I was thirty. I looked in the mirror and I looked thirty. When I came to here, to *Kannonji [a country temple in Iwate Prefecture, owned by the roshi]*, they say I look a teenager. I look in the mirror and I look like a teenager.

Sometimes mu is so beautiful. Kneeling on the bare boards, by the warmth of the wood stove, the day is a grey, snowy twilight. I'm mixing the soup around and around, brown into a foam, around and around. Breathing deeply and softly, a mu, I feel peace.

Five in the morning zazen. *Sutras [chanting]*, and our breath puffs steam engine billows of icy vapour. I look at these men, their hard, kind faces, and I love them. I then look at the old woman, bent double, who for the past ten years (since she gave the land on which Kannonji was built) has hobbled over to the temple every morning for sutra. A bare silhouette in the pre-dawn light, bent over her cane she shuffles through the snow. And before breakfast we are out shovelling the virgin white, and I don't even mind. Rice and soup, plain and hearty.

Takuhatsu, layer upon layer of clothes, sometimes ten, with our begging bowls and bells we walk slowly through the streets of Morioka, through the snow and sleet, in straw sandals, bells ringing, chanting. The little old women slide open the panel on their doors, drop a coin in a bowl and stand, with bent head and long apron, waiting for a monk's blessing. Sometimes they gasp in surprise when they see me—a woman, a gaijin. When I walk, just walk, chanting, not wondering what time it is or watching the doors, I am very happy.

Riko-san is very hard and very good, a man of precious metal. He walks through the snowstorms to get me warm clothes. He teaches me in simple broken English about Buddhism. He is simple and pure and has no doubts. So too is his wife. I love her. A temple woman asked in wonder whether I was a boy or a girl, then brought her child to kneel before me and kept taking my hands to kiss them. I wonder what she was saying.

There's been much fuss since I was interviewed on TV and in the newspaper. Now people point to me, want to put their offerings in my bowl, children follow me on the street. In jest, Taro-san calls me a goddess, Buddha of the caravan. Silly, because the fuss is on account of my being foreign and female.

The devout women of Morioka invite us to lunches. Oh, such food! They never eat with us—probably couldn't afford to—but reverently wait outside the room. With tears in their eyes they thank us for the privilege of serving us. I watch them on their knees bowing and feel weird to be in this role, especially in another culture from my own. At one luncheon it was decided that I had a Japanese face. Of course my face is as Irish as turf but it's all part of their acceptance of me. Several people have said that I don't seem Western.

When I was in South America I didn't feel estranged either; they said I seemed Latin. Quién sabe?

The woman in the fish shop served us hot *sake* and rice. It's warming, after hours in the snow. All around lie the bodies of fish, bodies heaped on bodies, with gaping eyes and mouths. I no longer want to eat fish. I wouldn't catch one myself. Shellfish and eggs I can handle. But then I eat fish for lunch because I eat what's given me.

JANUARY 13, 1980

Dear Family,

Happy birthday to my favorite brother in this whole world. Wish I could be with you. You've gone and grown up behind my back. Hope you like school and you're not showing off too much with all A's. An A- here or there would be good for the other kids. Right?

How was the Christmas for yis? I missed you. Christmas Eve was very cold and glum without a sprig of holly or a sniff of turkey. I was feeling decidedly on the wrong side of the Pacific. Word went around the monastery that I was down in the dumps, and they all rallied round. One monk did my chores for me. Another one wrapped me in a big woolen coat (it was freezing), popped head-phones on me and played tapes, his prize being hymns from Notre Dame. The abbot went out and bought a "Christmas cake," and the cook bought champagne. They were going to give me a Christmas party. Well, it was the funniest looking Christmas party I ever saw. Five monks and the cook huddled in the cold around four wooden benches. The plastic tree and yule log looked strange sitting on a "Christmas cake" of whipped cream and fresh strawberries. They lit birthday candles on the cake. Don't all Western cakes have candles? But they didn't know what to do with them, so they turned off the lights and patiently waited for the candles to melt down. Then they played "Silent Night" in Japanese and took turns singing English songs. Then Tetsuro-san leaps to his feet in full monk's regalia, hips swinging, and in choppy Japanese accent he does his rendition of Elvis Presley. Then there was "Home, home on the lange." Great cheer all around, though you could see everyone's breath as each sang his song. The party ended at 8:00; we all had to be up at 4:30. It wasn't quite Christmas, but it was certainly the Christmas spirit.

All the while there was the build-up to going begging this month. A couple of days before we were to leave for the north, one of the monks came to my room with an armful of bandages.

I asked what they were for. "Your wounds," he replied solemnly. We both consulted our dictionaries to make sure bandages *and wounds were the right words. They were. I closed the door and wondered just what I'd let myself in for this time. I felt as if I was going off to war.*

I've hit the news again. Aren't you glad it's not a demonstration this time? Everyone was amazed at a girl and a foreigner going begging. It looks hard, walking for hours through the snow in straw sandals (with socks), chanting and ringing a bell. "Severe training for a boy," they say, "but for a girl?" and their slanted eyes widen. So they interviewed me on TV; then the newspaper for this prefecture came around. I don't know what they wrote. The reporter couldn't speak English, so one of the monks told him all about me. Suddenly I had a public. People in buses would wave and point; children followed me in the street; people chased me to put money in my bowl. Today the newspaper came round again. There was such a response that they want another article.

It's funny, the begging isn't bad at all. I wear literally ten layers of clothes and once the fingers and toes are numb, you don't feel a thing. It's nice walking through the streets singing at the top of your lungs. It's like going Christmas caroling every day. Then the little wooden door rattles and slides across, and an old woman, bent over, clutching her shawl, shuffles in the snow to drop whatever she can in your bowl, then bends her head reverently waiting for the blessing I can't give.

Most days families from the town invite us to lunch. It's a big occasion for them, and they go all out. We wear our ceremonial dress. They put a feast before us. I'm trying all kinds of Japanese delicacies I could never have afforded otherwise. They're on their knees pouring out their thanks to us again and again for coming to their homes. If you could see the old women with tears rising to their eyes, holding the abbot's gown and thanking him. It's so strange to be in this respected position. I'm not used to it in my own culture, let alone this one. Fellows my own age passing in the street who normally would try to chat me up instead join their hands as if to pray and bow deeply. All the while I'm trying to keep a straight face.

This amulet that I'm enclosing was especially commissioned by the abbot for you. It is a New Year's blessing to bring health and happiness to the home. On the right is our name, on the left is the temple and the monk that wrote it (the same one that did Elvis on Christmas Eve). They say it should be hung in a special place.

When you mentioned coming to Japan, I must say, selfishly, I'd love you to come over; it'd be great to see you, but in fact if you're going to spend the money you'd get better value anywhere else. Prices are ridiculous. $20.00 for a steak, $13.00 for a melon, $1.50 for a cup of coffee . . . it's all true. But then you could eat tofu and mandarins and drink green tea instead. Little was left of old Japan after the war; now it's mostly ugly concrete rabbit warrens, but for me it's grand because I'm living in thirteenth century Japan *and it's fascinating. But I must say, of all the countries I've been to, modern Japan would be low on my list of "must come back to's." However, I'd still like to see ya.*

Love, M.

KANNONJI TEMPLE
FEBRUARY, 1980

It was *daikan [great cold]*. The great, coldest, coldest weeks of the year, coldest prefecture of the country. Go Roshi was delighted that I wasn't used to the cold—better training. I told the temperature by whether the offerings were frozen or not, and often they were. So, wiping a metal cup, the cloth would freeze on. Washing in the morning isn't cracking the skin of ice on the basin but taking a blunt instrument and bashing it. Perhaps the hardest part was not the takuhatsu itself but sutras in the morning.

Up and run to the little wood stove in the kitchen. A few minutes respite from the cold, then into *zendo [meditation hall]*. I was first, sitting alone in the predawn dark. The rustling of the robes to the rhythm of running feet, and the bell rings; wood resounds a dull thud. Slowly incense wafts through the zendo. I am more asleep than awake, struggling to incarnate, meditations usually frazzled. Tekkan-san's cushion is always there, so I wonder if he already sat. Tessai, Tessan and Jiko-san all gurgle, splash, spit toothpaste, then drift in one by one. Tachibana *sensei [teacher]*, the village English teacher, and his ten-year-old son. Could I, can I ever do that, lead a layman's life and still attend to my meditations?

From zendo into *hondo [hall for chanting and teaching]* where it's even colder. Sutra clouds of frozen breath. At the end, if I have the control to touch my baby fingers together for obeisances, then I'm glad the day is so warm. Sutra chanting ends and we scurry, run, laughing in the darkness, dashing towards the warmth of the hearth.

Jiko-san, chafing his hands together "Itai, itai" through the chattering of his teeth; Katsuko-san, round, cuddly dumpling, smiles sympathetically; Tessai announces the temperature. I squat among the sticks, my long robes flowing carelessly across them, huddled over the stove, warming my hands and watching the red flickering in the slit. Hypnotizes. Soji for breakfast. Soji—we run, bare feet seem to stick, slightly frozen, to the tatami. We sweep out the snow where it has drifted in the cracks, laughing all the while, more to keep warm than from amusement.

Breakfast is hearty. I hold high my rice bowl, blue bears dance across it. The kerosene fire glows warmly in its ceramic reflection. The rice steam curls mu and I am at peace and thankful.

Crossing through the snow in the dawn twilight, I look at the stars. Some days I'm happy, skipping, tingling, other days muttering, promising myself never again, consoling myself—I love you, Maura, you can do it, Maura; it's only X more days, wanting to linger in bed with a cup of coffee, or just once to sleep later than 4:30. I add a couple of sweaters and a kimono, then carry back my takuhatsu gear to the breakfast room. There, with Tekkan-san, I dress, Katsuko-san puttering around, kindly warming damp socks, straightening a belt or fold. Tekkan-san often seems gruff, "Noooo, this way," pulls, pushes, tightens my clothes, pulls my kimono firmly across my chest, just a straightforward arrangement of clothes. Then a few minutes' space before we have to leave, a quiet time. I sit, trying to be empty, to only sit. Sometimes in simple English with many pauses, Tekkan-san would tell me something about Buddha, about life, or read sutra with me. "You must learn to read Buddhist book," he says.

PART III

Tokyo

Yesterday I bought books. I read about mu, read that mu is not a mantra, don't just repeat mu but struggle with What is mu? I went upstairs to zendo mu. I am mu. I am nothing, nothing, nothingness. I do not exist (though I do). But nothing, absolutely nothing. Something trembled near my eyes. I wept, lay down on the tatami and wept huge, heaving tears. I was nothing, my dreams, my hopes, my conceits were nothing. I cried funeral tears. I was at my own funeral and no one else had come. I was crying and crying and crying and. . . .

Downstairs, it was time to make toast. Tetsuro-san asked what was wrong. I am nothing, and it's very hard and very sad and tears pricked. "Honto? You are near enlightenment. You must go to dokusan." I know I'm not near enlightenment but I would like to go to dokusan. I do mu, a deep total mu. Afterwards my vocal cords hurt. Roshi says keep with mu 'til *sesshin [an intensive week of zazen]* and then I will attain enlightenment. (As for that "will"—try "may.")

After dinner, Roshi says "put an ad in the paper for a new cook." He doesn't like my cooking. The fish was too hard (two weeks old, I scraped off the mold), the salad too hearty. It was true. I wasn't that put out. It was true. Though I liked cooking, wished it had been good. I felt too drained to really react, to be really hurt. After all the tears, I had heard the shock of Tekkan-san's possible dismissal by the people of

Morioka. There seemed to be an enormous web of conflicting saying and thinking. Morioka people had seemed so warm, generous, and appreciative of Tekkan-san, yet the dear little old ladies deftly stabbed him through the heart. Roshi dismisses us; the others say they're always hungry but grumble about too much food. I am tired, little sleep, and I am nothing—exhausted, spent. And Jiko-san says, "You are too simple and too honest." And for that time he is right. I can scarcely even feel bewildered, only wash the dishes and go to bed.

You must struggle with a koan, fight with it and for it. My energy in mu is renewed asking, What is it? Getting up in the morning is one of the hardest things for me. So I will get up even earlier and go to the hondo and sit.

FEBRUARY 22

> *I was not born*
> *will not die*
> *for I am*
> *nothing*
> *but please do not*
> *stand on my*
> *toe.*

If mu is mind, consciousness, it is nothing. I am always changing—not a thing. I am not the same person as ten years ago, or a moment ago, yet I am. But then where is I? A fish has the consciousness of a fish. I have the consciousness of a twentieth-century woman and no one before has had my consciousness. Where is rebirth? Consciousness changes. If reborn as a fish, I am a fish, not Maura, but a fish. Consciousness changes. Action and reaction, like a seal stamped on sand. Nothing is transferred, but the processes continue. Energy cannot be created or destroyed, only transformed. What is dead and what alive? He said, first and last thoughts. Makes sense. Plants and animals think. Has a stone consciousness? Is it conscious? If consciousness is energy, all form is, not has, consciousness. If we all are not havemind . . . huh? . . . what? . . . hmmm. Are things *mu [nothing]* and *u [something]*? Waves on the ocean are separate but the same. When the wave subsides it doesn't disappear, cease to exist, but does. It is no longer the wave but the ocean which is what it was anyway. Isn't that death? And mu is u and Joshu can say the dog has no Buddha nature.

Dinner was almost a fiasco. Jiko-san, at the last moment, added sauce and soothed my laments.

Does the first thought mean the beginning of a new life because thought is separation?

Roshi asked Jiko-san to place the ad [for a new cook]. He keeps changing his mind. He apologized and asked us to cook for a while, saying it's good to have cultivators in *tenzo [kitchen, or cook]*, then changes. Jiko and I were sitting eating the brown rice glue that we have dubbed jiko-mochi and that I love, I saying the only thing I like more than tenzo is the garden. I didn't look forward to the hours of dusting the clean altars I had dusted the day before. Then Tessan-san tells me my new job will be the garden. I can't believe it; I'm overjoyed.

Form is emptiness. It is never the same, always changing, so doesn't exist, is mu; but bang into the wall, of course; and form is form.

My life force is always being passed into new forms. Each cell born in my body contains my life force and each one that dies is dead. Is it so strange that it passes into a new body? Yet there is no "it." Nothing is transferred. It's the same with cells. I'm having a lot of trouble with this death-rebirth business. It's incredible. Cells divide. Then each one knows what to do. All the minute things, another me, all functioning. Miraculous.

The thing to which I am most attached, can least give up, least admit its transience, is myself.

FEBRUARY 25

I get up and go to zendo at 4:00. Not so hard. Sitting alone, trying the new mu that Jiko-san has taught me. It's more open; I prefer it. I raise and put back my head, saying mu. Someone turns off the light and comes into the room. Perhaps even Roshi. In the darkness I make out the pattern of the doors. It's a warm enveloping dark, a womb, dark, shared with I don't know who. It's peaceful and comforting. I will sit every morning in that stillness.

The figure is Tetsuro-san—Iron Wolf, prowling, always a little unsure, a little outside. His kindness and compassion to me have been enormous, an encouraging and humble word whenever I need it. He is soon to become abbot of a new temple and seems to be anxious. Jiko says he's neurotic.

He himself says he imagines people want to get rid of him. He startled me at the sink when he pounced. "Why were you laughing?" About him, he thought. "Joke, joke," he said. Honest in his weaknesses and nightmares. After all his generosity to me, when I had the chance to get him a takuhatsu hat, I did. It cost 10,000 yen but with my takuhatsu money, it wasn't that much, and money is for such things. He said he worried all night, distraught, asking himself why I had given him such a big present. Issh. He's so funny, so childlike, the way he opens his heart. He's poring over the newspaper.

"Aha." Face alight. "Olivia Hussey has married a Japanese."

"Oh, really?" and I add something forgettable about her, not sure of the relevance of the announcement.

"What do you think of international marriages?"

I approved.

"So you would marry a Japanese?"

"I'd need to learn Japanese."

Then he throws himself into excited jabbering with Mio-san, the gist being that I wasn't against marrying a Japanese. I love his innocence.

I was sitting up in zendo, and Jiko's words were in my ears. "When you are your mother, when you are Roshi, then you are enlightened." I didn't see how that was possible. If I wasn't myself, I certainly wasn't them. I kept telling myself: you are everything. Hard to conceive of. Then it hit me how totally arbitrarily we have defined our so-called self. I am my body, thoughts, perceptions, personality. So the thought of my mother is me but my mother is not. The real "I" I've defined as not me, and that which is merely the image and not real I have defined as me. Strange. The spit in my mouth is me. The air in my mouth is not. The food I take in isn't, yet somewhere it passes some vague border and becomes me. I myself was so arbitrarily defined—the thought is me, the spit and food is me, but the painting I produced, spawned from my thought, is not me, the tune humming though my head, me—and if I any way reject that definition of self as non-existent, can't I then redefine myself?

And I began. Each noise, sight, movement was me. I was tremendously excited, quivering, smiling. As if there was a statue, my physical body, with a cloth draped over it, hanging close around my body; it was what I defined as self. Now a tack through the head and cloth, someone is raising it and stretching it; it's still attached to my body but covers more and more, and that is me. How can I die or cease to be? I am eternal; I am process and thing. I am my mother. I am Roshi. I left the hondo, a new I; every noise and sight caught my notice, being incorporated into myself.

We went shopping. I cooked dinner, and soon my self-conception was back to its usual stifling structure. Does Roshi always feel like that? Before I admired him for having stared at his nothingness in its coffin and still being able to laugh. Now it seemed there was much more. Enormous.

After zazen, Roshi said something about *muji [the koan mu]* being everything and about the tenzo people (Jiko and I) working from devotion. So maybe it's not because he hates my cooking that he wants a new kitchen helper.

My relationship with Jiko has been interesting. I always oscillated between being amused at his childlike pranks and being irritated by his childish demands for notice. Constantly praising himself, yet as quick and enthusiastic in his praise of others. I don't believe he has ever criticized another's character—their habits, yes, but not their character. He often seemed to act uppity with me, correcting me on trivial points, straightening a wrinkle, this way, pushing me. It was annoying in a mild way. So I wondered how he'd get on in the kitchen. I can see how I've changed in my reactions. He often flaps around, does nothing, or fiddles with his dictionary while I do all the work. He asked me to do all the lunches since he "sometimes has business." Rubbish. My first reaction was, Hold on, make sure you're really doing more before you accuse, then point out how much you did, etc. Do the lunch and put up with it. Instead, I said no. If he had business I'd do the lunch and he could do it for me the next day.

I asked which day to put out the bins. "Today," he blithely said. "Where do they go?" Starting to resent. "Over . . ." He began to indicate. Before, I would have taken them off, fumed and forgotten it as unimportant. I ordered, "Come on." Not giving him time to take off his slippers at the door, I gruffly commanded, "Take those." He did, obviously meek and chastened.

In the kitchen I tell him to put things away if I feel put upon. In fact, now I can laughingly give him the towel or just shut up when he goes on and on and on and on, asking me to repeat the pronunciation of some word "merry," "merry," "merry," "merry." So no tension builds up. The moment it rises, it flickers, and so we laugh and joke and love working in tenzo.

He never takes the meals too seriously, which is good for me, though often disaster for the cooking. Every morning he makes mochi—a healthful, gluey combination of *komugi [wheat]*, beans, *gemmai [brown rice]*, peanuts or *goma [sesame]* or whatever comes to hand. We sip tea, eat slowly, and listen to his tiny radio. It's a simple, gentle, very great pleasure. He often adds charming touches, like serving on a special plate or with flowers. He does make me laugh so.

For Roshi's son's birthday party, the 27th, we had to prepare a big, sit-down dinner for fourteen. *Ok'san [Go Roshi's wife]* wanted two kinds of fish and a meat. I decided to positively avoid getting into a flap . . . three gas burners, no oven or even a grill. I had my part all ready by 10 o'clock in the morning of the 27th: chicken, fish, each separately marinated. Twice Jiko's rice came out too soft. I was helping him, so there was still a countdown tension but not bad. My chicken was very cold, being in the fridge, so I put it in the rice steamer and the outside went wet. I nearly died. My crispy delicious chicken. I quickly started re-frying and all went well.

Dinner—even I must admit—was delicious and beautiful. Roshi's son didn't show up. Roshi, from the other end of the table, beaming, said in English "Zank you verly much." He's radiant. "*Do itashimashite*" [*You're welcome*], I muttered, and all oohed. It was a success. Jiko and I hugged, shook hands, laughed, and after cleaning, sat down with flowers and finished the sake. Bejaysus it was grand.

In the afternoon I had time to spare. Tetsuro-san was cutting Tetsubun-san's hair. I shot some pictures and sat lazily in the sun, half in and half out of the big glass window. Playfully flicking the shears, Tetsuro-san teased, "Now, how about you?" I thought for a few minutes. My hair was growing, looking well, would soon be long enough to part in the middle. I had bought a hairbrush, thinking of getting a mirror. "How about you?" "Okay," I said. The day was warm; my hair was in the way; when would I have the chance to be bald again?

"Honto?" "Ii yo." Tetsuro-san jumped up and jumped down, asked Tetsuban-san, asked Jiko-san, put on his kimono to ask Roshi, then took it off, then put it on and finally shore off my hair.

Surprisingly, it didn't bother me. Of course, with no big mirror I don't see myself. The air and wind feel good on my head. It's a liberating feeling. I remember reading about light affecting some gland corresponding to a third eye in the case of shorn birds. Interesting. The next day it snowed. My bald head was very cold.

After zazen on the 28th, Roshi said it was sad to visit his family. His son took no joy in his birthday. All his family are in education and have no interest in zazen. How sad for him and sad for them. The opportunity they have let slip. I admire his emotional openness with us.

I feel very privileged to be at Toshoji. Roshi is a very great teacher and example. People think the life is hard, but I am grateful. Imagine, all my bodily needs taken care of and that which I most want to do—a very self-oriented thing—is not only tolerated but encouraged. Not a care in the world, no worries or regrets, only this enormous opportunity.

I wonder if every living thing doesn't have compassion—Buddha nature. All life has/is (not sure which) consciousness. Plants faint when an egg or shrimp is killed. Is this not compassion at its most basic? It will be argued that many people are bad. I have yet to meet the person whom I could point to and say "he has no compassion." Reflecting on all the goodness shown to me on my travels, I can only be humble, goodness far exceeding what I am big enough to repay.

These days I feel very conscious of life. Before, I didn't like eating meat because it was so toxic and I found rather insipid the sentimentality of "poor little things." Now it really saddens me to consume flesh, to see slaughter displayed in the supermarket. "Lashai, Lashai, Lashais," welcome. I feel remorse because of the extra wooden match I use, and though I must serve meat and fish to the others, I wonder where to determine my complicity in the crime. I would not by choice serve meat, but each time that I serve it instead of something else (as I must), must I assume this guilt?

MARCH 1

There was no answer to the ad for a new cook. Yesterday Roshi asked us if we would continue cooking. He said at first he thought we were trying to kill him, hard rice and dinner that smelled like medicine. I have to laugh; I love his frankness, but now he says everything is delicious. He thought we would soon tire of the kitchen, but we are in high spirits, and the kitchen is always clean. Jiko said that of course I would rather do the garden, but it's okay. It's still cold for the garden.

This morning, meditating, I couldn't still my mind for a moment. I kept thinking of different things to cook, etc. Was annoyed with myself. After morning sutra we had the ceremony where each person roars a question and Roshi answers. Tetsuro-san told me to go up.

"I don't know what to say," I whispered, flustered.

"Sit there," he said. So I thought I didn't have to ask a question.

Then Roshi calls, "Soshin-san."

I go up and wait for Tetsuro-san to tell me the Japanese I must say. Nothing. I look at him imploringly. "What do I say?"

"Ask your question." So I ask but my voice is small because of the awe and confusion I feel. "What is Buddha?"

I have so many questions. He waits a long time. I cannot understand the answer. Afterwards Tetsuro-san says, "Roshi said, 'You are silent, but your mind is like thunder.'"

I feel crushed. He's saying my mind is a storm; I have no peace. I think of that morning's scattered meditation, how hard it often is to keep my mind on things. He knows I'm so far from enlightenment, it seems like no use—I'll never calm my mind. I ask Jiko what he meant. "Only an allusion to the weather; never mind." I go again to Tetsuro-san. He says it is a common Zen phrase, no bad meaning, comes from a Chinese poem and is like saying, "the old man is silent but his life is etched in his face." I'm slightly consoled.

Chosan [morning tea at which Roshi discusses important things]. Roshi has been appointed one of the top teachers in Japan. How could I have been so lucky to stumble upon his temple, decide to stay (under the illusion he spoke English), be accepted, and have to pay nothing?

Roshi said something about when I was silent this morning. The other Roshi who came to announce Ban Roshi's promotion said he admired me coming as a foreigner and doing Zen seriously, that I was simple in my confusion. Jiko fumbles to translate, and Roshi cuts in, saying in English, laughing, "You are wonderful, number one."

March 2

Yesterday I went to enquire about my visa with Tetsuro-san. Watching all the people on the train, they seem lifeless; even Tetsuro-san was slumped into customary subway slumber. People's eyes are blank, or drifting across each other, creating a distance within the crowd by avoiding eye contact. I, too, am good at this. I try to catch the people's staring eyes so I can shatter the game with a smile. No use. They won't let our eyes meet or acknowledge the obvious that we are both there, three hours on the subways. The only one who would communicate with my eyes was a mentally retarded girl on a Saturday group outing. And she's the one defined as out of touch with reality.

Two little boys and their father boarded. They quivered with life and excitement, chattering, laughing, playing, looking at everything with wonder, yo-yos, and curiosity, eyes sparkling. How is it killed, I wondered. They asked their father a question. He ignored them. Another question, a mumbled response as he stares vacantly into space. That is how the crime takes place. And he is a good father; he takes the kids out on Saturdays. Watching them, I want to play— to play tip and tig, hide and seek, pirates, house, red rover, to pretend. Mothers are so annoyed when children return late for tea. How wonderful to be so engrossed, to so enjoy what one is doing that one loses all conception of time. If only mothers could rejoice.

Sunset was beautiful.

This morning Mt. Fuji was clear between the smoke stacks and the railroad tracks. 5:00 a.m. Go Roshi leaves for Iwate. I hope he brings back good news of Tekkan-san.

Everything that happens to me is a mixture of the circumstance and my reaction to it. Nothing can touch me purely without my filtering it, even if the mind is empty. By allowing everything in, I have affected the circumstance. The I-filter is constantly changed, too, by circumstance. "Karma means everything that happens, we directly or indirectly, partly or entirely, set in motion." At least insofar as the circumstance includes the I-filter, this is true, but possibly even the strong case that the quote suggests. You and outside you are not separate. If someone steals all my possessions and I am upset, I say something bad has happened to me. If I do not care, nothing bad has happened, yet it is the same external circumstance.

MARCH 3

Yesterday, sitting, the same question ricocheted round and round my mind. How are we all one? We're all made of the same stuff but that doesn't make us one. Kapleau says Mary hurt in Detroit, Joe feels in Rochester. But I don't. At least not consciously. Then I thought of the plants mourning the egg, excited when many miles away his owner came. I thought of how at Grandpa's death, Aunt Elaine got up in the wee hours of the morning, put on her coat, stumbled through the blizzard, and was with him when he went. Tears came into my eyes. There is knowing between minds. Perhaps (of course) it is usually inaccessible to consciousness. But that it happens at all, and that it is always present in plants, which don't have as complex a consciousness as we do, would seem to mean something.

In the afternoon I was very aware. Without an effort, I was just doing whatever I was doing, without distraction or forcing. Occasionally the thought would pop into my head "Hey, your mind is still." Then even that vanished. Because I was quiet, I was very surprised when Jiko said, "You are in very high spirits."

Today, business and flighty mind as usual.

MARCH 4

Yesterday I went shopping with Jiko. I bought a flash and tripod. I find myself slightly annoyed by his dilly-dallying, pulling and tugging at me, poking me to look at this and that. "*Ii ne, ii, ii*" *[That's good, isn't it? Good! Good!]*, on and on even after I answer him. I know we won't have time to do everything, and of course we don't. But I'm more annoyed with myself for lacking a spontaneity. Everything he shows me is marvelous, and we can do the other things another day. We did what was most important, the flash, and saw wonders. I feel perhaps am being too hard, asking him not to repeat, not to poke me. (Rather, I tell him it's okay for him to repeat but I won't always answer.) When I tell him that and he looks at me with the same expression and intonation as usual "*ii*" or "*oishii*" *[tasty]* and I don't answer or only say "mm," he persists and persists. He nags until I answer not just "ii" or "ishii," but "ii yo!" or "oishii yo!" and I wonder if he is dense or trying to annoy. I really don't think he has the meanness in him for the latter but hate to conclude the former. And of course it's equally my reaction. If I were more totally immediate, the repetition would not be annoying because each time would be as the first.

Last night I borrowed without permission one of Roshi's books. I felt very guilty and stayed up too late reading. I'm tired and grumpy this morning. Jiko tells me to come over at 9:00 for *omochi [rice cakes]*. I'm starving. He fiddles around for an hour and a half with the windows wide open, taking pictures and dropping my batteries. Then I'm freezing and starving. I'm disgruntled and more annoyed with myself than with him. Why should a change from what I had expected be annoying? I decide I'd better rest. The morning is gone.

Back to the kitchen to make lunch. No Jiko. The kitchen's a mess, his breakfast dishes still sitting, ten o'clock tea dishes still sitting. Of course, I had also left the latter. I'd hoped he'd put away the breakfast dishes, since he'd done nothing else afterwards. I can't say I do more work, because he spends more time in the kitchen, so though my work time there is more industrious, I have more free time. I'm making lunch. Still no sign of him. Well, the only help he is is to get out a few chopsticks. He had asked me to do lunches, and I virtually do, and don't mind as it's easy. But I didn't want him to take it for granted. I don't really feel over-worked, as there isn't that much to do and usually it was a one-person job. I do what's necessary, and if I feel resentful, I give Jiko a dish towel, usually with a laugh. I'm annoyed at myself for being so petty and decide I'm really tired and should sleep more.

Jiko comes in, all apologies. He'd been in a sound sleep. So he wasn't taking me for granted; it was an accident. I felt much better. Of course it was okay. He started going on and on about how I did much more work—still just fiddling with his dictionary while I worked. I handed him a tea towel and said it was okay. We're a team. There's no need to make comparisons, more or less work; we'll just each do our best. I'm glad the sentiment came from him, and really I don't mind doing more, so long as he does something. I also think he finally got it about the repetitions. We'll see. It is much better for me to be working with Jiko-san than with someone who never annoys me.

Reading that book, I feel so far from enlightenment. Not that it's so important for right now, but I'm on such a gross and sloppy level. Why can I not feel the unity of all?

March 5

Why can I not still my mind? Last night's and this morning's meditations were so scattered.

MARCH 7

The day before yesterday some psychologists came to test our skin potential, resistance, and breathing during meditation. Jiko was first. He came downstairs and told me how twice during meditation he had left his body and the researchers will be very surprised. I thought about my own meditations, how they are often so sloppy. In the afternoon I went up. A wire from my ear, two around my waist and five in my left arm. I really felt like a laboratory rat. I might have been peevish (as I was a bit for the news interviewer), this "probing a freak" bit, but the researcher does zazen himself so I wanted to cooperate. My meditation was deep. I was one with everyone and everything, including them. I felt strong love for them. At one stage I was their machine, and its rotations were my heartbeat. At the beginning and end we just sat naturally. They rechecked the apparatus and kept telling me to just be at ease. I thought I must be nervous and it was showing up.

At the end they came over, extremely excited, "*Subarashii, subarashii [splendid, splendid].*" "This is very rare data," they said. "We have tested many monks, 40-60, but this is very rare. . . . Your natural state is thirteen breaths a minute and in meditation three or four a minute; normally a good meditation is three to five." They want to test me again next week. I was very pleased, and it was hard for me not to tell the others everything they said, but I don't want the thing to seem competitive. I needed encouragement and it came. However, the things they are measuring are only by-products; they have nothing to do with my understanding, and it is this that I want.

I have been meditating now consistently for three months. (They couldn't believe that—thought it must be a year and three months.) I can perceive subtle changes. My posture is different, composure better. I'm more quiet. I remember finding Sean's silences unbearable and needed constant chatter and once had to stop myself from begging him to talk about just anything. I'm no longer compulsive in eating and drinking. If I do something, I like to do it properly, and I care less about others' opinions of me. I can even serve a bad dinner, feel sorry that it was bad, but not be upset to the core and watching each expression. I'm much better disciplined, but I don't know how permanent any of these changes are. So I am a bit afraid to go back to the "real world."

Mum sent a letter saying she was sad I had given up the idea of a Ph.D. at the Sorbonne (which of course I haven't) and appealing to me to help her sell her Dublin house in the summer. But I am finally doing what I have wanted and needed to do all my life and am afraid to break. I consider Buddhism my "religion," if it can be called that. On the other hand, I do want to continue with my outside life at some stage and finish the koans. So maybe I should find a suitable temple and get on with it, as I'll have to break from here sooner or later. I love, respect, and trust Roshi completely, yet I should not be attached even to him.

Toshoji, Tokyo
March, 1980

Dear Mum,

Many thanks for the parcel. Did you realize you had two of my favorite songs on the tape, in addition to "Raglan Road?" I don't know what made you think I'd given up the idea of a Ph.D. at the Sorbonne. For the first time since I left Trinity, I feel I'm making real progress on a would-be original thesis. Things are really clicking, and I'm writing notes all the time. As you know, I got very interested in theories of language, ideology, and the formation of the subject, especially Lacan's work. He is, of course, in Paris. Now learning my first non-western language and being immersed in oriental philosophy, many things are falling into place. As I'm sure you're aware, Zen has very different notions of the subject than ours, and grammatically the language is built to facilitate this. Or was it the other way around? Interestingly, most grammar books, in translating, do not make a direct translation, making the different concepts involved more obvious. But they also translate conceptually, so that the Westerner hears the Japanese phrase but can still think it in his own terms. Luckily, I have found an excellent book written by linguists from Yale that's extremely helpful. My ideas so far stem from Lacan's theories, but I've never seen them applied in such a case. In fact, I can think of a better way of confirming some of his speculations. It's very exciting but difficult, as I can only proceed at the pace at which I'm learning Japanese. I also need to study Shinto and probably linguistic changes that occurred with the importation of much of the Chinese written language, with Buddhism itself, and at the ideological level, with the attempt to introduce the Chinese political system, and how was all this reconciled with the emperor's god status—all of which occurred at about the same time. This is a huge subject, and it's the linguistic end that is most interesting and most original.

But it involves a load of work. I have to learn two more Japanese scripts, one of which is non-syllabic. Nonetheless, if I can pull it off it would put me in an important place in my field, though I'm afraid to get my hopes too high.

As I've said to you before, all this meditation has brought me many benefits, not least of which is much greater concentration and self-discipline. I really don't know if I would have been able to undertake a good thesis three months ago. I was so out of the habit of applying myself to anything seriously. Waitressing til three in the morning was not the most conducive thing to academics.

The other day some psychologists from some university came over to do tests on us and psychophysiological changes during zazen. They attached five wires to my arm, hung one from my ear and put on two respiratory monitors. They hadn't told the others anything about the results of their tests, but I resolved to ask them, because I was very curious. But after I finished, they came bounding over, full of non-scientific excitement and saying "wonderful, wonderful" over and over. They said they have tested nearly sixty monks but that my results were extremely rare and apparently I have been having deep meditations that are normally only reached after years of practice. So they want to do a whole bunch more tests on me and are coming back next week. Well, I was very surprised, though I have increasingly noticed changes in myself.

All of which brings me to what is my problem at the moment. This is the first thesis that has really absorbed my interest, that I feel I could put the necessary time and effort into, and that would be worth writing, in that it would be a real contribution. At the same time, I want to keep up my Zen. I was fortunate to end up with a really excellent teacher. He is famous (as are his books) throughout Japan and has just been given the highest recognition there is as a "teacher of teachers." But if I pursue the thesis, it would mean at least another year and a half in Japan. That's a heck of a long time.

The other problem is I don't have the books I need and it would be nearly impossible for you to send them, as I'd have to *search through bookshops, consult bibliographies, and probably be in touch with Brian Torode and Jim Wickham in Trinity. So I want your advice, i.e., "Mommy, what should I do?" Please try to be as objective as possible about it. I imagine your first reaction might be—two years or two and a half. I suppose I could manage. What do you think, you having been through the "get back to the books and really write" bit? But it is a long time.*

Love, M.

MARCH 8

Go Roshi came back from Kannonji yesterday; I really love him.

The day after Jiko slept through lunch, I asked him to put away the breakfast dishes, since everything else was done. I came in to find no sign of him. Half-way through lunch and he still hadn't appeared. I thought of someone else's words: "We are one, when a boil appears on your hand, you're not angry at it; you just do something about it." So I did. Jiko was moving rooms when I came in. He, of course, was engrossed in and delighted with the fun of it. I said "Come and help me make lunch." He said, "Oh," surprised.

A while later he came in. I said, "Jiko-san, I asked you to put away the dishes. I cleaned everything else. It's not so much to ask." I didn't like to make the comparison. I repeated myself; it often takes a while for things to sink in. Chastened, he did so. That evening he was all "May I help you? What can I do?" Next day he put away without my asking, but the following day he was back to normal. I hate to always prick his balloon. He is quite marvelous—a child's sense of fun, and what child likes to dry dishes? He is eager to cook new concoctions. "Ah, the joy of creation," says he. He goes to infinite trouble arranging glasses of water to play a tune with the radio. He meticulously cuts a piece of potato into a star, selects the right frying pan as a backdrop—the north star against a midnight sky, then pops it into my mouth. He truly has magic in his heart. I feel like Martha with Mary when I ask him to clean. I never thought of myself as a Martha. His strength also is admirable. I don't think I could ever fast for twenty-one days.

At last I am intellectually convinced of the indivisibility and nothingness of everything, but to integrate this into consciousness is so difficult.

Babies are never angry. Unhappy and hungry, of course, but not angry. Anger may be a learned emotion.

MARCH 9

Jiko-san asked Roshi if I should go home, as duty would dictate, or stay. He emphatically said, "Stay." He said, for peace in this world Zen is necessary, and he has an idea for me to start a *dojo [meeting place for Zen practice]* in Ireland. Hmmm. In the far future it's a possibility.

I felt a bit upset because I didn't in my own mind know what to do. Finally a good solution hit me. I'd stay two years with Roshi but go home in July to help Mum move house, see everyone after three years' absence, then come back to Japan. Seems expensive but a good solution. Mom needs help, and I can explain my ideas better in person. Or better yet, perhaps she can see changes in me. I wrote her a letter stressing the academic things I could do here but also explaining my desire to continue to do zazen. I told her how much I loved her and thanked her. I'll wait for a reaction before I mention meeting her in July.

I've been made "altar boy" now. It's more interesting but hard to remember everything.

Yesterday there was a death ceremony. I tried to put all my energy into awakening the dead spirit, and the outpouring was powerful. After the ceremony, Roshi was telling the people the news of Toshoji and praising me. He's very thoughtful.

Jiko-san and I have been having a great deal of telepathy lately. It's almost chilling. I'll think something and he'll say or do it, again and again. He too was amazed and kept saying, "Who are you? Who are you?" He says many praising things, but I'm really not at all extraordinary, and I don't know what to say. I'm trying to avoid making unnecessary distinctions and having to respond to needless praise doesn't help. I was practicing sometimes not using "I," separating myself from my emotions.

Tessan-san started going on about how Jiko and I must eat the same food as everybody else. We weren't eating meat or fish. I feel peeved. Reminding myself that it wasn't really "I" who was peeved helped, but I'm still very much attached to my ego.

I stood by the open window in the warm spring wind, washing noodles. They were wet, soft, moving between my fingers. The moment was eternal.

Jiko-san said I was an excellent Zen *obosan [ordained follower of Buddha]*, and I realized it was the first time I had been called an obosan. It was very pleasing. He said he wondered if I was an incarnation of an old Zen master. He sees good in everyone.

Go Roshi said we must lead simple lives. Apparently he said the researchers were bad because they left on the light when they went away. I hope he didn't really say they were bad—they're forgetful maybe.

March 10

My mind these days is so much calmer, still hardly empty, but stiller. The kitchen is such a pleasure. Two years of daily dusting dustless altars would have been impossible drudgery. Ah, but the tenzo—every day different, a creation. Two years would be not only possible, but wonderful.

Such happiness of late. But there's still attachment.

That's why there's the fear that if I left here the peace might also leave. When even the peace isn't clutched at, then there'll be peace.

Holding up my soup *chawan [bowl, also soup]*, steam curling, all of us giving thanks, the miracle became apparent, the daily alchemy. This had been life, killed and now made me, made my life. Humble beans and onions passing into me, supporting me, becoming me and I in turn passing into nourishing beans or maybe onions. Endless magical stream, not really of creation and destruction, only a flow.

Funny how in front of seventeen people, most of whom I don't know, I can, as altar boy, make mistakes, be corrected and feel no blush.

The notion of a nation is to a country what ego is to a body.

MARCH 12

Zenkai [also zazenkai; Zen meeting or class]. Up late. Didn't want to get up in the morning. Got up. Yesterday the meditations were terrible, hardly there at all.

This morning at chosan, Go Roshi said the kitchen was the best it's ever been, always clean and good food. He said he left the whole business in our hands. He also said he wants Jiko to ascend to the highest level of the Soto sect. Jiko says he's not interested; as an ordinary man he's more free. I think I am still attached enough to ambition that I would at least be pleased and would not refuse. Or maybe not. Who knows? Today Tekkan-san's destiny is decided. I'd prefer him to stay in Kannonji so that I could spend the summer with himself and Kas'ko-san.

It seems that at zenkai last night, Go Roshi was very critical of Japan, of education, of modern, free-loving women. He said the latter will die (but who won't?). I don't know how faithful the translations are of what he says. I'd rather not think of him as being so all-condemning. Surely all is neither good nor bad. But then, maybe that applies also to Go Roshi. Because I love him so much, I want him to be perfect.

MARCH 13

Tekkan-san came. I was very happy to see him and he the same. He kept shaking my hands and smiling and rubbing my bare head, laughing. I wanted to get him a present to bring to Kas'ko-san, but when I returned he'd already left. He must not have been happy with the results of the talk, for he left hurriedly without a good-bye to anyone. Mio-san chased him on a bike. This morning there was no chosan, so we don't know the results.

I mentioned that I might hitch a ride and catch a boat to Korea. Tetsuro-san's eyes grew round with horror and he told me fantastic stories of gangs with knives, who'd pump me with heroin and force me to do strip shows, or they'd throw my dagger-riddled, bleeding body into the sea. Jiko was not so vivid but insisted I'd need fluent Japanese or I'd get lost. They would never be able to really understand me.

Jiko-san is in many ways wise and a wonder. His koan (very awkwardly translated) means something like "everything is okay." When I told him that this sometimes seemed difficult to reconcile with Go Roshi's *"dame,"* [that's wrong] he said he didn't have that problem. The koan was okay; Roshi's talks were okay; everything was okay. He's no longer bound by the formal, logical requisite of consistency.

At zenkai last night, Roshi talked about mu. How one must be totally involved with it. Dogen sat for one thousand days with mu and ten minutes of only pure mu is a feat for me. Paradoxical, these ancient masters, because their desire is so strong that their ultimate freedom from desire is total. If I could only be so impassioned.

I got a letter from some librarian who had read about me in the paper. He's going to Ireland in May and wanted me to teach him Irish.

March 15

Tekkan-san's fate is still not decided. Tessan-san's pre-priest ceremony was held this morning. He may have to replace Tekkan-san. At the ceremony I messed up my part but strangely didn't feel embarrassed. Nor did I mind shouting out my questions in front of everyone at shosan, though last night at the end of my introduction, I blushed deeply. I was trying to express the gratitude I felt to everyone, but Jiko didn't even try to translate. Translation can be a problem. At this morning's *shosan [questions in front of everyone]* I asked, "What becomes of dead people?" It was translated "Why do people die?" Go Roshi's answer was rendered as: "You study more Buddhism and you will understand that they do not die." He smiled his eyes into my eyes so sweetly, but Ho-san told me that that was an inaccurate translation.

A man came from Kyushu. He sits sure and solid as a mountain. His little son came, too. He sat through meals, squirming, wriggling, slurping, watching with a child's wonder-filled eyes. I loved to see the spontaneity. We "Zenites" seemed self-conscious by comparison, though comparison is not really appropriate. Mio-san corrected him. Each morning of the ten days they stayed, he got up brightly, in little shorts, behind a dim flashlight, bobbing in the dark. Exercises and zazen, he does the lot. He sat last night through all of zenkai. Our eyes caught, and we were shutting and averting eyes like young lovers. He finally giggled, and I tried not to look. Afterwards, I was in the kitchen washing-up and he came in and we laughed and laughed, though we couldn't speak one word to one another. Children are such noble teachers.

MARCH 16

My moods changed so yesterday. Afternoon, lovely zazen in the sunshine. Evening, distracted, unable to focus. I got frustrated; I'm hopeless, useless. I waited up to give Go Roshi a late dinner. He beamed, really seemed to emit light, and I was elated. He said, "*Saiko*" *[The best!]* but Tessan-san was outraged. However I made it, he said it tasted like water. Just can't please everyone. All my presents backfired. First the curry for Tessan. Then I wanted to buy him a pastry, but it turned out to be bread with chocolate on top. I wanted to give the child a treat and left it beside him, but he didn't realize it was his.

MARCH 17

Listening to music in Masato's room, I went to another world, my other life. He is a kind of bridge, some thirty years old, long, scraggly hair arranged to cover the incipient baldness. He is gentle and silent, a voice that coos "zazen" with the tranquility of the wise. Yet he only talks about his stereo and his memories. Perhaps he thinks it's all we have in common. But his peace is real. He hitched across the States and Europe, can understand me, knows the road. The music is American. We drink coffee but sit on the floor. And it's very strange. The room is chilly, not cold, just so the skin tenses and tingles. Roshi is out, the music loud. I'm internalizing the music, really am the music, transported, transcending. I can't help smiling. I feel I'm bursting, vibrating up and down my spine.

Mio-san took photos. I looked at mine and was strongly hit by having seen it before. In Masato's room, looking at the albums, I felt I knew all these people well, but couldn't place them. Odd.

MARCH 18

Jiko-san out chanting sutras. I have tenzo to myself, everything fine.

MARCH 19

Again alone in tenzo. I give myself plenty of time to do everything and find the cleanup goes as quickly without Jiko as with him. In the afternoon I read and meditated. I come down to a very calm place. Thoughts aren't fluttering around unbidden and I just do what I'm doing. It's very peaceful not having to talk. Mio-san is the only one who is in. I find I like him very much. He used to seem so intimidating, as if he were looking over my shoulder. I know he accepts and respects me; maybe that's the difference.

Go Roshi brings us each back little cakes. I'm very touched. More than a big present, to have taken the time to think of us and want to give us a little treat, is so very kind. I spend a long, long time ironing his kimono. Could have waited til morning but thought he might need it this morning.

Today dawned totally different. I knew when I got up that I'd be grumpy. I felt I hadn't slept enough, though it was more than usual. Into tenzo and Jiko wouldn't shut up, spouting nonsense, and I forgot to take Go Roshi the kimono. The marmalade that I knew Mio-san was looking forward to didn't turn out right. I put out the wrong rice, but it was tasty. Jiko ruined it by boiling and boiling it. I washed my hands of it when he wouldn't stop boiling it, but he told everyone it was my fault for doing the wrong rice. I had been proud that when I did the rice it was always good. So I'm annoyed, and still more annoyed at being so petty in giving a damn about rice. Back to sleep for two hours and the world is brighter. Yesterday I was so together, calm, big mind; today so trivial and frazzled.

Keep at it, m'dear.

MARCH 20

For a day that started so awkwardly, yesterday mellowed out nicely. I like working in silence, watching my breathing. Mio-san and I ate lunch in the kitchen. It was much nicer than the cold, dwarfing dining-room. It's hard to talk to him (language), but his good nature shines through.

Yesterday was the first day of spring. Mio-san hung out the flag. Birds sang, and the air was warm and dancing. We opened the windows, and I sat with Nakamuro in the sunshine. He is one of the most unselfconscious, wonderful people I have ever met. He's twenty but looks fifteen and knows many different disciplines. Body straight and supple, he bends effortlessly. It's a pleasure to watch him bow. He's always laughing, always helping, but never in a martyrish way. Always the kind word, ready smile, and gusty *"ohayo gozaimas"* [*good morning*]. Goodness is no effort to him, just an expression of his nature. He gave me a book and a painted fan as one gives a conversation.

I wrote 'Who am I?' I amn't; I am. In some senses am

and amn't. What sense is what? Is there any sense? It's all so confusing. I wish someone could just tell me all the answers. But I don't, really.

Jiko-san came home late, tired, his voice hoarse from all the sutras. The last couple of days, I've been rather ignoring him, having enjoyed my days of silence. Last night I listened and chatted enthusiastically, and to see his face light up made me feel ashamed.

I feel timeless, a kind of happiness trembling.

The child came to say goodbye. He reached out his hand, giving me a western-style handshake, said in English, "Bye, bye."

MARCH 22

Another quiet, peaceful day. It's raining. Twilight in the kitchen. The gentle snugness of warm and dry while the outside drips. Doing the ironing in long, smooth strokes. All day my breath is very slow and very deep, and everything seems to be a meditation.

I sit in the kitchen with my Japanese book. Mio-san comes down from chanting sutras and is poking around. "You are a great woman," he says. "*hai*" [*yes*]. I am very surprised. People have said that before and I can laugh it off. I know they only say it for irrelevant reasons—foreign and female. But he said it not in a flattering way, more like one speaking aloud to himself, not concerned with my reaction. I was so taken aback that I blushed a very deep crimson and could only sincerely say, "Thank you."

Got a letter from Mom. I've been watching the post every day. I had put my involvement here in academic terms and sounded more together than I feel. I will get down to that aspect and must see about books. It made me feel very happy that she understands and is resigned to my being away for a while, though would like if it wasn't so long. Says she was touched by my thanks for her sacrifices. I should have thanked her years ago. Puts me at ease. I think it would be great to go back for Christmas, then come back here 'til after summer. Funny, though, I know if I'd shifted the emphasis of my letter to a more spiritual one, that she probably wouldn't have been so accepting. Yet that's so important.

MARCH 24

The researchers tested me again. They didn't say anything. Just as well.

Jiko and I read sutra at Tetsuburo-san's house. Jiko has such a sense of fun and festival. He decided to turn it into a carnival. We brought all the drums, bangers, and clangers we could find. Bremen musicians. Tetsubun-san loved it. Trying to read sutra, we kept breaking down laughing. Jiko bought sake, and we drank and toasted and watched TV comics. 'Twas a grand night. This morning I whipped into action. During the last week, I've gotten used to getting right at the cleaning and getting it done quickly. Jiko was surprised, and it's hard not to just ignore him and take over. He leans against the fridge: "I've forgotten how to do the tenzo jobs. You've gotten stronger; you don't need me." I must not be overbearing. The tenzo is for both of us. But still he only leaned. Everything was done but the putting away, and I hoped he'd just do it. I began the laundry and the rice and finally asked him to put away the dishes. It makes me feel like a sergeant. I don't like that role; it would be terrible to get used to it. Working with Jiko is good for me. I can learn much from him, and he brings out in me many tendencies that I don't like but then I can work on them.

Tessan-san suggested that I go to Kannonji as kitchen helper with him. I would love it. I couldn't possibly be happier if I tried. He said to tell Roshi, asked Jiko to tell him. He didn't seem enthusiastic, maybe afraid of how it would alter his situation. Fingers crossed, but either way is okay.

Chosan this morning for the first time in a week. Wonderful to watch Roshi again.

MARCH 25

Last night we catered for a party of twenty. It went off grand. Tessai-san came. I was very glad to see him. Strange. He only criticized. Not like him. Hope nothing is bothering him.

I had a great time with Jiko. I used to think he is the variable factor. He is the only one who annoys me, therefore it's his fault. But in some of my moods he annoys me, and in some he doesn't. So I'm the variable factor. Thus I'm at least as much to blame and a lot easier to try and deal with.

Go Roshi left for Kannonji. When he got to the end of

the road, he turned round and waved his hat like a young boy going on a holiday.

MARCH 26

At nine in the morning Tetso-san says, "Do you want to go to Kamakura?" Okay. And we're off, and a wonderful day it was. The sun shone. We went to see the big Buddha. There we were—in Buddha. I was very happy and excited, the blossoms' sweetness blending with incense. I felt a great yearning, a child calling his mother into the emptiness, hearing only the silence of his own voice. Oh, how I was aching for *satori [enlightenment]*. If only I could be a child and hear the silence of my own voice. Walking, there was only sunshine and fun. We were the only obosans, but their evidence was everywhere in perfectly swept paths. Bowing, they let us into the temples—free. Two excited giggling schoolgirls tried their English on me and asked for an autograph. We came back late.

PART IV

Korea

I packed my bag for my trip to Korea and went to bed, but slept little and got up early for zazen. Jiko-san very thoughtfully made me gemmai. Tetso-san rose from his bed (after a hard night's drinking) and drove me to the highway. He asked several drivers until he got me a lift to a stopover. There I'd scarcely put out my thumb when a family stopped. The father spoke English graciously and took me about 200 kilometres down the road. Though I knew it would be more practical to look for a long ride from a truck driver (the family kept making stops), I liked them and decided just to go with my feelings. He was interesting, a leftist who told me about Japanese politics and education. He had tried the monastic life thirty years ago but got too hungry. I was surprised at the imperialistic wave of desire to convert him, but I resisted it. The little girl, who never looked me in the eyes, practiced her high school English. On the Tomei expressway, we discussed the relative attractions of the Beatles. She was glad to speak English. They fed me, then drove me to a stopover to find me a lift. They invited me to stay with them in Sendai.

The next lift was with three guys, little English but much laughter. We stopped at a café, and they said there'd be few rides to Shimonoseki so maybe I should take the boat from Kobe. But I want to hitch, so they take me to a stopover near Kobe. There are no cars for Kyushu, so I agree, it's the ferry. While one buys me juice the others secretly get my ferry ticket. They write a note in Japanese to show people for directions, then ask the steward and my neighbours to take care of me. Tears prick my eyes. Sunset is beautiful.

After I arrive at Kyushu, I cross to the mainland, hitching. The driver drops off his load, then makes a special trip with me to the ferry. The kind man at the ticket office does mine specially; then I watched the sea 'til time to go. I talked to a gorgeous Swede (does acupuncture) but felt silly as his girlfriend was there. A Frenchman takes lots of pictures of me with sunset, etc., but his movements are sharp and desperate, and there seemed to be a terrible rage in him. He kept following me around, and there was something about him I didn't trust. I didn't want him to attach himself to me, but wasn't one obliged to help a desperate man? I didn't know what to do, so I left to do zazen.

Everyone in my section was kind, talking to me, feeding me. I fell asleep early but was wakened by the New Yorker on my left talking to the Londoner on my right. Larry was talking about women and wondering aloud if Buddhist monks were celibate. I didn't really want to talk to them but somehow, late in the night, I did, and found they were grand. Poor Larry is lovely, but lonely. They're going to Seoul. I couldn't believe it when Jack said he'd lived in Morioka two years, knows Richard-san.

When I arrived Saturday morning, it's raining and the visa office won't open til Monday, so I tried to decide whether or not to go to Seoul. Then I schemed, thinking that if I went to Seoul I could probably stay with Larry and

Jack, but they didn't invite me. They talked about people I should meet but only recommended a cheap place to stay. I'm surprised and then glad, because I had been scheming. It's better that a scheme should fail and that I should succeed innocently in something else. Anyway, I was sure that good things would happen. They offered to pay my train fare, but I wouldn't let them. However, I carried a camera through customs for them. The customs inspectors, of course, only bowed and waved me on, delighted with the gaijin monk. The money changers, too, were charming. With robes and a shaved head is the only way to travel. In the waiting room all the foreigners are clustered. By this time we are all friends, exchanging addresses and hugs. The Swede lives in Kyoto. I liked his girlfriend but he was inattentive to her. I decided to catch the cheap military train. Jack and Larry insist on paying for the taxi.

After a ride through magnificent countryside, we arrive in Seoul. A thin man with the eyes of a child asked me if I'm a Buddhist monk. When I say "Yes," he asks where I'm going, then weaving in and out of the crowd he beckons me, leading me I know not where. I follow him to a bus stop. Then from his briefcase he draws a slender black book, gold lettering, obviously often tenderly held. He writes in it, thrusts it into my protesting hands, and bundles me on to the bus. The girl lets me off as he directed, but I'm lost.

Spying a gaijin face, I ask him, does he know of Hillside House? He does and smiles a faint, impish smile. "Are you going to speak there tonight?" "No," says I, quite surprised. "I sometimes do," he says. He works for the U.S. Army. Another one, think I, a bit patronizingly. He soon dispels that, humbling me. It seems that he takes in street kids. (Makes me think of my street kids in Cuzco.) He spends $1500 a month of his own money on them. He makes them work or go to school.

I go home with him. The house is bursting at the seams with slightly scruffy, smiling lads. He tells me their stories, of street fights and prostitutes, pimps and gangs. They look like such innocent children. He chides them in English. They love the excuse to mock wrestle with him. A girl sits in the corner, a bouquet of flowers on her lap. They published an article in the paper about him, and he got a wad of proposals. This girl insists they're made for each other and keeps popping around with flowers. He ignores her. He tells me about professional matchmakers and how society is strictly hierarchical (status and age). One uses different word endings depending upon one's relative position.

He gets one of the kids to take me on the bus to Hillside House, but first he phones to make sure there's room for "a priest he's sending over." The divil! He didn't mention that I was female and Buddhist. Mrs. Francis looked openly horrified when she opened the door to me. No room at the inn. I offered to pitch my bag in any old corner. Then she relented. Hillside House is just for Army people and Christians. Well, you can't win 'em all.

That night, Saturday, was Bible night. There were a

bunch of straight middle-Americans and fervent Korean converts. Debby sat opposite me, kept staring at my hair (or lack of it). "Well, I suppose it's easy to take care of, but how could you shave your hair off?" she kept stammering, shuddering, gaping, aghast at my bristles.

After dinner was religious discussion. The subjects were naive and kept returning to the threat of Communism. The Koreans, though very ardent, obviously knew very little about Christianity. Afterwards they gathered around me, especially the Koreans, fascinated, bombarding me with questions. Of most pressing concern to them was not why I was Buddhist instead of Christian, but why was I a Japanese Buddhist instead of a Korean one. They repeated, resentfully, that they had had 36 years of Japanese occupation.

On Palm Sunday morning they invited me to a full gospel service with the largest congregation in the world. I'd never been to one, so I was game. Didn't the people ever stare! But the service was frightening. Thousands of people swaying, sighing. It made me think of a Paisley or Hitler performance. The sermon was interesting, making the promise best suited to an oppressed people, the promise of future rewards. "The Lord wants men with dreams," that is, men with desire. Forget this real world and dream. Be good and get yourself a reward—always "self." But the scale was awesome, simultaneous video and translation. Clean-scrubbed Pastor Malone, with piercing eyes and a limp handshake, approached us afterwards with offers of coffee. Downstairs in the coffee bar, the pastor who had been most stirring was surrounded by buzzing followers. She had risen at the end to exhort the congregation into a frenzied praise of the Lord. Catching sight of me, she knifed through the crowd around her. "Buddha, Buddha, Buddhist devil," she shrieked. "Out, devil, out!" banging me on the head, the back, the chest. Laughing, I assured her I was no devil. She'd recover herself, then flail at me again, tugging at my *rakusu [item of a monk's robes]*, looking imploringly for someone to confirm her urge to rip it from my neck. The Francises and Pastor Malone shooshed me out, embarrassed. They then took me to lunch at the base, that little oasis of imperialism.

Coming back in the afternoon, Miss Kim of the previous night was waiting for me to take me to see some temples. We went way up a mountain. (The bus driver wouldn't let me pay.) The setting was magnificent, in a niche between two jagged peaks, nestled among wispy clouds, a waterfall coursing down the mountainside. The temple itself is painted in many bright colours contrasting with the simple grey robes of the monks.

I was very surprised to see so many women, mostly old. It seems that, if they are divorced or deserted, this is a refuge for them. Good idea.

They have a custom of bowing before the Buddha; the extent of devotion is indicated by the number of bows but marathons don't interest me. If I was a Buddhist devil in the morning, in the afternoon I couldn't have been more welcome than the Buddha himself. They laid before me a vegetarian feast of Korean delicacies and invited me to stay. I declined, but these *bodhisattvas [helpful, compassionate persons]* were wonderful, their hearts so warm I could almost physically feel heat. Bowing, smiling, radiating good natures, they drew me into their room, urging me to put on socks. (A marvellous system of underground heating makes socks unnecessary. The cold is really the only thing that gets to me in temple life. . .)

There were two older-looking gaijins meditating there. I was intrigued. The man wore a Mexican jacket, his long white hair swept back, the air of an artist. The woman immobile in a subtle camel coat, silver hair in a tight knot. I thought they were leaving and rose. His eyes, startling blue, caught mine and we smiled at one another. When they came out, they told me that she was a Swiss swami who had studied yoga in India for 20 years. She was amazed that I had been accepted into a male temple with no fuss. She'd read that it is difficult. They offered to drive us down to the town, then offered that I should stay with them. When we were leaving the temple, the moon hung full and luminous. Mists curled around the temple spires. Over a loudspeaker we heard chanting, the echoes reverberating. The cliffs seemed to call to the forests, chanting in reply.

Virjananda and Jimmy (she called him "the dreadful druid") took me to their immaculate apartment, tasteful but not lavish. There were Persian cats, a balcony, azaleas, and a lemon tree. She was a truly ecumenical spirit—a blossom lay beneath a picture of her guru with palms beside it from

Palm Sunday mass. They were overwhelmingly generous, wouldn't let me pay for anything, kept trying to give me taxi money, lunch money, bought me vitamins and a T-shirt and wanted to buy more. She was a real inspiration, meditates four hours a day. She gave me many warnings and exhortations. We felt uncannily close. (She's sure we've been involved in a past life.) People used to take Jimmy for Irish because he was so droll. He also likes to drink, and I felt a great urge to join him in a bottle, but under Viraja's purer influence, I refrained. The Indians are really into renunciation, unnecessary as a permanent way but good training.

When I went for my visa (I had forgotten my passport!) I ran into many people I knew from the boat. One man came up to me, smiling a timid, Japanese smile, said, "I saw you on the boat; hope you're well." An American agitator leaps from the doorway saying, "You must be one of the people I read about." (Some foreigners in a Korean temple.) Next thing, he's telling me all about strikes, wages, working conditions in Korea. Interesting.

The visa people were charming, didn't even charge me. I even met an Irish bloke there.

Miss Kim and I met for lunch. The visa people had pulled apart the folded paper that Go Roshi gave me at my initiation. Underneath a lineage from the Buddha, Go Roshi had written something that neither Miss Kim nor her Buddhist father could decipher. Then the owner of the restaurant introduced herself as a Buddhist of some high rank, and she translated the words into Korean. Miss Kim's friend explained it to me in French, and I tried an English interpretation. Who knows how close my version is? It seems that Go Roshi chose the following phrases from Buddhist texts just for me: "The person who follows Buddha's precepts and laws will attain great enlightenment." Well, that could hold for anyone, but still there was a feeling of being in touch with something ancient, secret, almost magical.

I then bought a few gifts to bring back, got good and lost, but saw a lot of Seoul.

Jimmy came home from work, and we had a warm evening, sitting, chatting, drinking Campari. Reclining in luxury on the black leather sofa, we talked about austerity— a delightful way to do it. They filled me with determination. Viraja, by hand, strung beads which were seeds from the Bodi tree where the Buddha was enlightened. She laid them on a vial of Ganges water and other holy things (whose significance I didn't know), packed me a lunch and other treats. She tried to give me $20, which I refused but later found in my sleeve. We embraced. "We'll meet again; we have before," she said. She was soothing while I cried. "You have it," she said. I couldn't believe her heart. As I was leaving, she stood behind the bars of her iron gates, hands joined, eyes lowered, chanting a mantra for me.

How can I ever repay the world the goodness that has so guilelessly been extended to me? Surely there is no bad person in the world and so many with loving hearts. My eyes were watering. I was sad, but somehow not sad, as if I wasn't leaving and had always been there, and as if all the kind spirits in my life have been one, weaving in and out, so they were never far apart. Viraga is a wonderful woman with a deep and daily spirituality, a part of her every act. Yet somewhere she seems to feel something lacking, as if there was something she hadn't burst or a peak from which she had lowered. I thought, what if I'd gone with Larry and Jack? I'd probably have enjoyed it, but what happened was so much more important.

Viraja and Jimmy advised me to catch the train; that seems best, as I don't want to miss the ferry. Again, like a spirit, a little old man appears and takes me where I need to go, then disappears. In Pusan I get on the wrong road and lose lots of time, but I finally get a lift. It was a truck driver, a simple man. We had to wait ages for his cargo, while he kept talking about how I can sleep in his bed tonight. This makes me wary, but he's okay, takes a beautiful mountain road. It reminds me that Japan isn't all concrete and wire. It's exciting to be back on the road again but I have no regrets about returning to Toshoji. At 6 o'clock, with still a way to go and drizzle starting, I knew he'd let me out soon. I didn't worry. I knew from experience that something would work out.

He drops me at a terrible hitching spot, by traffic lights and nearly in town on the wrong road, but two women actually do a U-turn to pick me up. At the station the older one, who is from *Eiheiji [Soto sect's main temple]*, buys me an express ticket and presses 1000 yen into my hand for something to eat. The train is about to go, but again I have tears in my eyes. How are people so kind? I feel almost humbled before such generosity. I don't know if I'm capable of it myself.

I arrive at Toshoji at a respectable hour, not too tired. There's someone in my room, a new dormitory student, but this one is a woman, Mayumi-san. They put her into the kitchen for training with the idea that she is to go to Kannonji as cook. I'm also to go there, at least for the summer. Mayumi-san is tall and timid, often quivering like a startled rabbit. She's hard-working, quick to laugh, and a joy to have in the kitchen. But Toshoji isn't what she had in mind. She wanted time for zazen but instead is thrust into the kitchen. At first I too resented all the time not spent on the mat, considered it time wasted, but it really is only a greater challenge. Her hopes are pinned on Kannonji. The first few days she couldn't eat in silence; it scared her. She'd giggle and leave half her food. Now it's okay. It seems funny—she knows she's getting married in the autumn but not to whom. Go Roshi tried to fix her up, but she'd have none of it. I think she'd like to marry an obosan. She's 27 years old, has never had a job, was groomed only for marriage, i.e., cooking, sewing, flower arranging, and the tea ceremony. Eeyuk! I wonder what's behind her interest in Zen. Good on her for trying.

Jiko-san was to go to Tokyo, so Tessai-san's wife arrived to take his place in the kitchen. She had been kitchen helper for three years, and anything different from her style was "*dame*" [*wrong*] right down to the way I'd sit. Still, I had to admire her energy and orientation. She was basically right and not bitchy but only strong-minded and rough in asserting herself. At the same time, Yugi-san seemed too intent on corrections. She'd say the rice was too hard, he that it was too soft, and both would nit-pick about trifles. At times I could let it run right off me, but at other times I was definitely niggled. It's easy to see how little control I have and how firmly entrenched my ego is. These things couldn't have affected me but for the idea of "I." It helped to try distancing myself and to look at the conditions which caused each to be so critical. This is a point which I definitely need to work on.

I had great energy when I came back from Korea. I needed drastically less sleep. However, my meditations were very flighty, and I'd want to get up from them. I got a terrible pain in my left eye, and Jiko-san went to great trouble to find me a chiropractor and to bring me to her. She is excellent, and my posture already feels different. She's a spiritual person, though looking coolly efficient in her medical gown. Seeing my sewing in a plastic bag, she gave me a homemade purse for it.

PART V

Spring
1980

END OF APRIL

Last night after washing up and a very distracted zazen, we called on Tetso-san. Suddenly he says, "Let's go to Ginza." So we're off, himself, myself, and Jiko-san, cruising through the flashing lights, priests of the night. On to Roppongi, where we go to a bar, the Berni Inn. I haven't been in a bar since I lived in San Francisco. I feel I'm encased by this red wallpaper, English crockery, dart board, and the sound of "old boys" English interspersed with the clickety-clack of Japanese. Too subdued for a pub, it had supermarket music and more sherry than beer. "*Namu myo ho renge kyo*" *[the chant of the Nichiren sect]*, said someone as we passed—a strange sight, I suppose. Two Japanese approached us, bought us Irish whiskeys. Jiko-san was getting definitely looser, laughing, boasting of how wonderful Ireland was. Very comical. He was in his element, with whiskey and an audience. I enjoyed myself thoroughly, laughed and laughed. Tetso-san was quiet, seemed somehow out of things. He was drinking juice (was driver), but it wasn't only that. Jiko-san was a riot. Often as I've cursed the old devil, I actually miss him now that he's in Kyoto. When I was responding to circumstances with my ego, feeling put out by criticism, or when Takeo-san would lose his temper over nothing, I'd think of Jiko-san. "*Ii yo, nandemo ii yo. [It's OK! Anything's OK!]*." Totally unflappable.

This morning Takeo-san blew up at Mayumi-san because she was slow at making tea. At chosan she cried and cried. I could empathize but could also realize how ridiculous it is to be put out by one of his explosions. He's worried about his new temple and says himself that he's neurotic. Watching his face, I thought how truly wolf-like he looks when he pushes his mouth out like a muzzle. When he raises and knots his brow, adjusting his glasses, his eyes become small and beady. They're close together, like the eyes of a wild animal, and he jumps up and runs like a wolf. I went out of my way to be decent to him so that I wouldn't feel resentment over what I knew was my stupid "self-notion." It worked incredibly well. When they are barking at me, they are victims of causes and conditions, but when I am gentle and kind, they respond accordingly. Then they, too, are *yasashii hito [gentle people]* and it's impossible to bear a grudge. It's true that if you love your enemy you have killed him for he ceases to exist.

I thought I noticed changes since beginning Zen. It seems as if I'm laughing all the time, but I can't really remember how I was before. I think I've always laughed, but I don't remember laughing this much. Looking in my tiny, grease-stained mirror, I can never see all my face at once, but I think lines on my forehead have smoothed out. My hunchback posture has become straight. I was very surprised, though, when the chiropractor said, "You have an abnormal spine—it's perfectly straight."

Eshin-san said last night, "Your face is completely different from when you first came to Toshoji."

Takeo-san agreed and I thought, "Well, of course, I'm bloody well bald."

Then he said, "Your face is shining; it is an enlightened face. Your friends will be surprised."

I'm still trying to work out the best way to deal with correction and criticism. At first I thought, "Well, at Kannonji it will be okay because there'll be no one over me. That was one of the attractions. Or, if I have my own dojo, then I can do as I like, etc. Well, I realized I simply can't always be boss, so I'd better figure out how to deal with it.

Then we were folding covers for the monthly newsletter and I folded a huge stack in half, which was wrong, and I had nearly finished redoing them when they told me I was folding them too wide. I had to start the whole stack again. Eshin-san said, "Even Soshin-san makes mistakes, even excellent lady." Well, that seemed so funny compared to my own self-image (where I'm constantly making mistakes and being corrected by myself or others) that I started laughing and laughing. It really seemed hilarious. Then poof, all tension was released. Doing the stack all over again didn't bother me. And it didn't smart when Eshin-san said "Soshin-san is good with her head but not with her hands." All was well with the world. If I can divorce myself from my ego enough to laugh at my mistakes, then I think this will be the most effective response. Now I'm eager for criticism so I can try it out.

While I was waiting at a subway station in a seedy part of Tokyo, I was looking at the daytime dead neon light, the sleeping seaminess, waiting for night. It's an attractive world because it's earthy and grubby, alive, real yet totally false without the pretense of reality. Vibrant throbbing music and bodies. I thought about the alternatives that confronted me when I first came to Japan last November—the usual job as an English teacher didn't interest me. Either monastic renunciation or sensory wallowing drew me. A soul seeking surrender? It was either accident or providence that the former happened first. Either way was a search for liberation—freedom from inhibition, from other people's values, from their suffocating puritan ethic born from the delusion of a retributory hereafter. Or else the other option, spiritual liberation, but from what? This one was hazier. Those who suffer want liberation from suffering, but I seldom suffer. My life has been wonderful, blessed. Who could enslave me? I did as I wished when I wished. Now I feel gratitude that this Zen way took me, because I consciously, fervently, could not be said to have taken it. Now I feel there is no turning back.

I've been reading an excellent book that draws the distinction between positive and absolute *samadhi [intense effortless concentration]*. This makes many things clearer. I understand the Go Roshi of dokusans and sutras, the Go Roshi of chosan and daily life. I understand why soji is so important and have slipped naturally into positive samadhi in the kitchen.

Someone said that we must take care of things simply because they exist. This occurred to me as I was sweeping the floor. In the dust pile there were 16 grains of rice and two tiny crawling things that didn't need to die. It felt neither good nor bad.

I look at the clock. It is two o'clock. A long time later

I look at the clock and it is only two o'clock. It is always two o'clock. I feel a great peace.

Preparations are almost finished for Eshin-san's ceremony. Tomorrow he will be a priest. The ceremony is very simple and thrilling. Outside hondo the monks bow, then we file slowly in. Takeo-san beats the hell out of the drum in a heart-pounding chase intensity. I clack two pieces of wood. Eshin-san holds a fan. Ping bell, clack wood, bong deep resonant drum. Everyone bows. Eshin-san does various bows, receives the stick from Jiko-san and holds *mondo [the asking and answering of Zen questions]*. Each of us in turn shouts "Shak'shawan," and then each strides up, kneels before him, and addresses some Zen query. Then bowing, retreating, we roar "chincho." The loudness of my voice startled everyone, especially me. I enjoy bellowing out. My questions are: "What is emptiness?," "What is Buddha nature?" "What is man before he is born?" After having them answered, I'm afraid I'm still not much clearer in my mind. . . . Then more bowing. We each in turn offer our congratulations. Pronouncement from Go Roshi. We bow, and it's over.

Nakamuro-san sits with his fan, all athletic tension. Takeo-san once said that I was like a mirror, reflecting back impartially whatever was in front of me. But I didn't really know what he was getting at until, while watching Nakamuro-san, it became clear. He is beautiful. Sitting like that, he must be in deep samadhi. He's always happy and helpful, vibrant with energy while there so profoundly tranquil.

I was physically born in 1955. Can I die and be born this month of *Showa 55*? *[1979–80, the 55th year of the reigning Showa emperor, Hirohito]*

KANNONJI, IWATEKEN
MAY 2

The second day of the fifth month of 1980. Twenty-two days before I celebrate a quarter century.

Sesshin has begun.

Dokusan. I did mu with all my heart and all my soul and all my being. Everything was squeezed out until my head touched the floor.

"Is it your mind or your heart or your body saying mu?"

"I don't know." Tears are flowing without reason; I laugh without reason.

"What is the difference between I don't know and mu?"

"No difference." Go Roshi whacks me.

"Ouch!"

"Who feels pain?"

"I do."

Then, when I'm not looking, he jumps up, embraces me. "*Bikkuri shita!*" *[You surprised me!]*. I tumble backwards, laughing. He holds my hand tightly, my thumb.

"This is I don't know."

"I know."

"You must see mu in everything." I leave dokusan, crying and laughing, with Tachibana Sensei apologizing for his English translation. That's okay. He encourages me.

I go to dokusan with Kobai-san.

"Where does mu come from?"

"I don't know—how can it come from somewhere? It doesn't have a place."

Kobai-san is very fish-like, cold comfort.

"We've all struggled with the problem."

"It comes from me," I told her.

"If that's your answer, go to dokusan."

In we go again. Go Roshi says *"zenzen wakaranai"* [*"You don't understand at all."*].

I'm crushed, devastated. Roshi says, "Next time, come alone."

After lunch we rest. I'm crying, feel wretched, forlorn. I can't do it. Tessan-san has such strength in his mu; the fellow in white has such persistence. I couldn't keep on like him. (I take big pauses between mu's). He thumps his head like little Sandra [the most disturbed child at Glencraig], bleating and beating. I lie down, weeping and mu-ing and half sleeping. I resolve not to go to bed that night or any night until *kensho* [*satori, or enlightenment*].

Going into zendo, I hear Go Roshi say something about Soshin (probably saying, "I was wrong; she's hopeless"). I'm called to dokusan. I feel so dejected, empty-minded. It doesn't even occur to me to wonder why Go Roshi wants me to come alone.

"*Mu—do? [How is your mu?]*"

I mu for him with all my strength, raising myself high and squeezing every bit of breath into mu until my head touches the floor.

"Once more again," he says in English. (He doesn't speak English, but I don't register surprise).

I do so.

Then "Once more again."

My first and only thought was "He may make me do this for ages." Then he jumped at me, grabbed me—"This body is *muji [the figure of mu]*, this head, eyes, ears."

Suddenly I'm laughing and crying muji. I don't even realize "Now I am muji," but I simply was muji and everything around me.

And he hits different parts of my body. "This is muji." Count 20 in muji—20 parts of me, 20 muji in Kannonji, all around me. We're holding on to each other, laughing and laughing. "Heart muji," he says, thumping me. "And Go Roshi's heart muji," I say, belting him back. We're embracing.

"*Kensho shita [You have realized your Buddha-nature]*," says he.

I'm surprised. I was too self-conscious even to know that it was kensho. Only when I got outside and was looking at everything and really seeing mu did I finally know. Suddenly I understood why we must take care of things just because they exist; we are of no greater and of no lesser value.

At dinner the only words spoken aloud rang in my ears, "*Maura-san go kensho itashimashita [Maura has seen into her Buddha Nature]*."

At first I was so exhausted I felt neither joy nor sorrow, just relief. The next day I was ecstatic, couldn't stop smiling. Then all was as before—or at least, so it seems. Everyone tells me I look different. It's hard to be sure. I can't be bothered looking for big changes. I began the koans and flew through about twelve. Maybe they came easily because of my reading. I don't know.

After the kensho itself, a wonderful thing happened. That morning I had been fed from the strength of Tessan-san's and the others' mu's. Now that I had been "passed," as it were, I felt the desperation in their calling and I put all my strength into mu. With each breath in I thought, "Tessan-san is—" the huge breath out was "MU!" I called and I called to him. He went to dokusan and had kensho. There was still work to be done. Tessan-san and I cried and cried to the other monk. He answered, wailing. In harmony we shouted, trying to urge him harder and harder. I lost myself completely. I was him, Tessan-san, mu, all dissolved. But he didn't have kensho. I resolved that if he stayed up late, I wouldn't sleep but would urge him on. He didn't stay up. I was exhausted. Everything was expended. My throat was raw. I lost my voice, couldn't speak for two days. Still I tried calling to him the next day. The other head priest thought it strange and asked me to stop.

I wonder if Go Roshi judges by the right answer or how it's done. Probably both. I hope I'm not cheating myself by knowing some of the answers, but am afraid that I am. Koans were great fun. Go Roshi and I dissolving into laughter, he jumping up, careening around the room, hiking up his kimono to take a dive into a fictitious sea. It was so much innocent play. Yet I felt I wasn't going deep enough.

At the end of sesshin was Go Roshi's *teisho [Dharma talk]*. He spoke about me, said of the 20-odd foreigners that he'd helped I was the purest. He felt me to be like his child and wanted me by his side until he died. He said his plan was to make Kannonji an International Zen Centre for me. He turned to me beaming, "*Wakaru? [Do you understand?]*" (He never addresses the audience in teisho.)

"*Wakaranai. [I don't understand.]*" I had to reply. I love that man so dearly that I almost cried when Tessan-san told me what he said. Still, I can't see myself living always in Japan, being an obosan. Though it would be a good life for me, I'm just not that pure.

Go Roshi left and we began to settle into a routine. Tekkan-san and Kas'ko-san were still here. I fixed myself a room in the loft of a storage hut. I love it. Up high I feel myself to be a bird in my nest. All around the eaves birds wing and poke, calling. Two huge windows and sliding door give good light and ventilation. It smells so wonderfully of wood and now of tatami. Of course they all thought I was quite mad, but Tessan-san now says it's the best room. I climb in and out a window, commuting from the main temple.

One afternoon, on a whim, Tekkan-san took us up the mountains looking at blossoms. We picked many wild plants, brought them home for cooking. Gathering our dinner in the sunshine from nature's abundance somehow all seemed to be as it should be. Tekkan-san can be so gentle and always totally immediate and involved in what he's doing. This makes him brutally honest and when angered he is totally angered. It really annoyed me, though, to hear everyone putting him down, bitching behind his back. Not a soul stood by him—only Kas'ko-san, who could hardly be said to be a separate soul.

Tachibana Sensei took us (Tessan-san and me) on a grand outing. We went to another temple. It's much older and much more beautiful than Kannonji, but really made me appreciate Kannonji more. We're very free here, plenty of time for zazen. They do little zazen, only maintenance. We saw some very beautiful sites. I felt possessed, no longer human (or extremely human); an incredible energy was surging through me, sparking, flashing, a pure joy. He is an extraordinarily good and kind man.

Last night after dinner Tessan-san played the guitar. Me sitting on the floor, drab grey kimono, bare head, bare feet, doing my embroidery. He singing from the depths of a world of memories and dreams, his journey and love of life. Yet there was only that moment, rich and vivid. He made up a crazy song about Soshin-san cooking delicious pumpkin even if it was a little old and hard. We laughed like drunkards who can hardly remember why. He's so Japanese, yet a dropout (as he says)—two years travelling, playing his music, yet his ideal is the little woman on whose pretty face he can gaze as they both sit sipping tea. The dear little woman for whom he will fight all day so that he may relax, bathing in her innocence by night. Doesn't he need some education!

Women really are repressed here, forced into the mold of a giggling innocent. At first I rather enjoyed the surprise and admiration with which I was treated. Now I feel its oppressiveness, for it's only because I'm female. My heart went out to Kobaisan. She wished she could sit as freely and naturally as I, but couldn't. Such a simple thing. Always raised to sit like a lady, she was too self-conscious to be merely comfortable. It's odd, though, that she too said I look Japanese. I don't understand how so many people can say that. My eyes are distinctly round and coloured; if I had any more freckles I'd have a suntan.

The only change I can put my finger on since kensho is in reading *ookyo [the sutras]*. Now I love to shout in a big booming voice. Previously I simply could not. It's such a relief to really shout those sutras, lose oneself. (I could even sing at Tekkan-san's party.) I finally realize the value of ookyo, but it must be done loudly, then the breathing is very beneficial. The "screamers" in Ireland possibly did catch on to something effective, although they seem to lack the integrative benefits of a 2,500-year tradition. I can see shades of many therapies in zen. I've started chanting "*Kanzeon, namubutsu, yobutsu u in . . .*" *[the Kannon Sutra]* while I'm working. It regulates my breathing, and I can work with less distracting thoughts and a greater sense of oneness with the work.

I planted veggies, built a compost retainer, am preparing new beds. I feel such a peace puttering around in the dirt with all the wiggly, slimy, ugly little creatures. The creatures digging and fertilizing the garden and worth no more or less than I. I'm careful about them now; try not to disturb them, carry them to appropriate homes when they take over indoors. At first I was put out that Kobai-san was doing the kitchen, but it's worked out perfectly. I'm learning more about Japanese cookery and get to work in the garden. I'm very, very, very happy.

I stood in the rain for the longest time without getting wet. Nobody knew. It was my koan. The rain noises were on cement, on stone, on my plastic mac. The bird in the apple blossoms shook the moisture from its feathers and sang. I, in sympathy, shook in my mac and was silent.

To become is not to annihilate. To become the quarrel does not really stop it. It both stops and continues it. Wet and not wet. Is and is not.

How can one be Buddhist and not be socialist? How accept and allow the perpetration of a system based on desire? A system that functions as trigger and effect of the desire for money and commodities. A system that, to feed itself, must resort to crass commercialism and ever spiraling desire.

I wonder sometimes about Kobai-san's relationship to her own sexuality. She is staying with us until a husband can be found for her. She's apparently not worried about facing her future as the servant of a total stranger and has no idea at all of marrying for love. At first I thought perhaps she had come looking for a husband. She seemed to know nothing about Zen but talked incessantly about how hard it would be to marry someone without any hair. Tessan-san, she says, is her favorite but she told him that she didn't like men, that she was afraid of them. Often she would avert her eyes from me, or put a book in front of her face, laughing, saying my looks were too seductive. One night she said something to Tessan-san, using a word normally only used between lovers or close friends. He was furious, railed at her without letting up for fully an hour and a half. Banging the table with his fist, spilling the soup, stubbornly refusing to eat, threatened to call Go Roshi, and said she was welcome to leave. Kobai-san barely spoke. She sat meekly, eyes down, fiddling and folding a crease in her apron. She seemed neither particularly cowed nor perturbed. I, of course, couldn't understand and couldn't possibly imagine what could provoke such a reaction. Tessan-san's entire face was transfigured, almost unrecognizable, fascinating. His eyes burned into her. He seemed not to blink, every muscle in his body tensed, knuckles turning white as he gripped the table. It was all that seemed to support or restrain him. The following day she apologized and no tension seemed to linger on either side.

Yesterday Tachibana Sensei brought me to a jazz coffee shop. Good feeling to it. The waitress said, *"Mora-san desu ka?"* [Are you Maura-san?] I was shocked. How did she know my name? It turned out that she is a friend of the editor of the local newspaper, who apparently spoke highly of my English. The result is that she, her sister, and a friend will come every Sunday to Kannonji for English lessons.

It seems that many American jazz singers come and she wants to be able to talk to them. She was delightful and I think we may be similar souls—rare enough around here. She gave us free cheesecake and promised to take me to big concerts in Tokyo and anywhere I wanted in the area.

Funny. . . . I thought of ringing Richard-san; then I met him. I wrote a letter to Jiko-san and found his waiting for me. Then a couple of coincidences with Kobai-san. Now Kobai-san is convinced I can read people's minds. The telepathy between Jiko-san and me was often extraordinary, but I have certainly no special powers. Kobai-san asks me if I chant ookyo only for myself. Of course, for whom else? But she is trying to invest me with some kind of mysterious character.

MAY 24

My birthday: Working in the garden, sure that today would be like every other day, but not particularly bothered.

"*Gomen kudasai [What is called instead of knocking]*." I went to the door. A telegram. For me. I've never had one in my life before. In inscrutable *katakana [phonetic script used for foreign words]*, it said "Good Morning, Happy 25th birthday," addressed to Soshin O'Halloran Sama, from some woman in Tokyo—I have no idea who! How did she know my address, age, Buddhist name? Who could she be? Possibly the chiropractor. . . .

I made banana pudding. Tessan-san said, "What, no cake?" I pointed out the absence of an oven. The closest we could come was "hot cakey mix." He made a huge plate of plump, delicious, greasy donuts. He brought the stereo into the kitchen. There was great fun and love in the air as we prepared. Me in my long ceremonial gown dancing to Steely Dan on the tatami. We split one beer three ways. Tachibana Sensei remembered the date and brought me a radio. What a man! "Do you like jazz?" said Tessan-san. "Yes," said I, while thinking to myself, I'd like Phoebe Snow. Phoebe Snow it uncannily was. Often, with very simple things like that, I think of something I want and it just comes. Strange.

Sitting around the table we whipped a candle from an altar, balanced it in an ashtray. Tessan-san played the guitar. I sat crosslegged in my robes, smoking a cigar and laughing at it all. A grand birthday.

MAY 25

The next morning, Monday, Tessan-san and I had our

first disagreement. On Sunday we had gone to the hot springs with Tachibana Sensei. I had, as usual, bought a little something for his kids. Tessan-san muttered "Oh, I must get him something, too." Next morning he launched into a lecture on why it was bad for priests to give presents. They were only supposed to say "thank you" and take. I was furious. The cheapskate, trying to twist things around. He said priests don't have money except what is presented to them to spend on their needs. I have very few needs, and I would damn well give presents until I really did have no money, instead of not doing so because I shouldn't have money. I shouted and argued, tripping over myself with rage. Then he rambled on and on without connection about various things, never outright attacking me, but saying, "You will get sterner with yourself," implying but not saying that I wasn't stern enough. He divided and separated us by saying, "You still have your foreign ways" and "I hate to have these discussions with a woman." I was so angry I knew that if I spoke I would cry and corroborate the "woman" bit. So I glared, bored into him with every iota of anger I could muster. I shredded him with my eyes. Merciless.

Finally I had to start cleaning but couldn't stop mulling the whole thing over. Why had I become so terribly angry? It was really a small thing. I've seen him now, arguing with everyone, and Tetsuro-san had warned me about his "new-priest-that-knows-it-all" ways, so it was easy to foist the blame on to him. But my reaction was exaggerated. I needed release. He was on his way out to school. It was the wrong time, but I called him anyway. "I was very angry with you. I'm sorry. Sometimes you act as if you know everything and nobody else knows anything." I don't know if he caught the latter. "Your face was terrible," he said, "your eyes—" We laughed. It was okay. We're human. Since then I've purposely discussed Tachibana Sensei's present. Thankfully, no reaction.

I have so little control really. The day before, I was bursting with joy. Every twitch of the breeze, ripple on the mountain, whine of machinery, everything delighted me. Then, boom, I explode at poor Tessan-san.

MAY 26

Kobai-san has been having a heavy dose of *makyo [distorted perceptions from zazen]*. She hears footsteps, sees many priests, sees herself as a young girl in a red skirt among the flowers. Hears ookyo and our voices. Seems to have a fixation around ookyo. She can't do it loudly in the morning but since the onset of makyo does it loudly each evening. The obosans may have to do with her fear of them, as in Toshoji she feels there are people behind her.

Once she realized it was in her mind, she felt better. I slept beside her for a couple of nights. Zazen really does change consciousness. Just as consciousness-changing drugs may prod hallucinations, so will zazen. I'd love to understand the whole thing.

MAY 28

Kobai-san seems better now. Though I can't talk to her, I'm very fond of her. She is so honest and candid—inhibited but not too inhibited to admit it. She wants to touch us, but can't. I try to make light of it, chase her around the room, threatening to tickle her. She doesn't know what to do. She says I have many faces: beautiful, pretty, angry, child-like, frightening. People react to me differently of late. It's strange sometimes, my face is too bright, like glaring sunshine. The child said I look totally different and now look Japanese. The foreigners came and were fascinated, stared too long—perhaps it's the shaved hair. No, it's really odd. I look in the mirror and don't know. I don't know how I looked then and how I look now. It'll be interesting when I go home for Margy's wedding—hope that little sister of mine is doing the right thing.

MAY 30

I had my first zazen "student," Richard-san's English student. He came to meet me. Tessan-san invited him to my Sunday morning classes. It was a fiasco. His English is too good. I said I had no time. He asked if I had time to talk about zazen each day. That was my duty. I said there wasn't much to say; it was a question of doing, but I'd give him time before soji. He wanted to know all about English manners and customs. He came the next day. I talked Zen at him. He didn't seem interested. I felt tricked. He only wants free daily English conversation lessons. I'd give him a few more days and then get tough. Next day he asked me to teach him how to sit. I did. He was so enthusiastic, so hopeful, it gave me real pleasure. Then he stopped coming. I truly mustn't be a bodhisattva, for I felt a little relieved. Then he came again. I'm glad.

JUNE 1

For Tachibana Sensei's birthday I pushed my exhausted self, spent quite a bit on food and presents, cooked and cooked, decorated the sitting room. He phoned.

"Happy birthday," I said.

"But it's not my birthday."

"Ha, ha, you can't fool me; I remember you said May 31st, a week after mine."

"A mistake. I meant March."

What a laugh! So he went along with it and we had a smashing party. Then off to the jazz café. The atmosphere was of the wee hours of the morning, snug, not quite asleep, a warm cradling sensation.

The wasp and lady-bug invasion taught me plenty. *Busshari-to ["The Hall of Buddha Relics," where ashes of the cremated are enshrined]* was overrun with them. Tessan-san sprayed. I brought up the Hoover, but it seemed wrong to vacuum up the live ones and have them suffocate in its dusty bowels. What to do? One by one I picked them up on the shovel and put them outside. It took ages. Each time I cleaned Busshari-to, it was the same. It was annoying but I had to. Yet somehow, in an ever so slight shift of focus, it brought home to me that I am no more and no less than, and not separate from, a fading ladybug or a dying wasp. Respect life, not because it's right or good or moral, but because it is. It's a nuisance to pick up the sesame seeds one by one when everyone has finished eating goma *sembei [sesame crackers]*, to eat the potato peels that the others don't like, to chase and rescue even a single grain of rice. That the single grain of rice is all rice is all things, is nothing, is value-less, that there is no value and not-value great or small; only is. As I swept up the corpses in Busshari-to, I realized I was distinguishing life from death.

Each day in the garden I explain to the weeds that they do not really die; they change form, as they are doing any-way. Yet I distinguished. I didn't want to pick up the cadavers with my fingers. Clean-dirty, dead-alive, even plant-animal (for handling dead flowers caused me no qualms). So for training I made myself pick up all the dead flies, spiders, moths, and bugs that crossed my sweeping path. Not really so bad after all, though I'm still more inclined to use the broom. Have several times just forgotten and picked the thing up.

I love getting filthy in the garden. The others get dis-gusted. I had an interesting dream. Rushing to work in a place like Dunster [restaurant in Cambridge, Mass., where she worked in 1979], I jump off a bridge-like thing and land on a table where a nun is selling potato cakes. My filthy shoes first, then I sit on them. I begin to eat the ones I've destroyed; she gets almost hysterical: "You can't eat them; you stood on them, yuck, dirty." I'm in a hurry to work, trying to eat and explain that I dirtied them so I must eat them; no one else will, so they mustn't be wasted. She's in a flap. Finally she calls Reverend Mother, who is also upset, but acquiesces. I, thinking, how stupid, wolf the cakes, dash to work. I explain to the cook why I'm late. He laughs. Obvious dream elements—Buddhist/Catholic contradiction; the potato skins I made myself eat; Tessan-san saying my feet were dirty, the endless waste that revolted me at Dunster.

Sesshin Toki [time for intensive zazen]. Someone made a mistake on the announcements and hardly anyone came. Go Roshi was not perturbed but changed sesshin into zenkai, so fewer sittings of zazen. Pity.

It was a pleasure to see him again, an inspiration to watch him peeling an orange; he was deeply involved in the tearing of each vein. How many oranges had he peeled in his life, yet still enthralled! Watching TV. When I first came to Tokyo, I heard the TV from his room. I thought, "How insensitive his wife is," felt somehow superior to this soap-opera-addicted woman. She moved out, and still the TV blared incessantly. Roshi himself watched it. "Oh, well," thought I, not really knowing what to think. Now I could watch him watch. He is so totally engrossed, a child pulled right into the screen. Beautiful. I remember how the Ryans used to invite Scott to watch TV so they could watch him. Go Roshi was the same.

During the zenkai I was given a koan about a man digging a hole and not getting to the other side. Tetsuro-san's translation left out the fact that the question was "Why couldn't he get through after having dug the hole?"

Go Roshi said my answer was that of an unenlightened person. I was crushed. It tore open all my insecurities about whether I really had kensho or not. Later I gave a similar answer—that when digging there was only now, no after digging, therefore no through, only in the tunnel and digging. Roshi said that was the answer to a different kind of koan and explained that the man was universal and greater than any of his creations, therefore greater than the hole. Still, all my self-doubts were triggered.

He said the koans would get more difficult (a warning, perhaps), and he hopes I run away to Ireland (laughing). He asked me to stay ten years.

"I don't know," sez I.

"Nine," he bargained.

"Eight and a half," I offered.

He offered me his room at Kannonji instead of my loft.

"*Yuck, iranai,*" [*I don't need it*] I said, and he laughed. Always laughing. What could possibly disturb him?

During teisho, he said that I alone could become the greatest woman priest. (However, the competition is not exactly overwhelming.)

The final day of sesshin/zenkai, the TV people came to film me. They were fascinated and alarmed at my room. "Aren't you afraid of ghosts?" is the universal reaction. Even educated Japanese seem to be obsessed by ghosts. They eeked and ooed and generally fussed outrageously as they lugged the camera and lights up the ladder to my loft. They were funny. I liked them but felt silly talking about myself.

"Why did you do Zen?"

I told her the story about Ciaran [an old friend who became a Buddhist monk in England]. Afterwards, thinking about the question, it seemed like something I never decided to do but something deep inside that I knew I was going to do, not with a sense of determination but in the same way that I know Monday comes after Sunday. Inevitable.

Kobai-san was funny after seeing the documentary thing. She started calling me *Kannon-sama [Blessed Kannon, the Buddhist Saint of Compassion]*; she loves idols.

Go Roshi's 70th birthday-cum-book publishing-event was at a hot springs hotel. I barely finished my present for Go Roshi in the lobby below. Many masters had gathered for the occasion. They were beautiful men, radiant. Each gave a speech. At my turn I fumbled and blushed; how could I put into words what I felt? Lear's youngest daughter. Tessai-san's wife told me to give my present. I didn't want to in front of everybody, but I did while she blithered on about it taking three and a half months and me finishing while everyone slept. I was crimson. He passed it around.

The roshis were amazing, on the stage fooling around,

as innocent as babes. Those knowing sages, knowing it all, were leaving all knowing behind and just doing. There sure as hell is something in that Zen. Go Roshi, cancer-ridden, celebrating his 70th birthday. The night before, he chose his gravestone; tonight they hurl his tiny frame in the air, catching him three times. He laughs good-naturedly. I went to pour him a drink. He grabbed my hand, pumping it vigorously (they love an excuse to shake hands), saying, "Thank you, thank you," in English. I was crying.

I had to take my turn on the stage. Amazing—it didn't faze me to have to sing a song. I didn't use the mike but boomed around the hall with all the strength the ookyo had freed. I bobbed around making a fool of myself with the Japanese dancers. Okay.

Dear Mum, Margy, Scott, and Beth,

Phew! Am I exhausted! We had a sesshin where a bunch of people came to the temple. It culminated in a memorial celebration of

Roshi's 70th birthday, so there was a ton of work before and after the whole thing. The actual celebration was at a hot springs. So very Japanese, with the women all taking baths together and the men likewise. Then there was a big spread upstairs. Although I hadn't realized it, Roshi is very famous, and great Zen masters from all over Japan came for the occasion. (As usual, I was the only foreigner and the only woman monk. Only recently I learned how unusual my experience is when I heard of a German woman who bullied her way into a man's temple but was never allowed to wear robes or to be a monk. Interesting. Most temples won't allow men and women to study together.) Anyway, they're marvelous men, these old monks. They're like children, joking and playing. One old fellow gets up on the stage, a revered and respected Zen master, hikes up his robes, straps a pillow on his back and dances a strange dance about a "babe" on his back. Roshi just had a huge definitive book published, so that was also being celebrated and we were each given a copy. (Much of it is written in the script I've learned, so I'm struggling to read it.) They all took turns singing and of course I had to do an Irish solo. (Blush, blush). Luckily they didn't know how the tune was supposed to sound.

The ladies were all swaddled in pastel kimonos. Several of them did one of their abstract (to me) Japanese dances. Then I was dragged up to join them. I tried to imitate them but they resembled *fluttering butterflies, while I looked like someone shovelling snow. The difference was much more than a pastel kimono.*

There was no doubt that it was a Zen party when, at the end, we went around from guest to guest graciously putting their left-overs into our boxes. We're already sick to death of them after only one day.

It's nice to be back at Kannonji again and to be living in the country. Although we're near the highway at the front, out back rice paddies spread to the mountains, punctuated by bamboo groves. Less romantically, the buildings are full of creepy, crawly creatures.

In the midst of the preparations for Roshi's ceremony, we had an entire day of interviewing and filming for television. They came again this morning to film my room at the top of one of the wood sheds. It's really just a platform, and the women from the TV studio were terrified they'd fall over, so they clung to the wall. They kept mumbling that they were sure living in such a room was good for my ascetic practice. In August I've been asked to give three talks about Ireland and about my life, during a three day UNESCO confer-ence. . . .

Love, M.

JULY

My eye kept causing me trouble. Takehiko-san put in needles and electrified me, but the eye is as bad as ever. I went to an Occidental doctor, who gave me some drugs to mask the pain. I won't take them. I bought a massager. Maybe by loosening the shoulders I can help the eye.

KANNONJI, IWATEKEN
JULY 20, 1980

Dear Family,

. . . glad to get the invitation to Margy's wedding. It looks so official. Things must be hectic there. It's been that way here, too. We had dai-sesshin, the biggest sesshin of the year. However, the usual kitchen helper was called to Toshoji beforehand, and the other monk was busy learning to drive, so alone I did all the cooking, cleaning, weeding, flower arrangements, and sesshin preparation throughout this big temple. After all that build-up, I was exhausted, then did five days and four nights of zazen. But strangely, after the second

day of sesshin when I was most tired, I broke through a block and got a sudden, huge, unexplainable surge of energy, which took me right through sesshin, not tired at all. Now I'll take it easy for a couple of days before going off to the coast for this UNESCO conference. And soon after that I'll be heading off to Maine for the wedding. I leave Tokyo August 17th, so see you soon.

Last night, for a complete change of pace, some friends took me to a country festival. One of the mothers dressed me up in a kimono, binding my waist so tight I was sure my ribs were crushed. It was great fun, with all the little girls decked out in kimonos, beautiful origami chains festooning the streets. But it was so different from South American festivals, where everyone would get roaring drunk while they banged out the same tune on whatever would serve as an instrument, stumbling and stomping insanely til dawn. The Japanese version was much more restrained, prettier, understated, much bowing and fanning. Lovely, but I think there's a bit of the Latin in me.

After the festival the same friends took me to a jazz club in Morioka. The group had finished playing and were sitting quietly getting drunk by candle-light under the dark wooden beams of what could have been a Breton grenier. One of them was American and hadn't had a chance to speak English with a native in a month. When the gaijin in the yellow kimono with the punk haircut came in, he felt he had to invite us to join him. So we wined and chatted into the wee hours. We must have squeezed in an hour and a half of sleep before getting up for zazen and sutra. I'm writing this after breakfast as we await the arrival of thirty school kids coming to learn zazen. Should be funny. Anyway, must iron my kimono, change the flowers and whip up to the shops on the old temple bike. See you soon. . . .

Love, M.

JULY

My kid sisters, Kate and Margy, are both getting married! I can't believe it. I feel much too young to get married. Lately, I've been thinking of staying ten years to become a master. Then I wonder if I'll miss out on some love-type relationship. I'd be 34. But, really, I don't think it will be a problem. I feel that there'll always be men.

I worked hard on my koan and had a few really good sittings. I was wooden Buddha and flame. All must change, but nothing really changes, as it is always changing. As nothing really exists, how can it cease to exist? The flame is no more permanent and powerful than the Buddha. They are all muji. There is always change, change we perceive and that which we don't. We perceive change in relation to fixed ideas, but it's really not fixed, thus not a change. Words tricky, but inside it's crystal clear. A little breeze became a raging gale; it's changed yet not really; both are only particles of air in motion.

I did four nights of all night zazen, starting June 22nd, the longest day of the year and my longest night. It was incredible. The first night I kept thinking all beings are Buddha, could feel it. I felt totally purged, riding some high crest. The 2nd night I kept thinking no separation. The next day, pulling weeds, they were part of me but different, like the back and front of my hand are different but not separate. Taking a break, I drank a cup of coffee. It was like no other cup of coffee. It was me, like sucking my own blood, but more intense, as its familiarity was shocking. The third night "There is only here and now" reverberated in the corridors of my mind. The fourth night was bad; I kept nodding off. I love doing all night zazen. (I lie down for about an hour.) My eye went gamey on me. I want to do very hard cultivation. Already after only two days I've lost intensity and am as spiritually gross as ever (though I had a nice little samadhi this morning). I keep thinking that ordinary effort gives ordinary results. Before, I was looking forward to going home, but now it seems like an interruption.

I've been having some cases of telepathy. I got a beautiful letter from Jiko-san, full of Buddha and very supportive of me. He's going soon to his temple—Buddha and he are waiting for me—he underlined. The temple was meant for us, etc. He really is very pure, very good, but I wouldn't be into it at all.

Go Roshi came up for sesshin. I had been slaving. Tessan-san had most conspicuously not been. There were too many weeds. We were scolded. I couldn't stretch myself any thinner and resented Tessan-san, resented when I had to do all the work. All Kobai-san's and the little he had, was left undone until I did it. While he smoked, listened to music, I ceaselessly scrubbed, cooked, pickled, and did zazen, then hated myself for resenting him. If I was truly involved in my work, I wouldn't be looking to see what he was or wasn't doing, wouldn't be measuring and comparing.

Go Roshi asked if I could hammer. I said I could. Together we went out to nail up the donor plates. I did the top row, he handing me each one in turn. I was rather proud of how I handled a hammer. When we came to the bottom row, he did one. He licked the nail, and with two blows of the hammer it was firmly affixed. So we continued, I doing the top row—tap, tap, tap—he the bottom, strictly, smoothly. We laughed and giggled at my clumsiness. Each board seems funnier, our heads coming together like conspirators in laughter. Tessan-san came back from driving-school. He took the hammer from me.

"Man's work," perhaps he thought. He did it better

than I, so I relented but the fun dissolved. Roshi returned to his room.

I decided to do a really good sesshin and stayed up each night doing zazen. During the days Tachibana Sensei had to go to school, so no one could translate my koans. Sometimes I went to dokusan alone. One time Roshi asked me about my sisters' weddings and then when was I getting married and to whom.

The second night of sesshin, the young priest seemed near to kensho. He went to Busshari-to. I was doing zazen above him and came down to take a break. He and Nakanagi-san had joined one another in Jizo-sama's room [the room of the bodhisattva who looks after deceased children and prisoners]. As I gulped my coffee I felt a sense of mission. I'd help them that night. Going back in, their mu's were flagging. I started crying with them. All night we roared. When Nakanagi-san began to doze, I shook him, crying into his ear, holding him, guiding him to the window, anything that he might continue. The young priest kept going of his own accord. I had to stay strong, when we were all fading, had to bellow a mu that would resurge us. Mu seemed to throb in my *hara [belly]*, seemed to be a pump surging up and down. I became them, them me, all only mu. It was deeper than anything that happened to me before kensho, first time I'd done mu 'til morning.

Nakanagi-san had kensho next day, but the young priest finished sesshin without it.

PART VI

Resuming

After a long absence, I resume. Ireland over, weddings, ups and downs. Margie's not so good but Kate's was a laugh—parties, singsongs with Chris, the best man. Me playing the spoons, all of us battering, rejoicing into the night. Cooking for weeks ahead. Orange ambrosia and mushroom soup forced on all who entered. I'm extremely happy about Geoff. I couldn't stop smiling throughout the ceremony. Many flirtations and reunions. Comforting to know that men are still falling in love with me and friends are still close. But it was hard to walk home alone by the canals after the last pint, the last bus, past the strolling couples, their greasy late night chips steaming from yesterday's newspaper. I had a lost feeling, wistful, not knowing for whom or what, for my practice that's not as good as it should be, for the lover, so wonderful, that I've yet to meet? Or was it just the whiskey and the damp? Who knows?

And who cares, for as time went on I felt less frantic, less constrained to live all that I was going to live in those six weeks. There was much love, deep warm womb love, coming from those I was afraid had forgotten me. It took a little time to bridge the gap, the missing years and sharing, but it was all there still. Much to do. They wanted me to give a talk on Zen; some wanted to train; the politics pulled me. So many places to extend myself, but first I must train myself, and rigorously.

Back at Kannonji, I was surprised to find that Eshin-san had run away. The stories . . . In a way I was relieved. My training would improve and their terrible pressure to marry me off in May would be gone. Apparently in my absence this plan was even more formalized. Tessan-san is kind but severe, teaching me ookyo, screaming at me. I can't understand the Japanese, don't know what I'm doing wrong. Tears come but they are like sweat, an excretion. Inside I'm not really affected. I don't dislike him (though he shouldn't take pleasure in his role), am not angry or really upset. This is the first very definite progress I can see. I'm grateful.

Kannonji, Iwateken
November 12, 1980

Dear Mum, Scott, and Beth,

Phew! Back in Japan at last! You must be back in Maine by now, Mum. Hope your trip was less eventful than mine. I got to London with no trouble except for the ton weight of baggage. Then going out to Gatwick I made every mistake in the book and ended up on a train that sailed gaily through Gatwick, hurtling out into the countryside as my plane prepared for take-off. Arriving at the desk in the airport, I asked the attendant what was the next one I could catch. "Sorry," says she. "This is an Apex fare, good for one flight only. Your ticket is now worthless." I nearly died. She must have seen my face falling nearly into my runners because she took mercy and said she'd pretend I'd rung up beforehand to cancel. That way she would only charge me the cancellation fee. But that was still £37.75, and sterling at that. I guess my face didn't rise much because she finally took pity. "Don't tell anyone or I'll lose my job, but I'll reissue your ticket." What a relief!

Had a stopover in Saudi Arabia. I only saw the airport, but it was odd to see the men in the lounge in full desert gear and the women hidden in their long, black tents. Our next stop was Hong Kong. I had a whole day there, time enough to wander around and be glad to be getting away from it. It's a huge, hot, teeming city, totally Asian in feeling despite the Western-style skyscrapers. I thought I was beyond feeling squeamish at marketplace sights after a year in South America, but I have never seen so many slimy things writhing, wriggling, being slashed, scraped and gutted, in any such a tiny area. Everyone seemed to be involved in some kind of carnage, but the day of sunshine did me good.

When I arrived at Tokyo, it was the middle of the night. I knew the gates would be locked at Toshoji, so I decided to snooze in the station until it was time for the early morning train north to

Morioka. I found myself a bench and settled in. I suppose every self-respecting Japanese has a home to go to, so my fellow bench-mates seemed to be mostly down-and-outs and drunks. Just as I started to doze, one rather inebriated character decided he had to welcome me to Japan and to practice his English.

I can guess what his contact with the tourist industry must have been since all he knew was "Hello" "No, thanks" and "Get lost." Then one of the better dressed ones, who was a mute, set himself up as my protector; he wouldn't let any of the other curious or friendly bums within yards of me. The shock came at one a.m., when the train station closed down. All the subways had stopped, and all at Toshoji were asleep. Using signs, gesticulations, and little drawings, my mute got it through to me that there was an all-night cafe nearby. There, for the price of one expensive cup of coffee, you could try sleeping to the thump of Japanese rock music. That seemed to be what all the clientele had in mind as they sprawled across tables or hunched in their chairs. At four a.m., when the station re-opened, my escort accompanied me back, ascertained my train, and sat patiently for another two and a half hours until he saw me on to the train. I was so touched by his kindness—and we couldn't even talk to one another.

When I got back to Kannonji, I was amazed to find that the monk who'd been here when I left in August had run away. (They always seem to run away rather than give notice.) Another fellow has been sent, at least temporarily. In Tokyo this one always seemed *surly and very bossy, so I wasn't exactly thrilled. But I just do what he tells me. He works like a wild thing, which is great. Luckily my Japanese is still terrible, because there was talk of giving me a crash course in ceremonies and leaving me to run the whole thing! So we'll see what happens with this fellow. He doesn't know any English at all, but so far we're getting on fine. But facing into this eternal winter, it crosses my mind that I must be crazy or masochistic or something. Oh, well—it sure as hell is good training. The Army couldn't be much tougher. Anyway, m'dears, I must go gather wood for the bath fire. Think of me when you turn on the central heating. (I'll try not to think of you at such a time . . .)*

Love, M.

DECEMBER

December 3rd was the first anniversary of my arrival in Japan.

Shimo-san has been sick. Exaggerating. Looked like a pig peering from under the lurid pink blanket.

I went to dokusan. There was much questioning about letters and return dates. It seems that Go Roshi had a premonition I'd return before Kate's wedding. So much for premonitions.

I passed the koan of the big and little mountains. Now am free from desires, ambitions and attachments, can do real action, not just reactions, being led by the nose. No longer does he accept blindly but is free to accept or act because he can accept. It's real because it's the action of the real man.

The snow has started. It's still novel enough to be beautiful. It lies a white cushion across the mountain and rice fields. Somehow the world seems new, an infant, untainted, quiet, sounds absorbed by the snow. The mountains echo a deep silence pierced only by the occasional cry of a crow.

DECEMBER 9

Hondo—dust, shoji and sweep; *Ue [upper levels]*—feather-dust & sweep; *A-Genkan [entrance where footgear are left]*—sweep; H-wind *Roca [hallway]*; Zendo —dust, shoji and sweep; kitchen, roca and dai-genkan—sweep, *renshu [practice]*.

DECEMBER 10

Busshari-To 2, 3 and 4: Vacuum and do stairs, damp towel but not take down, dust walls.

Shimo-san has gone to Tokyo for 10 days. Whether he is here or not is equally okay. I'm amazed. In Toshoji he was the one spoiling influence for me. I didn't want to be stuck here for the winter, didn't want to be with him, didn't want to do takuhatsu. I wasted much valuable time and energy pondering how to avoid doing these things. Now I've asked to do takuhatsu—even alone. (I'm sure there'll be times I'll regret that.) Life with Shimo-san and winter are fine. He was sick for a few days and rather repulsive. The combination of his expression and Asiatic features gave him a distinctly Down's Syndrome appearance. After he recovered from his sniffle he was marvelous, always laughing, writing me little songs, helping me at every turn. I have to admire his hardworking nature and generous heart.

Tachibana Sensei had me over at his house on Sunday. We sat under the kotatsu watching an old black-and-white English movie. It was bliss. Cream cakes, apples, and brandy. There was no more in the world to ask for.

These last two days, alone, I slept later than usual. The first day I forgave myself. "It's merely conditions; you'll get down to it." Today I was disgusted with myself. My zazen is not good or strong enough for nonsense like missing a sitting. In fact my zazen seems very bad. I know that is only a thing of my own creation—"good zazen/bad zazen"—but it reflects where I'm at, which is a pretty unadvanced state. Nuts. Get down to it!

Dear Mum, Scott, and Beth

. . . *Back here the picture is still unclear, but will undoubtedly sort itself out. The new monk here has a bit of a chip on his shoulder, as he's been a zen student for five years but hasn't managed to have kensho yet (the initial breakthrough). So he feels that all the younger trainees who've had kensho have to be shown that they're not as great as they think they are. At Toshoji all he did was argue, so I decided to make things easier for myself up here by doing things his way from the start. The first few days he pampered a cold, sat all day beneath a pink blanket, looking for attention. I'm afraid I was less than sympathetic and Florence Nightingalish. However, he recuperated and attacked the wood-chopping with admirable vigour. Soon my attitude towards him completely changed. I did as I was told, so there were no arguments. We actually had great fun in broken Japanese. Then this monk had to go back to Tokyo on business, and I was left here on my own. I was managing morning and evensong in dubious Japanese. (The lengthening or shortening of a syllable can change the whole meaning, so who knows what I was saying?)*

Last night, just as I was finishing dinner, a shout came at the door. A monk had arrived from Tokyo to keep me company for the next ten days. He's a bit of a character. I remember that last summer he asked to become a priest and Go Roshi threw him out on his ear.

I wonder what happened in the meantime. He talks to himself and grunts a lot and does everything the opposite way from the other monk and insists he is right. I wish there were some definitive authority on the subject. It's confusing changing everything around with every new face. Next month will be the begging, so there'll be a bit of a gang here. Maybe by then they'll have found someone else.

The weather has turned quite cold, but I wear my Goodwill duds under my kimono and scarcely feel it. I look a big lump, but who cares? Tachibana Sensei [the local high school English teacher] *takes good care of me. Last Sunday I went to his home. We watched an old Gary Cooper movie, ate cream cakes, and drank brandy. I was in my element, loved being with a family on a Sunday afternoon. Of course nowhere nearly as good as my family, but still very warm and kind. . . . Happy, happy, happy Christmas!*

Love, M.

DECEMBER 11

I finished dinner and was reflecting on the fact that it was one year to the day since I became an obosan. Led to the inevitable pointless analysis of change, progress, etc., getting nowhere fast. Then a shout came at the door. Go Roshi had sent help! This bloke is a right character. He does everything differently from the way Shimo-san does them and insists he's right. He was here last summer, asking to be an obosan. Go Roshi got rid of him—yet here he is and apparently knowing it all. He's obsessed by food, continually grunting, groaning, smoking, and talking to himself. His breathing (significantly?) is really quite strange. I was sitting in the kitchen doing zazen, basking in the warmth of the wood stove. He was inside, laughing away good-o to himself. "In this Zen, it's marvellous," thinks I, "anywhere else he'd be thought quite mad." Ah, well. His smile is great and he's good about soji. Either way, it's only ten days.

DECEMBER 13

Shimo's really quite a character, still snorting and adamant over tiny details. He's advanced a lot in koans and I can see why. He has the talent of losing himself totally in what he's doing. He still has a very sharp ego but that only proves to me how much of an ego I still have. If I didn't, I wouldn't be bothered protesting when he insists I do something I know is unorthodox. However. . . .

I could have punched him out last night when we went to Sasaki-san's. That dear old woman is always giving us food and help, so much so that I'm embarrassed to go down with him. He goes down (she's busy, but he plunks us there anyway), and the first thing he says is "Obachan, there are no flowers in Kannonji," with a big peal of laughter from him. She is mortified, apologizing, explaining the price of flowers, the price of the train, wringing her hands, telling him to ask Jakuda-san, not her. She keeps bringing up the subject, obviously disturbed. She tries to tell him some story about the temple; he's only laughing insanely, she shrieking "Listen to me, listen to me." In desperation she tells me the tale. I pretend to understand. She gets out her precious goeka instruments, is playing us a tune. It's beautiful, the expression on her face, mellow, intent, holy. He laughs, halfway through, "We have no more time; must go." For a fraction of a second she looks crestfallen, quickly recovers, finishes her tune through his departure noises, and then she mutters on again about the flowers.

DECEMBER 14

For the last two days I've been able to enter a shallow samadhi. The exciting part is that I have some measure of control over it. As Sekida [in *Zen Training*] has pointed out, it's fundamentally connected with breathing and posture, though his exact methods don't work for me.

Today I feel rotten. For the first time I feel like quitting. Other times I've felt like leaving, but always in the future at a definite date. Now, because the future has no definite date, I just feel like leaving. I won't, of course. I know it's only a mood, and it's quite obvious what's brought this mood to a head. Last night Tessan-san was to phone for takuhatsu information. I left the information and went to the *onsen [hot springs]* with Tachibana Sensei. It happened so quickly I hadn't a chance to think, but about two miles down the road I regretted going. Sure enough, Tessan-san was annoyed that I wasn't there. Knowing that threw me into a kind of wretched mood—totally stupid, the kind of thing I thought I had gotten over. I thought things no longer disturbed me, or at least, only affected me on the outside. Nonsense, another disillusionment. Every time I think I've progressed, I seem to mess it up again.

I volunteered for, insisted on, takuhatsu. Now it seems so ominous. They predict this year to be very severe weather; this time no gloves. It's been nice sleeping in the living room while Shimo's gone. When I'm feeling down, I try to cheer myself up with little perks like that. It would be nice to have someone I could talk with. I don't actually feel lonely but do enjoy company betimes. Before, I always used to console myself with the thought "Ah, well, it's good for me." And it is, yet I feel I could live a more natural life in the West and still continue training. Bah, I know this is just a mood. It's infuriating to be such a victim to moods.

DECEMBER 15

Such a day as yesterday I wouldn't like to go through again in a hurry. My mind was in such a whirl and confusion it's hard even to recollect my thoughts.

I hated him [Shimo] for a thousand little, insignificant things. The fact that they were trivial and insignificant made me hate myself. One year of ascetic practice and I seem to have got nowhere. I sliced through my finger, through the nail; the tip was held on by a sinew. He grudgingly bandaged it, asked nothing about how it felt, only grumbled about my not watching the fire. I felt vaguely hysterical. Did I need stitches? Would I be fingertip-less? Hating him was only a projection of my mind. What blackness was there in my mind. I lay on the floor, cold, tired, still pumping blood, the room so smoky my eyes stung, and I cried. For a long time.

Tachibana Sensei phoned; he was alarmed to hear my voice. He took me to Morioka. The poor man didn't know quite what to do with the sobbing female but was wonderful. Just to unburden myself, to have someone, anyone, to talk to. We drank coffee between philodendrons, his eyes heavy with concern. "There, there, it only proves you're human. Human relations are important." It was a combination, I guess, hating Shimo and his bossiness made me unduly upset at having angered Tessan-san (by missing his call), my finger, the oppressive greyness of the weather, shoveling snow. . . . I felt trapped for months in the cold, and was secretly dreading takuhatsu.

December 20

On the 15th I looked at the calendar and could scarcely imagine lasting the five days until he left; the first five had seemed eternal. He even spoiled the thought of returning to Toshoji, for there I would be with him again. I comforted myself, trying to see the bright side—like the fact that I could sleep in the living room. Big thrill.

But he left yesterday and by then all had changed. I knew it was my mind's projection. We talked; he drank sake, his face turning red by the fire. He never offered me, the guest, any, but it didn't matter. I couldn't understand most of what he said, but that didn't matter either. The warmth was there between us. He said I seemed an extraordinarily happy person. That made me laugh and laugh, having tormented myself so over the last few days. He was earthy. He showed me innocently how to work, to throw oneself wholeheartedly into one's work. (I'm practising Dokusan with some minor successes). More than any koan, he was a living koan, singing and hearty.

Me and my day of sobbing was all only mood. Now it's gone, released. The pressure of the resentment I felt towards him was checked from anger, so flowed down in tears. Yet it was so encompassing—my very being. All the while I knew it was my own creation, that I was free to rid myself of it, but I couldn't. I, me, my ego-self, was the mood; now it's over and that self is over. The "I" constantly mutates. It has no "essence." Yesterday, alone, I felt very happy, very at peace. "What is it that I lack?" Nothing, absolutely nothing. But that is equally a mood. Because it is more pleasant, I would like to see it as somehow more real, truer, always there behind, but in the same way it will come and go.

Things are resolving themselves nicely. I wanted eggs—expensive, I won't. Then Chiba-san brought them. Tessan-san told me to buy *geta [wooden platform sandals]*; Chiba-san says that for a New Year's present she wants to give me geta. I dreaded no longer sleeping in the living room when Shimo comes back, but realized that if I sleep in the little room I can easily warm it. That was a real weight off my mind, one of my greatest sufferings (amn't I weak?). So I feel sure that takuhatsu will be grand. The dread is gone. The trapped-by-winter feeling is gone. I don't mind at all doing all the work by myself. I'm surprised. Soji just doesn't bother me any more, and I feel no urge to skip or shortcut. I have things organized now; there's time for the temple and for me.

Eshin-san wrote again, a beautiful letter. His love is so pure, sincere, and loyal, much truer than I deserve. In my reply I told him about Killian. It only seemed right. Not that Killian is by any means "the man," but I still do not feel committed.

DECEMBER 22,

Still alone and happy. Winter is very much here. In the mornings, getting up at 3:25, it's extremely cold. During the first few days and leading up to the 14th, I strongly resisted the idea of winter. I felt trapped, fed myself lines like "this is the last winter," "Tekkan-san and Kas'ko-san managed," "Only four months," etc. None particularly helpful. Now, strangely, it's changed (not through any heroic efforts of mine.)

In the morning, delivering *buppan [little rice offerings placed before Buddha statues]* at 4:30, I warm my feet on the cooker afterwards, hands like clubs; the same during ookyo. It stings to touch the metal door handles; the buppan are frozen. These days I feel cold, but that's all. There's no comment; my self isn't resisting it nor having to persuade it. Like the koan about not getting wet, I'm cold; of course, I'm cold, but not really cold. Takuhatsu will be fine, and I've wasted so much energy worrying about winter.

KANNONJI, IWATEKEN
DECEMBER 26, 1980

Dear Mum, Scott, Beth, and Jane,

Hard to imagine that you're basking now in Florida sunshine as I look at the falling snow. How was your Christmas this year— beaches and coconuts? Probably as different from our Park Avenue ones as my one was. (Somehow Park Avenue always seems like it was really Christmas.) I have been minding the temple alone of late until the beginning of next month, when a bunch arrive up from Tokyo to beg. The first couple of days seemed a bit lonely, but when I felt a little lonesome I made myself go do some cleaning, and then I was fine. Now I really like having the place to myself—perfect peace and quiet, no one bossing me around, I can do things at my own pace.

Christmas Eve we had a small blizzard. At the start of the blizzard, I took off into the woods, not to be daunted from my celebration, and lopped off the top of a little pine tree. Between the prints of two celestially borne Buddhas, on top of the telephone table, I set up my tree. Trimmed it with old bits of ribbon and some "things" I cooked. No oven of course, so I deep fried and frosted some things with a texture reminiscent of doughnuts and a shape like Christmas balls. (I tried stars, it took all my trigonometry to cut out a pattern for one, but I guess I never got far enough in physics, 'cuz damned if they'd keep their shape. So much for Christmas and higher education.)

Meanwhile, the snow got more insistent. I was doing evensong—the introduction "Dai hi shin dharani" is followed by an impressive drum crashing. Right on cue as I thumped the drum, the power failed. I finished evensong squinting in the twilight, then whipped a candle off the altar and hightailed it back to the kitchen.

I stoked up my fire, sat down to watch the snow fall by candlelight. It was very quiet and peaceful. It had the "peace on earth, *good will to all" quality that Christmas should have. All that was missing was you guys, but you were in my mind. Not able to read or do much of anything, with no light I settled down to meditate for a while.*

Hardly had I tucked up into a lotus, when Tachibana Sensei burst in like Santa himself, bearing a bag of goodies. Behind him his two sons, like Santa's little elves, came bumbling in ready to tuck into a feast. Tachibana Sensei, bless his heart, brought not only crackers and sweets but a little naggin of whiskey (for the cold, of course) and a Gateaux "Molly O'Rourke" fruit cake. I was stupefied, made right in Dublin. Someone had given it to him five years ago and he'd never touched it. (Must have known a Dubliner would be around for Christmas sooner or later.) I was a bit wary of it, Gateaux cakes at their freshest can often taste like they're five years old. Didn't know how this would be, but time cures all ills (or something). It wasn't just good, but the best fruit cake I've ever had. Must have been the whiskey. Cake with a vintage!

So we sat round the stove in the winking candlelight, chatting and laughing. The kids were delighted at the Christmas tree; it looked better in the low lighting of a one-watt candle.

Christmas morning after breakfast I sat down (with another slice of fruitcake) to open my presies. Thank you. Bethie, I opened yours first, as I could guess what it was, and I played it while opening the rest. A very nice choice of music, it made me feel like I was back at home. I was dying to dive right into the book, Mum, looks great, not only Rome, D.C., and Korea, but the hero spent part of his childhood in Dublin. I've heard it's very good and someone else said I really should read it. Thanks. I hadn't the chance to sit down for a good read, as I had people coming for a ceremony and a heck of a lot of Christmas Eve blizzard to remove before that. It was the first ceremony I've done alone, but it went well. Christmas was a spectacularly gorgeous day — blue skies, virgin snow, and that savage piercing winter sun that transforms everything to crystal.

Last night I was exhausted and ready to call it a day early. Didn't feel much like cooking, so my Christmas dinner was a simple rice gruel and piece of tofu. At least no worries about Christmas calories! (Actually it was very tasty.) Did you have all kinds of tropical treats? I suppose you ate out, hope it was good. Takes all the work out of Christmas, leaving all the fun bits, I hope.

LATER

Well, got in my western Christmas-cheer bit after all. A bunch of the Morioka gaijins got together for some traditional fun. Had a bonfire, sung carols in the snow (snowballs and all). For dinner everyone brought a dish. We were American, Irish, English, Afghani, Iranian, and Indian (no Japanese at all!) so the dinner, far from turkey and ham, was very exotic, but finished by mince pies. We all regressed, as we reverted back to childhood memories and party games—even pin the nose on Santa. Great fun altogether.

I'm dying to hear about your Florida festivities. My love to the Sweeneys when you see them. It'll be great having a holiday with them. Richard, who gave last night's party, says he'll make some tapes for me. Thanks for the blanks and the vitamins; they'll be good to keep me fit for begging. I've been holding onto this, hoping to hear from you, but no news. Hope that means you're having an excellent time. I'll pop this off (and probably hear from you immediately).

Love you all dearly, M.

P.S. *To Scott and Beth, my heartiest congratulations on your report cards. Those were excellent grades, but even more important than the grades themselves was how they pleased Nana. She wrote telling me how proud of you she was. Making her happy is even better than being top of the class. Anyway I'm proud of you both, too (but don't get swelled heads or I'll bash 'em down). Love yis.*

DECEMBER 27,

I told Tachibana Sensei about Eshin-san's proposal. His reaction was shocking. It almost frightens me, the suddenness and depth of emotion with which the Japanese can respond. You feel you're always sitting on a potential explosion. He talked nonstop for two hours, carried away, repeating himself, then recovering himself. Eshin-san shouldn't be allowed back. The hara-kiri mentality—He explained he was of the old school, but . . . I was a bit shocked at the end of the session. I was afraid ever to have anything to do with Eshin. Mentally I prepared to write him a letter of rejection. The next evening he phoned.

He declared his love, sounded as if he were reading lines from a play, though I'm sure he's sincere. When he hung up, tears came into my eyes. Why? After talking to Tachibana Sensei, I'm worried about his coming back.

Christmas Eve I was a little lonely at the edges, so I packed myself off to do soji. It worked. Then I lopped off the top of a pine tree during the blizzard and covered it with colored ribbon, then deep-fried overiced "things." The electric power failed. Dinner was by candlelight—gruel and cabbage. Watching the snow fall, so soft and firm like a mother patting her baby to sleep, by the gentle glow of a single candle, I felt quite still and at one, in peace with the world. No Christmas Eve celebrations, and it didn't matter. The lights were out, so I settled down to meditate by the wood stove. Tachibana Sensei burst in like Santa, bearing a bag of goodies. Behind him, his boys tumbled in like elves. He brought a naggin of whiskey and the best fruit cake I've ever had, made right in dear dirty Dublin and enjoyed in Japan. Looking out the window, the candle seemed to glow inside me, but the wood fire seemed to crackle from inside, too. Felt so happy, so simple.

Christmas Day saw loads of snow to shovel and a little unwrapping ceremony while I had my fruitcake breakfast. It made it seem as if the family were here. The day was too sparklingly, spectacularly beautiful to feel homesick or lonely. The sun, dazzling on the virgin white, was elating. In the morning I did my first ceremony alone; it went well. The rest of the day no one came around. Christmas dinner was tofu and rice gruel. Very delicious. No complaints.

Being alone these days, I can work at my own pace. The division between work and rest seems not as sharp and, interestingly, I get flashes wherein time actually feels subjectively different—where it is now totally, not overshadowed by other. Never realized before how very "not-now" my ordinary consciousness is.

Two gaijins are coming for the takuhatsu and Tessan-san will do tenzo. Wasn't I daft to have been worrying? And isn't life grand?

JANUARY 6, 1981

Takuhatsu has begun. I'm tired, but it's okay. Last year I could only survive by promising myself never again. Now it hurts just as much, but it's as if it doesn't matter. I feel I could go on and on. I'm working hard. In the morning I do buppan or *chokka (ino)* [morning prayers], walk for three hours, rest a half hour, then soji, practice ookyo at 3, at 3:30 collect buppan, at 4:00 do *banka [evensong]*, then every second day I cook. Up in the morning at 3:30 for zazen; evening, too.

Shozan-san has left. Tessan tortured him. He was slow, slow of wit and body, but quick to laugh and share a biscuit. He was always apologizing, grovelling, smiling. He used to be a taxi driver; it shows in his servile manner. Tessan grew impatient, wanted to teach him, and the only way he knew how was by shouting. He picked him up on any little thing, roaring, swiping, even throwing a soup bowl at his head. He left, driven away. Then a poor innocent came who'd never done zazen. He wanted to stay a while. Each took turns exercising ego at his expense. He lasted a night and a day. It was interesting to see how Tessan's relationship with us depended so much on having a release. Shozan-san was his fall guy, and we were marvellous. Shozan left and he laid into us. Shimo-san came, and the foreigners became excellent, whereas Shimo was crazy. But he'd hold his own in a fight. The first night they roared at each other (the night the innocent newcomer came for his first taste of the monastic ideal). Tessan-san seemed pleased—an ally in his camp. Together they bitched about Tessan, and it provided release, but Tessan-san missed Paul and Galli-san. "At least they were normal," said he.

We did have fun with them here. The western youth in me that lies dormant so much of the time in this male, Oriental temple life came out. Galli-san whipped tuneless, heartfilled songs from the guitar; I played the spoons. (Paul composed one about Maura of the mountains and a great one about "I hate takuhatsu, I hate the snow, going back to Tokyo.") After Shimo came, Tess' reaction was to go mute, hang his head, and be as surly as possible. At first he maintained his pleasant disposition towards me, but after a while, during the day, that disappeared too. He wouldn't answer my greetings, made huge fusses about nothing. There were periods, then, when he had to take out his frustrations on me, and he'd blow his top over trivia, especially if I did something like give Tess a cup of tea at an inappropriate time (i.e., anytime). But at least I could understand that it wasn't really me, that he just needed a release. Usually it was grand, though at times I, too, needed a release and cried. It was all so obvious, one bouncing off the other, none with real control, a series of moods, pressures, and repercussions squeezing back and forth in a box. (But at night he usually became charming again.)

Tess did carry *kanshugyo [practice in the cold]* to extremes at times. He wasn't doing it himself, admitted he disliked it. (One of his favorite lines to me when anybody made a mistake but I was to be blamed was "You wanted to do takuhatsu; you wanted to." Although I had never complained, it seemed a fixation to him.) Food would be hidden away. He'd stop me from cooking anything vaguely interesting. Tessai-san was suffering from acute war pains but would sit freezing in his room rather than come in to Tessan's company. I really had to beg Tessan and use all my influence to get him to let Tessai-san use a heater (paying for the oil himself).

Meanwhile, Tessan slept in the warmest room in the house, snuggled into the *kotatsu [a quilt-covered foot warmer]*.

As for us taking turns at tenzo, he did take advantage. His errands were always on my days off, and several times he just plain told me to do his turn. I didn't really mind, though. It's better training the more I have to do. (Bed by 9:30, up at 3:30 to do zazen). But although I didn't mind the work, at times his bitching got to me, and I must admit that when the backbiting started, while I didn't really join in, I also didn't try to bring about reconciliation. That was wrong of me. I feel it strongly. Ultimately, in a situation, it all doesn't matter. Whether we criticize or praise, it all passes, it's all empty, all phenomenal, so I might as well try to make peace in those situations. I, too, was just reacting to situations—or rather the tentative "I" is merely a reaction to different events. All during kanshugyo I was very aware of the passing, phenomenality of circumstances and people. It was so obvious and made everything easy.

Truly this takuhatsu seemed to go fast and was not hard, yet my frostbite was terrible, bleeding and oozing pus. (Though I could have worn gloves, I only did so on a couple of excruciating occasions.) My room was freezing (no heat). Paul came in and was really shocked by its size and temperature. (What with my head in the closet and my feet at the door . . .) Working most of the time, just no problem.

Last year, however, I suffered more. Trying, subjectively, to recall, it seems as if I had more highs off takuhatsu last year. This time it was just something I did and got on with it. There were some lovely moments, though. Sometimes you could actually feel an energy of givingness and purity from the people, and I'd feed off it, feel it surging through me, my voice becoming loud and untiring. Sometimes after *tenjin [a refreshment after takuhatsu]*, sitting by the altar, soft candles glowing and warm welcoming home, having done *choka [morning sutras]* before dawn and walked, roaring, all morning, then offering ookyo again, a wonderful peace seemed to pervade. I was not only here and now, but the whole universe was, and stopped. Everything was very, very still. (Often in the distance, especially when we'd come home, I'd hear sutra-chanting—usually "*Namu ki e butsu.*" ["*I take refuge in the Buddha.*"] Strange, as we weren't chanting that. And one time I heard the Kanzeon Sutra with Paul's voice; mild hallucinations).

Then, on several occasions during our breaks, people gave us tea and senbei, toast, okashi, or pastries. Oh, but they tasted good! Incredible. I wished I could always appreciate each bite, each sip, with such relish. At times I felt guilty—all these people giving, giving. Little old ladies running after us in the snow, people stopping their cars, young children on their way to school, workers on the upper stories throwing money out the windows, giggling. And why? So we can live. They'll never come here, never be refreshed by the peace of Kannonji, by a good sitting in a quiet zendo. They're all so unselfishly giving only so that I can carry on my practice. I owe them a debt, the debt of my self-oriented (though there is no self!) practice. It's a huge debt, one I'm inclined to shirk.

I got a cat, Gion-chan. At first I felt like a new father being handed twins, awkwardly holding them—"Now what?" But she's lovely. She rides on my shoulder while I cook and keeps me warm at night. Sometimes she's obnoxious.

Tetsugen-san wrote me three letters and sent two parcels. He comes on the 8th. I think it will be good. One of the ladies said my complexion has changed. Tachibana Sensei says I look younger and seem stronger. I think I only look plumper from eating loads of sweet mochi rice cakes. Tessai-san, because of his dislike of Tessan, was inclined to exaggerate the extent to which I've been working, so now everyone thinks I virtually carried takuhatsu. But it's not so. I worked, but not very much more than usual. It just was no problem.

JANUARY 8

I realize how easily people are fooled in spiritual affairs. They want to believe people have attained depths and to feel associated with the extraordinary. At Jakuda-san's, after dokusan, a new woman was seated with us on the floor around the kerosene stove. They were all devout old women, religion the most important issue in their lives. Transposing cultures, if I were with these same kind of women in my own Ireland, I'd represent the antithesis of all they devote their lives to. Here, in a culture totally foreign to my old one, I not only sympathize with them but am even more involved

159

(fanatical?) than they. Strange. . . . The new woman asked questions about me, and they began talking about me, not telling untruths, but the things they selected to point out made me seem special, deep—even the shine in my eyes. The woman seemed almost infatuated, holding my hand, gazing into my eyes, saying how glad she was to meet me. It made me wonder if there are hundreds of unscrupulous people with as little insight and understanding as me, masquerading as being in some way developed and capable of teaching. Irresponsible.

During takuhatsu I got a letter from Jean-Luc. The first time. I hadn't heard from him in almost a year. I dreamt he came to Kate's wedding; the next day this letter arrived. I was thinking how I'd made a bit of a fool of myself writing five postcards but with so little response. I sent him a Christmas card; he didn't answer. Then next day, this letter. Lovely. He's very interested in Zen, wants to be my student in Zen. He signed beautifully in English, Spanish, and French. I allowed myself the luxury of daydreaming about him a bit. He's spending next month with his girlfriend.

Many times during the past year I wondered if I wasn't somehow missing out, vaguely feeling that by the time I re-entered my old world everyone would have settled into couples. Those feelings aren't there anymore, partly from having gone home when I did, partly from feeling there will always be men, and partly from not caring whether there are or not. It just doesn't seem to occupy my mind. I suppose now that I've said that, it will become an obsession. It seems as soon as

I recognize any change or progress, its opposite makes itself apparent.

January 10

Tetsugen-san arrived and seems gentle and undemanding, helpful and appreciative. He has a quiet nature that is at times tinged with sadness but he is usually smiling. His kidney has been removed, and twice a week all his blood has to be cleaned by machine. He has been practising for ten years and seems to me to be much more of a true priest than Tessan or Shimo. He has no need to assert himself egotistically. In fact, he is perhaps too humble, saying that he's disappointed with his progress so far.

I didn't realize quite how basic Tessan-san's and my life here were until Tetsugen-san came. Even in the depths of the northern winter, we didn't use a heater and only lit the wood stove a couple of hours a day. I was used to doing breakfast and buppan with numb fingers in temperatures of -9°C. I couldn't believe it when he offered me a stove for my room. (However, I refused.) He even buys food. For months now we've been surviving on a basic diet of *daikon [Japanese radish]*, cabbage, and rice. Tessan-san didn't want to use even brown rice, because it took an extra five minutes of gas to cook and that was a waste. There are little things, like the fact that now we don't have to keep boiling the same tea leaves all day, so they were only bitter. I used nearly to blind my eyes trying to make out the tiny *hiragana [phonetic Japanese characters]* in the morning dimness; now we can use a light.

Yet Tessan-san provided a good training, for now I really don't care one way or the other about such things.

JANUARY 12

I feel very glad to be young, not just mentally (as I sometimes feel) but physically. After shovelling snow in the sunshine, my body felt strong, straight, and young. It was wonderful striding through the snow, shovel on my shoulder, breeze in my hair.

JANUARY 15

Buddha's *inaku naru day [the day Buddha entered Parinirvana, left this world]*. I tried doing zazen all night. Very cold. Not very good.

JANUARY 16

I'm amazingly untired. All day and when I'm falling asleep a voice resounds in my head, "I am empty, I am impermanent." There's a peace about this voice; it keeps other noisy thoughts from entering.

After his trip to the hospital, Tetsugen's arm always hurts, though he says that otherwise it's not really painful. When he comes back he looks weak and drained. Often he looks grey. His eyes are close together, so from the side they're scarcely visible. He stares into space and seems colourless, eyeless, lifeless. Other times, he's full of energy but talks little. He's very good to Gion-chan, who lately has been driving me bats. She's been bringing out the worst in me, so I imagine what it would be like to be re-born as a cat and try to treat Gion as I'd want to be treated.

We're having a spring thaw. Beautiful—a black old man pushing a black barrow, etched against the wintry fields. The mountains breathing greys, blacks, whites in mists of *sumi-e [ink]* paintings. Coming home in the dusk from the onsen, I wanted never to stop. . . .

Dear Mum, Scott, and Beth,

Glad to hear you enjoyed your holiday. Lucky divils. Sounds like you finally got the Christmas you've been wanting, Mum. Scott, how was your birthday? What did you do to celebrate? If you took any pictures, I'd love copies. Any more good ones of the weddings? I thought the photos in the paper were good, though not Geoff's best angle. Beth, how are your rabbits? I got a new kitty; she's all black and full of mischief, and I'm mad about her. (She's sitting on my lap right now trying to capture my pen.) She keeps me lovely and warm at night. I gave Mu-chan your letter, Wiggs. She was very pleased, but it took her three days with a dictionary to read it. She promised that she'll answer you, but she may be slow. She wants to go to school in Ireland and wishes you'd come to Japan so that she could meet you.

Back here, begging has started, and the temple's been like a 3-ring circus. Of the people who came for begging, two have run away completely from monastic life, and two returned early to Tokyo. That leaves me with three very strong-willed monks that don't get along with one another. It can be like treading on eggshells. Each one takes turns being wonderful to me as I am the neutral party—or should I say "referee." But so much tension builds up that at times I get my head blown off for no reason, so I keep a low profile. It's pretty comical, really, and at times it's hard to keep a straight face. After all my worrying about the cold when begging, it turned out quite grand this year. The clothes are a big help, but even at that I must be more used to it or something, because my hands are still bare and frostbitten yet the whole thing doesn't take anything out of me this time . . . a pleasant surprise and relief. I've been on television again, three times, local and national. Mum, I'm sure you were disappointed by the videotape of the program that I sent you, but they shot for a day and a half and from that cut out all except the image they wanted to create. They chose to edit out everything about you guys, my studies at Trinity, and my "bourgeois" background. They had an idea of the poor little monk that they wanted to push, hence the shots of my room and my tatty sandals. . . . There have been quite a few lunches out during begging. The local people put on these wonderful spreads. This time I've been taking notes and asking for recipes, so next time I see you guys I'll make a big Japanese feast. Meals here at the temple are mostly cabbage, daikon, and rice. Any good recipes?

Much love, M.

KANNONJI, IWATEKEN
FEBRUARY 12, 1981

Dear Nana,

Happy Valentine's Day and happy spring. I hope the winter so far hasn't been too harsh for you. Here we're just finishing "daikan," the great cold. Yesterday we had mamemaki [bean throwing], *something akin to Halloween in so far as it is a day for driving out evil spirits. Everyone throws beans and peanuts, shouting to scare out whatever evil may lie in store for the new year. Then we had a big party. Go-Roshi, the teacher, was up from Tokyo, and all his students came. It was great fun, as everyone helped out—but we'll be eating leftover seaweed rolls for weeks! There is a new monk coming to stay here next week. He has been training in the temple on this card [Sojiji] for four years. Seems amiable. All my best wishes. Be careful of the flu.*

Love, Maura

MARCH 7

Galli-san has come and gone. He was meant to stay two or three days but gradually it extended to about two weeks. We had fun, sheer, innocent, can't-stop-laughing-over-nothing, really funny fun. He said that in Tokyo he had been very angry and upset.

We talked a bit about muji. He was suffering the same way I had from not really understanding what he was trying to do with it and there was no one he could talk to about it. I told him just to lose himself in his work, to throw himself into it, and he is muji expressing itself. This idea he seemed to grasp for the first time and thus totally. He did a commendable practice, diving in with energy and enthusiasm. Having spoken with him and seeing his efforts, I was re-inspired to heed my own words. Our *gaijin ookyo [foreigners' sutras]* in the morning strained at the rafters. So we did muji yuki kaki, muji soji, muji dancing—all the while laughing and throwing snow balls and sipping *umeboshi [plum]* tea. At times we felt sorry for Tetsugen-san. He went through a dark period for a few days, when he scarcely spoke or even answered the most mundane of greetings; meanwhile, we could scarcely restrain our spontaneous mirth. At times it infected even Tetsugen-san, and he giggled. Up on the roofs, we abandoned ourselves to shovelling snow in the sunshine, conquering each new piece of ice, slipping, catching, victoriously detached slides, down, down. . . . Back on the ground, pulling the waste from the outhouse, carrying it in reeking bucketsful to the fields, or building a snowman, walking, singing, to the post office. He was very Italian, emotional, easy to bring up. Poor Jiko-san would watch his hands, waving a mile a minute, like a dizzy puppy or a kitten waiting to spring.

Jim gave a party and we went. Galli threw himself into dancing with the same vigour. He was taking muji very seriously.

He danced on, oblivious to the small clutch of females now gathering around him, subtly dancing for him. I left the room and found another scene—people sitting on the floor, playing guitars, less frenetic, very warm. It only occurs to me now that the same thing happened to me as happened to Galli; a little group of inebriated admirers gathered, fawning. We danced and sang 'til very nearly zazen time. I grabbed a couple of hours sleep but scarcely felt tired.

Jim came to begin my sculpture. We were standing in the chilly corridor, my hands turning shades of blue and purple. He was shocked and insisted on bringing me to the hospital. I was embarrassed—they seemed so much better. The infection had gone inside and was erupting in mounds of pus. I remembered all the mornings when I (like the little match girl!) clawed at the twigs, my hands red and oozing, trying to shake off the snow from the sticks so that they'd light. I realized I must have been carrying an infection for two months. They gave me an antibiotic, and it's nearly gone in just a week.

I went to dokusan. I had to repeat the koan about "All this universal law is like a dream, a vision, foam, shadow, dew, thunder. This you must realize." I did a mirage; he didn't understand. For my foam, Go Roshi burst into laughter as I blew it. For shadow, he loped around, trying to kill his shadow. (I had merely sat still, one hand following another.) For dew, he hiked up his robes, stalked through the fields, heaved a heavy stone to find himself drenched. (My dew had disappeared with the sun. I'm still too intellectual.) For thunder, he banged and tumbled to the ground. For "this you must realize," he said I must roar it, thumping my leg. He asked for the meaning. Originally, I had explained that it was all my daily activities, but I thought he felt this was wrong. So this time I said I was empty and impermanent. Tachibana Sensei, trying to translate this, looked puzzled. I explained I meant myself and all things. Go Roshi said it was my everyday activities.

He asked me to stay at Kannonji until Tetsugen-san

married. (He used to laugh at that possibility.) And then he'd have me come to Toshoji. Either way is fine with me.

I thought, one day, of my father. I loved him. He lived 43 years, died, and is no more. It made me sad. He was such a wonderful man. No one knows him any more, loves him any more. He can no longer touch any one, move people. Lived, died, and gone like so many hundreds of millions. As I will. Galli-san says he loves my father; for that I love Galli-san. He really had a feeling for him, kept asking about him, reminding me to give him his photo.

"I want to meet your father," he said.

"You can't," I said. "He's dead."

"I will. You will be my father."

Perhaps the reason that I love Galli-san's love of Dad is not so much from my love of him as of my own frail, human shunning of my own mortality. Yet I do not exist. There is nothing to lose.

Dear Mum,

*. . . They say the most pleasant months to visit Japan are
May and December. May would probably be too soon for you.
August isn't nice, and June rains a lot. I'm presuming I can get free
time. As soon as you're definite, I'll ask. Except for sesshin times
(about 5 days a month in summer) I should be able to get some time
off, if I know in advance. I may be here at Kannonji for some time
yet. As I guess I told you, the present monk really can't manage
alone. They're looking for a wife for him. It's so businesslike here.
Until then, I've been asked to stay and help. I gladly accepted.
Spring and summer are so much nicer here than in muggy, big city
Tokyo. Our normal quiet work routine was disrupted for the past ten
days when Galli-san, a hilarious Italian who lives in the dormitory
section of Toshoji came to visit. He's vivacious and animated, also a
big help. The poor little mute monk here didn't know what to make
of him but had to giggle. So the temple mood was decidedly different. Things are always happening here. That was fun, but this peace
is also wonderful. The only sounds are the birds calling and the
dripping of the melting snow (though actually we can usually hear
the nearby highway). Next month we'll have the first sesshin of the
year. I'm looking forward to it. They're like a transfusion and I can*

make progress on my koans. Now that you're reading so much about
Zen, these terms probably make sense. Have you heard of the
Mumonkan collection of koans? I'm beginning those now. . . .

Lots of love, M.

MARCH 11

Coincidence—I was thinking of how I no longer have
to teach English and was glad. Then I was thinking about
how Chiba-san wanted to learn English once. Just such silly
light thoughts. Then Chiba-san came and asked me to
resume the English lessons.

My zazen is rotten. I read in Dogen Zenji's piece that if
your mind is contemplating Buddhahood and Bodhisattvas,
the deep meaning of the sutras, etc., it's no good. But as soon
as I sit down to meditate, I'm filled with thoughts of what to
cook for dinner. Before my koan comes to mind, it's
thoughts of soup. I know good samadhi concentration is
really important, and I don't seem to be able to concentrate
at all.

MARCH 13

Yesterday I spent the day sewing at Sasaki-san's. She's an incredible woman, 70 years old but simply bursting with vitality. She ascribes it to hard work and going to the temple for ookyo at 5:30 each morning. Even through fresh snow she wends her way to Kannonji, bent double across her walking stick from years in the rice paddies. She's always talking excitedly, breathlessly, hands animated, gesticulating, bouncing on her worn legs, cocking her dyed black head flirtatiously—70 years old and irrepressible. While sewing and cutting, she can't suppress the smile flowing from her joy in life. Too frank to play games, she freely "praises herself and chastizes others," all the while laughing and working. The sun streamed in. We sat on the floor, stitching, her wrinkled hands as nimble at the needle as in speech. She wears a thimble like a wedding band. In and out, in and out, in perfect rhythm, every stitch straight and of equal length. She plies me with goodies, says "hurry back," and I scarper through her little oriental garden of pools and rocks and tapered shrubs. I half walk, half skip (she's infectious) past the snow-covered apple orchard with its single black crow on a naked bough, then back to make the lunch and to stretch out with a cup of tea. The mountains look higher, more nebulous. Life is wonderful. Truly, what is it I lack? Nothing. It's so simple.

MARCH 15

Jim came. He asked me many questions about Zen and consciousness,etc. I felt reluctant to answer. I knew my explanations could only be shallow and his approach only intellectual. So we talked. It was hard to explain on a level he'd appreciate, which means, of course, that I was intellec-tualizing, too. He's forming a little *benkyo'o-kai [study group]* for reading and discussion. As he was leaving, he kept saying that he really hoped I'd be able to come. He had obviously found our discussion stimulating.

So, shortly afterwards, as I was walking down the hall where he'd been sculpting, with buppan in my hands, the thought flickered across my mind: "Jim thinks I'm interest-ing." Then, CRASH, I hit the door with the tray, spilling water (nothing broke) and I suddenly woke up and felt very ashamed. Humiliated. He thought I was interesting because of what I was saying about Zen—bandying about "no-mind" and "emptiness" and the like, and here I was, not only think-ing and intellectualizing, but being vain, too. Am so ashamed.

Then there's the cat. She really had been bold of late, dirtying my bed, stealing food, climbing where she knows she not supposed to. We figured we'd have to train her while she's young, but we just seem to be punishing her too often. She ducks if you move your hands suddenly. She doesn't drive me crazy any more. (I've got used to her shrieking and pouncing on my shoulder when I'm concentrating.) I only punish her when she deserves it—which I still think may be too much. But Tetsugen-san upsets me a bit, because he punishes her cruelly, unnecessarily. He is always jumping at her, teasing and tormenting her, shouting, locking her out. He used to be kind to her, kinder than I. Now she's afraid of him.

Perhaps he feels guilty. He had a dream in which I took her away because he was always getting angry at her. I feel awful. She's here because I like cats, yet she must feel miserable. It's my responsibility.

MARCH 17

I'm disgusted with myself. I'm dawdling in my practice. I'm resolved to get up in the morning promptly, eat less, do four hours of zazen daily, and not stop until I reach complete enlightenment. No more fooling around. I'm trying to work with "What is this mind?" It's teasing and frustrating.

I've been thinking about Dominique [an English girl, teaching in Morioka]. I feel a sense of responsibility towards her. She really wanted to do zazen but has never gotten around to coming. I've told her the bus but never gave her the extra little push of offering to meet her or arranging a time. She was so excited at the possibility. I must arrange a definite time.

Dear Mum,

Happy St. Patrick's Day. Your card arrived today and I wouldn't have known the day but for Beth's nice decoration. . . . Go Roshi gave me a surprise a while ago. You recall my telling you the plan for his daughter, Mariko-san, to marry a priest from Kyushu and then inherit this temple by way of dowry. Temples are passed on in that way. Well, I guess poor Mariko-san didn't like the monk; anyway she refused. So Go Roshi stripped her of the dowry and in dokusan suddenly floors me by saying that if I marry a good Zen man, he'll give me the temple as a wedding present with which to build an international Zen dojo. I was very touched by the offer, after I got over my shock, but had to turn him down. They're so matter-of-fact about marriage here. People are obviously beginning to worry that I'm getting long in the tooth, and they really find it hard to credit that I don't want to get married! By the way, you came into the master plan, Mum, you and any of the kids would be brought here to live and would be taken care of! . . .

Winter is jerkily giving way to spring—can't believe it went so fast. Life has settled to a lovely pace and a peaceful routine. Plenty to do, but not too busy, and things seem so quiet. The air is fresh and pure off the mountains, smelling of pine trees and spring thaw. The birds are returning and chirping away.

After I go to sesshin in Tokyo, I'll be going to my first ever Japanese wedding. The second Tessan-san who was here (can you keep track of all the names?) is getting married. The whole thing still is hard for me to conceive of. They've met once. He wasn't even all that impressed, but she wasn't bad, and he liked the temple that came with her and really wanted to get married. So the date was set. As business-like as that. One puts more effort into buying a new car. Strange, then, how well many of these marriages turn out. Perhaps they're not going into them with all sorts of illusions and expectations. Glad to hear that Kate and Geoff sound so happy and are working hard on the new house.

Mum, you said you've been reading about Zen and Japan. What have you been reading, and what do you make of it? I'm very interested. You should practice sitting on the floor, because most people don't have chairs. We have 2 or 3 stowed away somewhere, but for example you couldn't eat, as they're higher than the table. In Japan it's considered polite to sit up properly on the legs, but it hurts most foreigners at first. . . .

Love to you all, M.

MARCH 18

Spring Equinox. We go to different houses to chant sutras for their dead for one week around the equinox. I try to really contact them (and Dad) so that perhaps in hearing ookyo they may be liberated. Yet often my concentration fails, and I wonder what's left to call to or to be liberated. What does happen at death? Who am I?

It's lovely going around to the houses, being welcomed in, chanting, chatting, warm and snug in kotatsus, served tea and sweet cakes. Abe-san was chatting animatedly, a soft light behind her through the paper door. Perhaps it was the light, a sort of funeral parlor subtlety, but suddenly it struck me— she will be dead. So alive and vibrant now, then dead and gone. First they'll chant sutra for her and remember, and gradually not even remember as the ripple subsides into the ocean. As we went along through the traffic, all the faces seemed to me to be death masks. . . .

I'm so impressed with these zenkai ladies. There's something in their eyes that dances. I began to wonder if all Japanese were like that (since they are mostly the company I keep), but they aren't. Galli-san noticed it at once as kensho. That was on his mind, but I'm sure he's right.

Jacuda-san was talking. I could only make out a part of what she was saying. She said something about one time in dokusan there was light coming out of Go Roshi. The fact that I couldn't fully understand her was not so important. She held me with her eyes. They didn't seem to blink or flicker but seemed to swallow me up. I felt an intense gratitude towards her. As the head of Morioka zenkai, she has taken care of so many sesshins, made it possible for Go Roshi to give dokusan. I felt not just my own thankfulness but that of every *unsui [monk undergoing Zen training]* she's nourished, every sesshin she's catered for. She mentioned Dogen, and tears began to rise to my eyes. I'm grateful to her, to Dogen, to all the Buddhas and patriarchs. But there was power in her gaze.

MARCH 21

I've been socialized. I don't know how or who did it (I suspect Tessan-san) but now I jump up, get the tea, fetch like a servant or a dog or a Japanese wife. It is a real socialization because I wasn't even aware of it and don't really mind. But thank God I wasn't born here and will never marry a Japanese man. (What am I saying? Never marry. Period.) *Chonans [eldest sons]* are the worst.

I've been re-reading a bit of Freud through the light of Buddhism. It's interesting how his concept of the wish ties in with that of desire, instinct with craving—craving to live, craving to die—theos and eros. This craving leads to a new reincarnation (without soul), like being born with instincts but as yet no personality.

Freud thinks telepathy may be primitive pre-linguistic communication. That makes sense if the universe is really one fabric. Plants, of course, have now been shown to possess consciousness. Why do we say rocks are not alive?

MARCH 28

Dominique came. She cycled out from Morioka
through rain and then sun. Good on her. We talked and
talked, 'til I was embarrassed to have talked so much. She's
still not sure. One thing that really pierced me somewhere
sensitive (we were drying dishes under the dim kitchen light)
was when she whirled around and said, "You shouldn't be
here. You should be with children, with people, where you
can do some good. Look at you. You're radiant. People
shouldn't have to cycle miles to see you." And of course I do
love children and love people, but I'd hate it if people looked
to me when I'm so immature in my practice. I'd hate to fall
off. Even to her I spoke too much, saying some things I'd
read rather than experienced. I felt ashamed. I told her to
forget all I'd said, that I was still shallow. I could see that she
took it as false modesty on my part. That night I read in
Dogen that he said we shouldn't act like enlightened masters.
I felt personally chastized. What can one do? In the koan
"the man up the tree" I always felt he must just display his
Buddha-nature. That is what Go Roshi does. But what
about when it's still so dull?

Funny things have come up in my meditations—day-
dreams, bad concentration. One idea is to have a Zen commune attached to a monastery so that lay people could also
do training, with child care facilities so that terms of 100 days
at a time would be possible. Then people could also train at
least three years, but if they didn't want always to be monks
they could pass on into the commune.

APRIL 1

Sesshin. I must do a good one. [Kyogen], my koan, not good. Kyogen is all sounds. But sounds and I are not separate. I am Kyogen.

Now, after sesshin, I had an excellent session. I entered Mumonkan. I made new resolves. I'll try sleeping without lying down, do more soji. On the first night of no sleep, at around 11:00, I felt very tired; around 1:30, my mind became crystal clear; I could only think of my koan. Unfortunately, I guess I overanalyzed it. As I was working with it, I got so involved that it was like a dream. I even had trouble remembering it. I began imputing motives to the people in the koan; they would have been my motives. Go Roshi wasn't impressed. The second night I slept. The third night I slept about two hours sitting up and on the zendo floor. I found my knees ached, so I sat on Go Roshi's step with Mumonkan on my head so I wouldn't fall asleep. (The book on the head is very helpful.)

PART VII

New Resolve

Dear Mum,

. . . As I was quietly sitting here minding my own business writing to you, this monk just asked me to marry him. At first I didn't understand. Anything vaguely romantic is so far from the tone of our strictly partnership relationship as to be inconceivable. The Japanese language allows sufficient ambiguity that at first I thought he was talking in the abstract, i.e., would I ever marry someone? I answered with what I thought was appropriate indifference, and by thus not initially refusing outright, I got a whole plot laid before me. He says that Go Roshi had said, if I wanted to marry this monk, it would be fine by him. He presented the proposal, if it could be called that, very practically. As he was sick, he needed a cook and we could continue life pretty much as before. My God, are they businesslike! I was almost too shocked to speak. He offered to support you and any of the kids here and said I could go back to Ireland every so often. I was still speechless and bumbled and stumbled and said I'd write to you. Meanwhile, Go Roshi had told me that he wanted me back in Tokyo, where I could train better with him. He had apologized profusely that I had to mind an "invalid" and promised that by July at the latest I'd be back in Tokyo. He said that if I stayed for the 3

years' course of study (I'm half-way) that then I could go back to Ireland and teach. (I know he'd help finance a dojo.)

I made a lot of progress at this last sesshin (just got back). The monk who was translating for me said that in three days I did as many koans as he in six months! Go Roshi and I work well together and it would be difficult to find someone as good. So here are my options—give me your advice. In the midst of my stumblings with Tetsugen-san, and after he'd said "Well then, it's decided. Let's marry" (At times like that my Japanese seems faulty. What had I said?). I, frantically searching for an out, said there was a boyfriend I still hadn't given up on and wanted to write to. I really hate this constant pressure to marry. Everyone worries that I'm getting old, etc.—it's only meant as kindness. But what I might do is accept this nebulous boyfriend, stay until the end of autumn (that will be two years), then go to France, find another Roshi, and do post-grad work.

The other option is to calm down (I am inclined to bolt terribly when people begin talking about marriage), then go back to Tokyo, finish my term of study properly, i.e., the three years, and get the whole training solidly under my belt. I do risk messing things up by breaking too soon. What do you think? Actually, having written to you I already feel calmer. Big deal—if everybody keeps pushing me to marry I can just refuse. I just get to squirming as if there's a noose there. Tetsugen will get over it; it's not as though he's in love *with me or anything. But anyway, what do you think I should do? Try to be objective—not just thinking another year-and-a-half off in Japan, but thinking also about my qualifications for the future. Tell Nana not to worry. There's absolutely no way I'll stay in Japan. Cripes, at this rate they'll drive me out!*

Anyway, sorry to have gone on at such length, but he just now sprang it on me. As I said, I'm just back from sesshin in Tokyo. It was excellent; I'd say the best one yet. Toshoji has changed a bit from my days there. Someone found out about the cheap dormitory accommodation they offer to Zen students and advertised it in an English paper so now there are four foreigners, even one woman. It's much less isolating, I should think, than before. One of the foreigners, a Jewish student from Pittsburgh called Paul is over here doing research on Japanese theatre. He got free tickets for a recital, so I went along. It was fantastic, and the best part was having a guide who could explain the various styles, techniques, and meanings of different gestures. It was called a dance recital, but they also did many pieces from Kabuki and Noh plays. They're marathon performances, starting at 12 noon and going on into the night. People drift in and out when they please. The pieces are unrelated, so they don't miss anything. The audience chats, shouts encouragement, picnics, and generally relaxes, having a good time. Watching them all decked out in magnificent, special occasion kimonos was almost as entertaining as the performance.

The other highlight of my Tokyo sojourn was going to Tessan-san's marriage ceremony. It was my first wedding here and unusual in being Buddhist. Weddings are usually Shinto. They had only met a couple of times before the wedding, yet both were cool as cucumbers about it. She looked gorgeous, serene and radiant, as she sat waiting on a throne. Her head was covered by a white hood in deference to the superstition that women have horns! Her first outfit was white silk; then she changed several times, the number of changes being an indication of the wealth of the family. Poor girl, though—she had so many layers on she could scarcely move and couldn't touch a bite of her dinner. There's another custom which says that no one may mention parting, good-bye, or separation during the day. If they do, it's meant to bring bad luck, and the couple may split up. So everyone drifts away without good-byes.

The actual ceremony is very simple and beautiful (no promises of love!). They used a lacquer set just like yours to serve the bride and groom during the ceremony. Then, with sake poured from exquisitely ornamented gold vessels, we all drank to their health and prosperity. After the ceremony, a lot of sake flowed with a feast that made our weddings look like Saturday night's reheated leftovers. It was sumptuous (cost about $80.00 a head), and they even weighed us each down with presents as we left. As they were getting ready to go off to Kyushu on their honeymoon, they looked a funny pair. He wore western clothes instead of his monk's outfit. Having no hair with his navy-blue suit made him look a bit like a con-man; she with her tight, prim little suit could easily have been the social worker turned warden. We all went as far as Tokyo on the train together. The newlyweds sat in separate compartments without even a pretense of romance. Thank God I'm not Japanese.

So now I'm back here at Kannonji. I've just been out digging my vegetable patch, and there's great satisfaction in getting all the preparations done. I've calmed down a bit since my proposal. I'm sure Go Roshi did not suggest it, which is the impression Tetsugen-san was trying to give. Go Roshi always says he wants me back in Tokyo, where I can train more intensively. . . . See you soon.

Much much love, M

APRIL 20

A bit of a gap. Let's see now. I stayed in Tokyo until the 10th. It was a wonderful time. Sesshin was excellent. There were no major kensho-type breakthroughs, but several nice little "Ah, so desu ka" jerks. Go Roshi asked me to stay in

Kannonji until July at the latest, then back to Toshoji. He says if I want to marry Tetsurai-san, that's okay. I wish he'd drop the marriage thing.

Yesterday a letter from Paul and Galli-san. They said that Eshin-san has become a monk again. He may well fall in love with Sochun-san. She's marvellous, like spring sunshine after a bleak winter. She's always laughing, always bustling around working, overflowing with joy and energy. I was very touched when she wrote me a lovely letter saying how I had inspired her. If only she knew how she had inspired me. She could teach me much about true Zen practice. All during sesshin and the days that followed there was an uplifting sense of *sangha [community, congregation]*. It's something I miss here. The crazy gaijin and Yokokawa-san, with her huge sensitive eyes and poetry, and Jiko-san, as daft as ever, racing down the train platform, holding the carriage. They're wonderful.

Paul-san took me to a Japanese dance performance. I saw my first bit of live traditional Japanese culture and had my first *obento [lunch in a box]*. I've only been here one-and-a-half years! Paul couldn't believe it. It was a marathon, beginning at noon and continuing until evening. He explained many things to me. There's Noh, Kabuki, and puppets. Noh came from the Zen mind, he said. It's very simple, with different gestures having pre-ordained meanings, like a language. Pine trees in the background of the stage mean that it used to be performed at Shinto shrines. Kabuki was a reaction to Noh. It's much more flamboyant and fast-moving, almost gaudy. It's often preceded by a striped curtain. Kabuki is a family monopoly. A few families get all the lead roles. They don't allow women, so a boy is trained from childhood to be an *onnagata [female impersonator]*. Japanese dancers usually have a repertoire of about one hundred pieces, any of which they'll do at two minutes' notice. So rehearsals are few (same pieces, over and over). If one's mother is sick, one can cancel at a moment's notice; it's not like the cutthroat competition in the American theater world.

The audience was fun to watch. In the afternoon it was mostly old ladies, elegantly clad in their silk kimonos. It was like a picnic; people ate, drank, chatted, shouted encouragement to the cast. Occasionally, a pair of hands could be seen moving with it, obviously a dancer who knew that piece. By our standards, it could scarcely be called dance, just movement. The women were totally constrained in their girdle-like layers of kimonos. They kept changing costumes on stage with the help of little men dressed in black that the audience literally didn't see.

One day, Jim took me to a fancy hotel. We drank endless cups of coffee, watched the bureaucrats dressed to match each other, and the decor, in tasteful, subtle, banal non-colours. Then we slowly meandered through the galleries, poking through the streets of downtown Tokyo. I really felt like a country bumpkin who'd come up to the big city. Everything was exciting, a thrill. I could scarcely contain myself.

All during that sesshin, I felt a joy bordering on ecstasy, a huge love for everyone around me. I could scarcely keep from smiling. There was an affinity with everyone, people with whom I'd never even spoken. When someone would have kensho, it was I that felt relieved. Sitting in the corridor, the young lad beside me heaved great tortured "mu's." Each one went through me, until tears dripped down my face with his anguish. This sense of sangha that I said I lack in Kannonji was not at all from need. I can manage quite well, peacefully alone. But it was rather from love. All this love welling up inside was begging for an object. I ask myself, why can't Tetsugen-san be my object? He is there. But with the language barrier and his inhibited personality, it is difficult to have a real relationship, and intimacy is hard even to imagine. But he is good and kind to me, though in other moods he is bossy and demanding. Tachibana Sensei says he treats me as a thing, a temple attachment, but that is only his manner, not his heart.

When I came back from Tokyo he asked me to marry him. I thought he was speaking of marriage in the abstract and said either way was okay. He said it was the same for him, so we might as well marry! I was aghast. He was practical. He needed someone to cook, clean, etc. His sickness pension would provide. It was all so calculated. He ran down my benefits in the contract—I could occasionally return to Ireland, he'd support my mother, etc. My stomach was turning, my mind racing. I began not to understand Japanese, and I thought I was postponing the decision, when he triumphantly exclaimed "So, then, it's decided. We'll marry." I gulped, then backtracked frantically, trying not to hurt his feelings, forgetting that feelings weren't really part of the offer. Since I happened to be in the middle of writing a letter to Mum, I stalled, saying I'd ask her.

The next few days, I felt claustrophobic. He was charming to me most of the time and a cruel bastard to the cat, tormenting her, hitting her, locking her up, inventing nasty teasing games of intimidation. I'd look at him and feel blackness. When I found her locked overnight in Busshari-to, I wanted to scream at him. How could I ever marry a man who'd be so cruel to a cat? The blackness was in my heart. Where was my lofty love for mankind? I felt trapped. What he did physically to the cat I felt emotionally as me (maybe I overreacted). I resented that he could dare to think of dooming me to the banal existence I'd have with him, he who had scarcely enough life in him to look people in their eyes. But surely I should be indifferent. If I really just took a day at a time, then anyone, anywhere, any life should surely be okay. I pelted myself with recriminations. I wanted to run. Any excuse. Aagh. Then a letter came from Mum. She still hadn't received mine, but I used it as an opportunity to make my refusal plain. He took it well. After all, he had little emotion invested in the whole thing. I was amazed at how relieved I felt—amazed and vaguely shocked. Get your act together, kid!

Dear Mum,

Happy birthday to you. Omedeto gozaimasu. Tanoshi tan-joobi da to ii desu ga. A wee package is on the way but will be late. Gomen nasai, ne? [Sorry!] *You'd better blinking well make it over to Japan. As soon as you have a definite date, please tell me. I'm still assuming that I'll be able to get free time, though if I'm in Toshoji, as is the plan, it should be easier. Go Roshi is coming here to stay for a while in May. I'm looking forward to it so I can advance with my koans. You're right that Nana seems to think I'm getting too involved. I got a come-back-home but very nice letter from her. . . .*

By now you must have gotten my last letter with my almost hysterical reaction to Tetsugen-san's proposal. Poor fellow. I did calm down, and he wasn't at all put out that I wasn't interested. I was amazed at my almost allergic reaction to the mention of marriage. . . .

I went the other day with Mu-chan's mother to see the cherry-blossoms. They're lovely. Underneath the trees sit little parties of "Ohanami no hito," people who've gone blossom viewing. You imagine pastoral picnics, quiet family outings with Oriental tranquility. They're mostly mobs of rowdy drunks out with any excuse to

share a bottle of sake and some songs. Still, they look as if they're
enjoying themselves: "Blossoms, what blossoms?" And the Japanese
need these chances to let themselves go. Anyway, m'dear, the very
happiest of birthdays to you. . . .

Love to ya, M.

MAY 4

Tessan-san came with his bride for the night. Though
there were times I thought he'd drive me batty, I really do
feel a love for him. When he shows his good side, it's like a
winter's hearth. The two of them seem to be doing well by
each other, both a little chuffed at being married and each
aware of rescuing the other from the shrivelled, cobwebby
shelf of spinsterhood. They seemed positively playful with
one another, she tapping his newspaper. (Why can't the
Japanese touch?) They could even have married for love.

Where Christianity preaches original sin, Buddhism
preaches original enlightenment.

May 13

Yesterday had dokusan. Phew. Go Roshi gave a big speech about how he'd never met a girl as diligent as me (hasn't met many girls in training). About how I was the same calibre as the old priests, the likes of Dogen. (It's more a reflection of the low quality of present-day Japanese priests). The upshot of the thing is that he wants to make me Kannonji's *jushoku [head priest]*. I nearly died. Wants to get Tetsurai-san all trained (provided he doesn't run away) and then marry us! Leps. I glugged.

He said only my children were fit to be successors of Kannonji, and though he had looked all over Japan, there wasn't a man worth me. Great, so runnerup for the stud contest is Tetsurai-san. But I finally clicked on the reason for all the marriage bit: My purpose is to make kids.

Kneeling in dokusan, the smell of incense sitting heavily in the air, made everything seem old and already cured by time, as if it all didn't matter. He was glowing, enraptured in the excitement of his plan for me and my children, he and his "baby," Kannonji. I found myself nodding—everything, anything was okay. Then I caught myself. Wait, hold it, no, that's not what I want. Stop. I thought of my ego, of discriminating consciousness, etc., but still, it's not the life for me. I told Tachibana Sensei that in Japan people don't want to do zazen; in Ireland they do. I wanted to build a dojo over there, I said. Sensei was squirming in his seat; he obviously didn't want to be the one to present Go Roshi with disappointing news and asked why I didn't call everyone over here. That's all I needed, him confounding me when I was so reluctant and so insistent. Go Roshi was laughing, said I was a plane and could fly to Ireland. Tachibana Sensei seemed to be putting things vaguely when I needed to be firm. But it'll all work out in the end, I'm sure; Go Roshi is always changing his mind.

At first I was a bit disappointed not to be going back to Tokyo, but when I came back here it was so overwhelmingly beautiful, the life so pure that I couldn't stay disappointed.

KANNONJI, IWATEKEN
MAY, 1981

Dear Mum,

A very happy Mother's day . . . . Are your Japanese plans any more definite? . . . More people are coming to Kannonji now that the weather's improving. Busloads of little old ladies doing the rounds of the temples. A group came yesterday and chanted ancient sutras, ringing bells. Many could no longer carry a tune, but their cracked voices wavered up and down with touching determination. Hope you get to see some of them. Do write soon, Ma, and have a good day. After six of us, you've earned it.

Love ya. M.

MAY 14

Lately and today specially (I was alone) I've been getting flashes of *tada ["just"]*. Doing something and it's all there is in the entire universe. These arise spontaneously but are so refreshing and different that they attract attention and immediately my discriminating labelling consciousness jumps up to say, "Hey!"

MAY 15

Tachibana Sensei got really angry with Tetsugen-san. Says he treats me like a thing, a temple attachment, and shows no gratitude. That's an exaggeration, though he treats me often like a maid. I think it's part of the way Japanese men are raised to treat the women in their lives. Now, pretty much I just say "Hai" and do as I'm told. I reckon in the long run it's I who gains and he who loses, I who'll get my ego battered and his that will grow more entrenched. Nevertheless, once he told me to plant *kiku [chrysanthemums]*. (I was already weeding in the rain, right after breakfast, while he sat around digesting.) I quite firmly said I'd go to Sasaki-san's and get them, but I'm not planting them today. He looked shocked and giggled nervously, a bit embarrassed: "Why?" I said I had other work to do. I didn't feel or sound annoyed. Pushing the wheelbarrow down to Sasaki-san's for the kiku, I felt, "Hee, hee, hee, I'm a bitch, I'm terrible, but chuckle, chuckle, I enjoyed that." Then I saw her—skinny, 70, down on the floor vigourously scrubbing the already gleaming wood with such earnestness she didn't even hear my call. I felt ashamed. She trundled into the garden and dug me up kiku from the ends of the rows she'd already neatly trimmed, thinned, and transplanted. She motioned me into the shed, all the time half running, her stooped back parallel to the ground like a cyclist angled for speed. The shed was dark, smelled musty. She took the lids off various barrels, pulling out all manner of salted and preserved vegetables and stuffing them into bags for me. Then "sayonara." She was off about her work. Ashamed, thoroughly ashamed, I bought an ice-cream and pushed my barrow past the rice fields with the radios, the many bent bodies at their jobs. I wondered what they thought about, if they thought at all. Were they all like so many Zen masters, living their koans—digging and digging and only digging?

MAY 18

Yesterday I was in a bad mood. No reason. Felt if there was anyone to interact with even a bit that it would quickly be dispersed. My bad moods usually are. Tetsugen-san came back from the *onsen [hot springs]*, thrust the kettle through the window at me. "It leaks, put it in a bottle" (using the most brusque form of Japanese commands). "When you're done wipe the kettle well or it'll rust." (Again, very curt). I bristled. Who did he think he was, telling me to fill his bottles in a manner like that? I was about to lash out, but before I could remember the word for slave or servant, he turned on his heels. "Next time, next time," I seethed. I'd had enough of him and his arrogant ways. I'm sick of silently resenting him; it's better for both of us to air it, even if he is my superior. Didn't I feel small, then, to discover later that he'd brought the kettle, filled it, and returned with it, not for himself, but for me.

Today it's pouring rain, but I'm in a great humour. Even yesterday, though, it was totally clear how all these moods just arise and fade, are empty and impotent. Yesterday I felt completely empty. Frighteningly empty. There simply was no me. Not the kind of universal me I sometimes feel— but nothing at all. Void.

Yesterday Ojii-san came on his bike, like a gentle spring breeze that you mightn't notice if you weren't paying attention. He's old and bent with a gait like a fisherman wading out from the sea. He lit incense and bowed to Kannon sama. Then walked very slowly, as if he felt the weight of the sunshine, across to Busshari-To. In his stocking feet he smiled, a golden smile of sweets and dentists and irrepressible good will. He climbed the stairs, doing one thing at a time. Every movement seemed to command his total attention. "No, no tea this time. Next time. Sayonara." Onto his bike. It was green, creaking down the tree-lined alley. The carrier sparkled in the sun. One white butterfly flickered across his path.

Am reading de Beauvoir's biography. Thus far she doesn't appeal to me much as a person. Very arrogant and seems quite cut off from her feelings, or maybe they're just not the public's business, which is fair enough. De Beauvoir and Sartre had no friends and few relationships, she said. I wonder if that kind of isolation is necessary to achieve anything (I know, I know. There's nothing really to achieve, but until I really realize that, I must go on trying to achieve, though really realizing that there is nothing to achieve.) She spoke of a woman (Camille?) who was writing from 12 p.m. to 6 p.m. every day. It prodded de Beauvoir, and I think, if she's putting in that kind of energy and devotion on something like a novel, how much more I should be putting into my training?

I was thinking about Mariah and how she sent me the cigar two years ago. Was wondering where to get one this birthday when what arrives but a big 40¢ cigar. She's great. I'm still giggling from the card. She also is trying to remember if I'm 27 or 28 (26!); it's a relief to me. Two years ago I felt very old, very afraid of growing old. Now I feel 18; I don't look it, and no one else thinks of me that way, but the world and my relationship to it feels like when I was that tender age.

I'm relishing growing old; as my body decays my spirit is only going to soar all the more.

MAY 19

The morning was rain. Not like yesterday's heavy, pounding rain, but a soft, grey vaporous rain. Went to Sasaki-san for daffodil bulbs. It was cold, we agreed, not like May. Ojiichan loosened them with a big fork. I cleaned them off with a trowel. It took all his strength to lift and aim his blows but each one was perfect. He gave me purple rubber gloves for my bluish hands. He smiled and continued down the row. We filled two boxes with daffodils and narcissi. They were heavy. I washed the rubber gloves in a puddle and gave them back. He was still smiling. I picked my way back in the rain, now more like airborne dew. The mountains were scarcely visible but very present, at once rooted and wispy (like the driving instincts that show themselves as dreams. . .)

Today no post. Pity.

Last night I tried to stay up all night doing zazen. But I dropped off for an hour or two. I was really annoyed with myself because I missed that time of lucidity that comes after the tiredness. Felt very annoyed. However, today all day long "this mind is Buddha" which I read in the *Shobogenzo [writings of Dogen]* struck reverberations in my thoughts. "This mind is Buddha, no mind, no Buddha" suddenly became very clear. They are only echoes of the one.

Strange and charming that in the technologically advanced Japan such anachronisms as the bill collectors exist. No one has a checking account, so they come around on their bikes and scooters collecting. It's much more human. Just now came the waterworks collector on her bike, her little one on her back. He bravely gave me the change. I like him better than the bank tellers.

Circumstances are forever making a fool of me. I should say "teaching me" but I'm a slow learner. Sometimes I bitch about Tetsugen-san and stupid trivial things, the way he jeers when he thinks I'm doing something wrong or silly, how he never closes the door, no longer notices what I cook even when I make his favorite dish. I mused—he has no emotions or heart. It would never occur to him to bring me home a treat, for example; that kind of spontaneity isn't in him. Of course as I thought the thought, he closed the door behind him. Yesterday he brought me home a piece of cheesecake (Yuriko-san had said I like cheesecake), tonight raved about the curry and comfrey tempura I made. Oh, well. I've accepted that once I get to know people they're always good; I always like them (even the Shimoshinge-sans of the world). If only I could actualize Sono's "Thanks very much for everything. I have no complaints whatsoever." Truly each situation is its own perfection. I wish I could uproot the bitch in me that knows, even as it bitches, that it's nonsense and destructive.

I love the cat. (Actually, it just hit me that there's another example. The cat drove me crazy for ages; now she seems the best one I've ever known.)

I've been gathering wild plants and mushrooms. I love strolling with my bucket, seeking them out and bringing them back. Each one has its time of perfection, its tricks in becoming edible. Soak with the bath's ashes, boil three times, grate through the slit in a daikon. . . They have no fertilizers or spray; they're free and it's the same thrill as rescuing the battered chair or leaky pot off someone's rubbish pile. The scavenger, gypsy, make-do renovator in me revels. I was standing by the rice paddies with my pail. The wind was still and the waters unruffled. The sun was streaky through the clouds. Indigos, emeralds merging. Only one violent splash of yellow—huge dandelions reflecting in the water. I was dumbstruck and drawn into it. The cat ran over to me, rubbing my leg, and as I re-emerged it came as a relief to realize that I'm not separate from it. I remember the times I battered the flowers with my pleas to be let inside. Now, for moments, there is no inside and no outside.

I was tired after staying up all night. The tiredness dragged across a couple of days but seemed also to drain my usual discriminating mind. There were many moments of pure absorption. These are still rare, but it's the first indication I've had that my consciousness may actually be changing. I actually enjoy working. The first time that thought flickered across my mind, a voice, almost a reflex, quashed it—afraid someone might hear and take advantage. But Go

Roshi is right. Working *isshoken mei [with all one's heart and soul]* is not work.

MAY 26

The other day Sasaki-san came on her bike. She looked ravishing. She sat on the step where I was scrubbing the floor. A white scarf was draped like the Virgin's veil, draped carelessly on her head. She still has all the mannerisms of a young coquette, darting her eyes playfully, laughing flirtingly into her hands. As she so often does, she brought us some of her good home-cooking. She wanted to play goeka music at the ceremony on the ninth. She prevailed on Tetsugen-san, employing every measure of her female charms. Her eyes were beautiful, pleading and winning. His eyes were on the floor. He often seems to be fascinated by something inanimate when a person's eyes are too intimate, or even real. I wondered if perhaps he was listening with everything he had and if that was why he had to focus on something as undistracting as the concrete floor. She paused, straining for his reply. For a moment he was silent. Then: "Don't wash this floor like in Tokyo or the water will seep underneath and freeze in winter." A short soliloquy about cracked concrete and he lapsed again into silence. She took no heed and continued as if there had never been a gap in the conversation. I could have dumped my bucket on him. How could he be so insensitive to her?

MAY 28

We went to collect plants from one of Sasaki-san's relatives. It was early morning. Misty. The rice fields had not yet been planted and formed spreads of square lakes into the distance, reflecting mountains and clouds, that day a patchwork of blues and greys. We were putting the plantlings into a box. I was handling them rather roughly, thinking more that he was being rather grasping in asking her for more and more, and thinking that I'd have to plant them. My mind was far away from the plants. One tiny one went under the next sod I added. "It's alive, it's alive" she said, not in alarm, not scolding, but as if a self-evident truth were speaking itself while her lips moved. I was ashamed.

My birthday came. Tetsugen forgot. (On his birthday I'd gone to a lot of trouble to make a special cake; he only said it was better to buy one. Sometimes ya can't win.) In the morning I scrubbed windows, smiling that it was my birthday even if the world forgot. But it didn't. I was overwhelmed, tears actually brimming, with the kindness. Tachibana Sensei with four presents and a bottle of German white wine. Chiba-san made me a beautiful *samuè [work outfit]*, loads of underwear, and a strawberry cheesecake. Dominique showered me with presents and good will. She seems to be getting more and more into Zen. Hope she can suspend her intellect a bit.

Life is great. Actually, my body's in bits—a cut that

keeps bursting on my toe, a shin all bruised from falling through a stool while window-washing; during the cold my frostbite re-emerged. Some weird rash or biting is gradually spreading, first my arm and stomach, now legs, neck, and chest. Strange. But the old *atama [head]* is ill. Am working very hard these days, about 12 hours a day without a break. Still the place seems dirty.

MAY 30

A quiet day. A day of wind and weeds and dirty windows.

KANNONJI, IWATEKEN
MAY 1981

Dear Mum,

. . . I asked Go Roshi if there would be any time when it would be most convenient for your visit. He got very enthusiastic and said "anytime," even if you came in time for next month's big ceremony (when I'll be run off my feet), that would be okay. But

watch out. I'm sure he hopes you'll fall in love with Japan and we'll
both stay and live here happily ever after. . . . As for my leaving
here, I'm still not sure when. Your point that I should expose myself
to Zen as it's adapting itself in the West is, I think, very valid. My
problem is two-fold; one, how to break it to Go Roshi and second,
whenever I see him actually in front of me I just can't imagine want-
ing to switch to another Roshi. He is so excellent and now under-
stands me and my level in a way that would take ages to re-establish
with someone else. Still, as he's not here right now, I do feel inclined
to go back closer to home. Hmmm.

. . . You're right. Things were a bit awkward here with
Tetsugen-san, but they've rebalanced. Soon at least one and maybe
two from Tokyo should be staying here, which will break up the cou-
ple set-up. . . . My plans are still so nebulous that I can't say with
any certainty even what continent I'll be on next spring. Anyway,
I'm busy these days. Soon Go Roshi, his wife, and two others arrive
to stay. Then for the ceremony on June 7th (this temple's 10th
anniversary). We're expecting over one hundred people with top
Roshis, politicians, reporters, etc. from all over Japan. I always
thought I kept this place clean, but I see it now with new eyes and
little nooks that haven't been disturbed at all during those ten years.
Ah, well, I've nothing else to do but clean, so I'll have it ready in

time. Am dying to see you. Do practice your Japanese. You'll be
grateful for any little bit you have. . . .

Love, etc.

JUNE 1

Tetsugen-san made me a *zenpan [chin rest]*. The wood smells beautiful. The chin is curved; the board is carved. He inscribed my name and an old Zen exhortation that from ancient times people have done such hard training and attained *daigo [great enlightenment]*. It hangs by a royal purple string. Holding it in my hands, I feel a sort of reverence for all the hard training that has gone before. However, that didn't do me much good last night. It's hard to sleep on the bloody thing.

JUNE 2

I wonder if the Japanese have a higher incidence of paranoia than Westerners. People are so reluctant to say something offensive that it helps me understand better why Tetsuro-san was convinced everyone was talking about him behind his back. On the other hand, it's refreshing to be allowed to be naive, to expect the best and see good. Our culture sponsors a cynicism even in its humour.

This morning I read Dogen's commentary on Gensha's one bright pearl. During zazen, I kept repeating, "The entire universe is one bright pearl." I felt luminous. Everything really was a divine light. Couldn't help smiling. If that had been a koan, I'd have to say "There is no pearl, no universe, only BRIGHT."

KANNONJI, IWATEKEN
JUNE 15, 1981

Dear Mum,

. . . . Here things have calmed down a bit after the 10-year anniversary ceremony. So, Mum, are you definitely coming to Japan? Your trip to Ireland in September is right when I was expecting you. Maybe you'd be best getting one of those "round-the-world-with-

stopovers" tickets and come to Japan from Ireland. Otherwise the £99 London/Hong Kong standby deal might be your best bet. Do let me know as soon as you're definite. It's a pity you couldn't have been here for the ceremony. It was quite impressive. There was a woman priest (first other one I've seen) who told marvellous stories about when she and Go Roshi were young and training together. She set off at 20, walking around Japan, chanting "Namu myoho renge kyo" (the practice of another sect) and visiting various Roshis. She ended up trying to visit my Roshi's Roshi (Harada Sogaku Roshi), but was kidnapped and kept locked away by priests of her own sect. She escaped by climbing out a window and went to Harada Roshi's temple, where they all took her for a boy. She went on and on with great adventures and funny anecdotes—a podgy, little woman, full of vigour. . . .

For the days building up to the ceremony, I'd been working literally non-stop, sleeping just a few hours a night. But somehow the rhythm of everyone working together engendered new energy, and I didn't feel at all tired. So even if you decide to marry all the rest of the kids off in one huge ceremony, no problem—I'll cater! Then, after the ceremony, we did the civilized Japanese thing and went to a hot springs to relax. We all spent the night. (Go Roshi paid everything for me.) Had a big feast and numerous soothing dips in the springs. But then I just went poof. Suddenly, when it was time to enjoy myself, all I wanted to do was sleep. They made all of us give a little self-introduction and sing a song. I got a mischievous pleasure from seeing all the dear little Buddhist ladies oohing and aahing and clapping when I was singing "Take her up to Monto."

Tetsugen-san must have overtired himself getting ready for the ceremony. People, like him, with kidney disorders are said to be prone to depression, and the following week or so he went into a depression black enough to make any of Margy's look like amateur theatrics. I was ready to tell Go Roshi that it's him or me but not both of us! However, to my relief, it wasn't a permanent character change (or the real hidden self), and if anything, since then he's been brighter than ever.

Love, M.

P.S . *Guess what's for dinner tonight? Whale and chrysanthemums—these were looking stale on the altar. I feel awful about the whale, but he buys it because it's cheap. Aren't you looking forward to Japanese food, Mum?*

JUNE 22

A gap. Much has happened. We prepared for the ceremony. Paul-san and Yokogawa-san came. I saved the wine from my birthday to welcome them. Paul extravagantly gave me Japanese and Zen cookbooks that cost a fortune, and he struggling to keep the shirt on his back and rice in his belly. We toasted and tasted with the wine. It sparkled, but the occasion didn't. There was a tangible stiffness between them. Paul later told me they'd had a falling out. She had been in love with him, a fact that seemed to irritate rather than please him.

The next day Go Roshi was coming. I was busy with last minute preparations. It seemed as if I had been doing nothing but cleaning for weeks and still all around me were little dirt traps, black holes. I finished Go Roshi's birthday cake in the midst of the chaos. It took ages, a challenge to my ingenuity. A cake with no cake pans and only a tiny toaster oven. Paul said it sounded like a koan—"Bake me a cake with no oven." I built tin foil pans, held the door open with a Biro, performing culinary gymnastics of twisting, piercing, covering, and exposing the batter. The result looked decidedly unstable, taller than wide or long, three uneven layers each straining to slide in a different direction. Feeling warm towards Jacuda-san, I saved her some mediocre doughnuts from the day before. She embarrassed me thoroughly by distributing a half each of the by-then-hardened rings to the Morioka *zazenkai [gathering]*.

Dominique came to dokusan. She seemed excited. Go Roshi gave her muji—intriguing. Then Tachibana Sensei took us out for coffee.

My own dokusan was incredible. We only talked about the koan, nothing personal as we usually do. But Go Roshi was so beautiful, so radiantly beautiful, he really seemed to shine. Our eyes met, and truly there was no separation, but it was I that was drawn into him. He told me that my training in Kannonji was the best possible, just to throw myself minute by minute into each job. When he said it, it seemed obvious, and I wondered how I could have contemplated training elsewhere. I think I promised to stay three years. I'm not really sure, as I was mostly trying to hold back the tears that promptly overflowed when I left the room. I don't know where they came from. I certainly wasn't sad, but neither was I crying from joy. It just seemed to be an expression of the nameless emotion that had overwhelmed me. The following dokusans only dealt with koans. In "Seizan, Alone and Poor," he gave me a very emphatic full marks. In "Joshu examines the hermits," he said I couldn't even imitate Joshu. Either way is okay.

In one of Paul's dokusans, he encouraged him to help me found a dojo in Ireland. I was thrilled. Maybe he's accepted that alternative.

That evening Go Roshi returned to Kannonji with us. The next morning I was waiting in the dokusan line, alone, the sun soft-shining across the tatami. After breakfast, Go Roshi announced that it was his birthday party. We got out my wobbly cake and the warm beer that Paul had given him. He distributed both. We joked warmly about blowing out the candle, but the universe would be in darkness. "Thank you beery much" to Paul. "Thank you cakey much" to me. We were all laughing.

The rest of the time 'til the ceremony was work without respite. But I didn't even want to rest. I had loads of energy and was riding high on the excitement of everyone being there. All had great spirit and helped tirelessly. Jacuda-san oversaw everything and yet saw to the little things, like that everyone got a cup of tea. Oku-san was there, but Jacuda-san seemed much more Go Roshi's wife and Oku-san a dear sister, whose relationship is rooted in the past.

Yoko-san, too, slaved away. Every time I saw her, she was sweeping or scrubbing a floor. When I called her Kannonji's Cinderella, she put her hands on her hips and leaned back, her teeth seeming huge as she laughed and laughed.

Paul, too, worked with every ounce he had, singing boisterously numbers from the musicals back home as he scrubbed Busshari-To's windows. His job, washing windows, had been started by a young Japanese lad the day before. He'd come asking to stay. Tetsugen was out collecting Go Roshi from the station. I said he should ask him when he got back. He volunteered to work. I gratefully accepted the offer. Things got hectic. He, Paul, various workmen all asking questions and in the midst of it all Naifari-san arrives for ooyo and tea with all the time in the world. The lad worked hard. Tetsugen returned and ordered him to clear off. He wouldn't look at him or explain but merely shouted over his shoulder as he strutted away. I insisted on feeding him lunch. He was quiet and soon went out to continue work on the windows. Tetsugen began abusing him again and ordered him off the premises. Paul and I were furious. We were all going to Morioka for dokusan. I said we should at least take him to Morioka, but Tetsugen refused to take him even as far as the bus. We pulled out. Tears of rage were in my eyes. We live by other people's kindness, and yet he couldn't even spare the kindness one gives a mangy dog in one's path. Paul was equally incensed; his eyes flashed black with what looked like hate, although I don't think him capable of that emotion. Then he cursed Tetsugen for his dictatorial ways, also for not eating the lunch I specially prepared for him. When we returned to Kannonji with Tachibana Sensei, the police were moving the lad away. He had sat down in zazen, refusing to move. Wonderful. Just like the priests of old. Then Tetsugen half convinced me that he was unbalanced, but in retrospect, I don't think so. Paul reminded me about the lad that had been driven away during Takuhatsu. We both sighed and shrugged.

So we worked and then worked. Morioka zazenkai women came and took over the kitchen. They kept asking me where things were, but I didn't know.

Paul's birthday was the 6th. He had left behind invitations for friends to come to the ceremony. I wanted to do something for him, but where was the chance? So at 3:30 in the morning I started baking. Only time for one layer. I went out before the dawn to gather herbs for the cake. The grass was wet with dew of last night's rain, the air misty and cool. Gion-chan followed me, jumping through the long grasses. The mountains were shrouded, revealing yet mysterious, in webs of grey sinking to black. In all the business of preparations, it was a time of stillness, of total quiet. Everyone, even Go Roshi, was asleep. It was my own little oasis in time. Then back into the fever and fun of work.

Tetsubun-san arrived from Tokyo by surprise. Before, my Japanese was never good enough to talk with him, but this time we got on famously. He likes to work, to laugh, to drink beer. His heart is very young for his 50 years, younger than Tetsugen-san who prides himself on his youthfulness (prides himself with all the showiness and trappings of one desperately reassuring himself, as he fades through time).

After it was all over, Tetsubun-san and I sat drinking soda in the summer afternoon sunshine. He said he felt no difference in our ages. But when he said it, 1) it was true and 2) it wasn't to emphasize his youth but an attempt to attribute it to my "mirror zen." Incredible man. Also the only Japanese that I'd call really sexy. When he was leaving, after a couple of beers and blushes, he asked me to say "goodbye" the European way—with a kiss. I was delighted to oblige.

That reminds me, Oku-san's face nearly burst when

Paul kissed me "hello." He's still completely natural about such things, but I'm getting self-conscious with the Japanese. When he found his birthday cake and gifts, I was working in the kitchen. He came upon me from behind, whirled me by the apron strings and kissed his thanks. My first reaction was flustered. Imagine! But also I was very conscious of Yokogawa-san, who could have felt hurt.

Go Roshi was also keeping up a hectic pace. Because of my height, he'd asked me to stick up various bits of paper from above. I, of course, wanted to "really do" the thing, but was so self-consciously "really doing" that the tape stuck to my fingers and things crinkled and split. Sweeping the corridor, I met him popping through the window, one leg in and one leg out, kimono hoisted rakishly. We both dissolved into transcultural giggles.

The night before the ceremony itself, we had a small party. As it was also Paul's birthday, he was heavily toasted. They asked him to sing a song. He opted for a belated "Happy Birthday" to Go Roshi. I crowed along. Go Roshi loved it and called for an encore.

That night we had *bansan [evening sutras]*. Go Roshi didn't come, sending instead the message that he had drunk too much *tamago sake [sake with egg]*. I loved him for that. He never gets drunk or even tipsy, so it was marvelous on the eve of this momentous occasion that he could be so unattached to his image as to send the message that he couldn't come because he was drunk! Jacuda-san was well on, waltzing around the kitchen. In fact, they all seemed to be well-oiled; I'd been doing the washing-up, but that didn't last long enough to account for the fact that I was stone cold sober and they all at least flushed.

Paul came into the kitchen. Everyone must have been pouring him birthday drinks. He looked pleased with himself, pleased with life. But then he blurted out, "They're burying you in there; they don't understand; they love you and are taking turns around the table praising you, but they'll bury you. Go Roshi's not saying a word, but he must be thinking to keep you in Kannonji." He was almost moaning.

The sake must have made them sentimental. Those praises used to really upset me. They made me feel as if I was living a lie, because I certainly wasn't all the wonderful things they say. Now it just seems as if they're talking about another person, and I find it amusing. It's just the Japanese way. (One of the things they must have said is that now I look Japanese. Two different people said so lately—it sure is as if they're talking about some other person.)

The ceremony itself went off grand. I rang the bell as they filed in. A few roshis came, but not as many as last year. There was a small, pudgy woman monk. Her face when at rest looked like a surly old man nursing the ulcer he deserved from an overindulgent life. Her bald head and unfeminine features but girlish voice combined to give the impression of an aging eunuch. Then she spoke. She came alive. I couldn't understand all the words but couldn't miss her spirit. She seemed to be popping. Her sentences were punctuated by excited dashes of her fist and comic sweeps through the air.

Her tiny frame seemed to balloon as she'd stretch, illustrating some yarn.

Tetsugan-san also came to the ceremony. Go Roshi thanked him for publishing his books. He was, as always, absolutely radiant. Dom saw it too, a light from him that is almost blinding.

After the ceremony we went to the onsen [hot springs]. Then a terrible tiredness flooded over me. I slipped into the hot mineral water with every cell in my body drooping. I was scarcely able for the party, a bit of an anti-climax.

Perhaps Tetsugen-san overstrained himself, too. He went into a black depression that seemed endless. Didn't talk to me except to ridicule me and give orders in the gruffest possible Japanese. The common greetings that mean nothing but symbolize a multitude, he dispensed with. I was biting back the resentments, chastising myself for my intransigent ego. "Good morning"—a deaf ear, still tongue, where's the difference? Tetsubun-san had stayed an extra day to help. Tetsugen-san was the soul of cheer and humour for the moment. They both exuded the fun and laughter of school-boys on the bounce. Then suddenly into the pits of gloom. He confronted me.

What had I done? I wracked my brain. I tried to be light and normal, which he seemed to find very irritating. I almost respect him for that, for refusing to be seduced by my false entreaties. False they were, as I was choking with hurt, yes, really hurt. That "non-existent" ego was bleeding.

During that time, I spoke with no other living soul. Gion-chan tried very hard to bridge the chasm to humanity. She ran if he so much as picked his nose. Ten long days. Ten days of thinking this was his true personality; this was the future mapped out for the next year and a half. I was ready to tell Go Roshi I'd take care of Kannonji alone, that it's me or him.

Then it broke. As suddenly and completely as it came, it cleared. Last spring (about the time he proposed), he had ordered me a new set of summer robes. They arrived, and with great pleasure he gave them to me. With great relief I received them. His first civil words. I thanked him profusely, but it was less for the robes (which I didn't need) and more for reprieving me.

Sasaki-san phoned. I nipped down on my bike, by the brook and across the rocky roadway. She motioned me into her dark kitchen, the bare wood beams glowing. She was rubbing salt into large fresh sardines (iwashi). That room always seems timeless, as if nothing had changed since long before she was born, but she was bouncing up and down on her hunkers, flapping her hands and telling me her schedule in a hurried voice. Up at 4 o'clock, cleaning, light the rice, clean the altar, go to Kannonji, make everyone's breakfasts and lunch bentos, then o'soji [cleaning]. Yet she always finds time to come to ookyo and to give us her goodness. Suddenly she grew quiet and still. She was no longer speaking from agitation, looked me straight in the eye, unwavering, and says "All I ask is that when people come they say the old lady is kind." My heart wrenched. She knew all the backbiting that Morioka's zazenkai deal her even though she had donated the land and is so devoted.

I love the very same ladies that do it to her, but those pleading eyes. . . . "That's all," she said, "and then I can be happy—now these sardines are secret; the young ones will be annoyed that I'm giving them away." She was sure I understood. I was choked and couldn't think of words. I could only bow deeply, then up and off on me bike.

Chiba-san invited me to a concert where a Japanese woman was playing the harp, Irish style. They said it would go on late. This was all a ruse so that I'd be allowed to stay the night with them. Chiba-san asked Tetsugen-san, who said they were to bring me back after breakfast, but when she asked, he said I should be back by five in the morning. Nonsense. He just didn't want to get up and do service. The concert itself was so-so, but then we went back to their house and ate dinner and drank beer. The rain was falling and the air smelled sweet. He opened a sliding door, lit an oil lamp, and in the flickering darkness we listened to the pattering of the rain. We sat drinking and chatting. It was a bit nostalgic, a thing I always love, just to natter with good friends. Don't often get the chance. The dictionary required squinting in the dark but somehow we managed, in fact til 3:30 in the morning. I'd been up for 24 hours by then but felt incredibly high from their warmth and the occasion. I don't really mind having to do the dishes, but not having to do them, not cooking (though I did that before I left), plus a steaming mug of percolated coffee, all thrilled me. Things I used to take so for granted. There was no way I'd be back before breakfast. Chiba-san, who makes no bones about disliking Tetsugen-san, just told me to take things easy. It was a rainy morning. Coffee and toast for breakfast and fresh tangy yogurt. We looked at pictures, smelled roses, discussed the twittering sparrows and shedding dog. I knew Tetsugen was probably getting more and more annoyed, but I didn't give a tinker's damn. Whether it was from tiredness or from joy, I don't know, but that whole morning I was in some kind of blissful samadhi. "Moment after moment." If that's what it's all about, then it's worth it. Nothing could bother. Everything, from the rain-glistening mountains to the dog's filthy pawprints on my clean kimono, was wonderful. It grew later and later. Chiba-san still didn't ring. Ah, well, might as well be hung for a sheep as a lamb, I thought, as we headed, not homewards, but to the tamago farm.

They had been telling me about it for a long time, but still I was unprepared for how it would take me. They had brought me to my place, to my life. It was drizzle-pouring. Black hens bespeckled the place like some insistent mildew. Everything I looked at was dotted with them, and each dot would be not one but a cluster, on steps, stools, stones, an abandoned wreck, a tumbly shed, haystacks, anything stationary—strutting, calling, laying, and reminding me of my childhood. They guided me into the large dark old farmhouse.

The first room had a mostly dirt floor with one raised

section of black wood beams. It smelled of the good damp earth. In the centre was a huge tree trunk turned into a table, and every surface was covered with bouquets of fresh or dried flowers. The man of the house spoke deep into my insides. What was it? Maybe it was the way his eyes never wavered, so that I was barely aware of what he said but only absorbed in the depth of him. The sitting room was also dark, the darkness of soot and wood. A huge square open hearth had no chimney, so the smoke curled up, up towards the ceiling, but wearying on the journey, sifted downwards. Our eyes stung pleasantly. Then he carried in a huge pile of kindling bound with straw and fed the fire. His smile came straight from his hara. The woman twinkled, dimpled, wiping her hands on her apron, smoothing it across her sparse hips. She made *mat-cha [tea]* for us, a long ritual of wiping and whirling the universe into a bowl. She knelt by the fire, dipping water from the soot-encrusted cauldron. Slowly, almost caressing her utensils, she poured. Her features were dim in the soft light of the room, but one side glowed colours thrown up by the fire. I was drawn into her every movement.

I knew we should be getting back. Tetsugen would probably freak, but truly time was hardly conceivable. Could there really be a future or a past or anything besides this room, this woman with her frothy tea?

It was the anniversary of his mother's death. We did ookyo before a little altar reeking of incense. Chiba-san finally decided we must leave. Pity. The woman was busy making mochi. I wanted to stay, wanted to work hard for them.

The scenery coming home was spectacular. It was still rainy. Tetsugen was still in bed. He wasn't too angry. We were so very late, it was such a complete affront that he was already beaten. "*Dameda [no good]*," he said.

They put me on the radio. The interview was in Japanese, and I didn't understand one of the questions. There was a very long (for radio) pause, awkward (for the interviewer) silence. Well, that's a difficult question, she said. I wonder what it was. I had to laugh.

Tetsugen went into another depression. First he was just nasty for a few days. He scarcely spoke, and then it was always curt and mean. I was getting fed-up, but was trying to tell myself that it was only my ego. Then one time—again it was trivial, and I was revolted by my pettiness—he was snapping orders. I always obeyed, but under my breath, murmuring "I hate you; I hate you." That shocked me. Listen, Mors, you've never hated anyone in your life. You know full well he's decent. It's not him you hate, but the way he treats you. Whatever it is, this isn't healthy. So I blurted it out to him, gently, apologizing, saying, "I just don't like the way you treat me. I'm human, too, not your servant or a dog." That doesn't sound gentle in retrospect, but at the time it seemed inoffensive, perhaps only compared to what I was feeling. He laughed, in embarrassment, I think. By the time I'd finished banka, he'd gone to bed.

For three days he stayed locked in his room. At first I thought maybe he was dead. I felt shockingly unperturbed. Several times I called to him. He answered that he was okay, but he didn't come out. Was he trying to punish me in some way or just so sick of everything that he wouldn't come out? It was peaceful. When he finally appeared, he was surly, his skin a sickly grey, stubbled. For the next 48 hours, he only snarled at me to wash my filthy feet and get him the Sensei's money. But something had snapped in me. I didn't care about him anymore, so I was free of him. He could say what he liked to me, hate me if he liked. It didn't matter so the whole thing became rather amusing. I felt a bit of a cruel bitch to be laughing at his misery, but it was a lot better than going under with him.

Then he came up from it.

Go Roshi came for zenkai. Dom came to consult with Go Roshi and asked a million questions, wanting everything to be rationally amenable. It wasn't.

After zenkai, coming home, the light was on in the kitchen. Strange. A bald head. It was Shimo-san. I couldn't believe it. It was late and I was tired, but I managed to throw something together for him to eat. The next day, early, Tetsugen phoned Go Roshi, who said to throw him out. Easier said than done. He had no money, he said. Tetsugen brought him to the station, but Shimo was back at Kannonji before him. There's something in him I admire. He's a very free man. Doesn't give a damn about much of anyone or anything. But his being there made allies of Tetsugen and me, us against him as it were. We sat on the roof chopping stray branches and laughed about mad Shimo-san. They say it's Zen sickness, that he used to be normal but overdid his Zen training and went a bit bonky. He was marvelous, though. Here we were busily throwing him out, and he had guts enough to do banka. I do enjoy that kind of guts. I stopped feeding him, and he left peacefully enough, first ascertaining exactly when sesshin would be.

It struck me that cats can do no right or wrong. Is that because they have no ego, or because right and wrong are our mental constructions? Even when Gion kills, it is not wrong.

July 11

Several mornings of samadhi. For the first time I woke up, still actually sitting. Got the news that Galli-san was coming early to prepare for sesshin. He came and we had fun. Tetsugen went to hospital and left Galli a pile of wood and an electric saw. We climbed a tree, listened to the wind blow and the rice grow. For lunch I made an improvised spaghetti with *soba [buckwheat noodles]*. We sat on the veranda of the founder of the Soto sect's room, looked across the rice paddy, and toasted each other with lunchtime saké and ice cream. Then he went back to work and I pulled weeds. I heard him shrieking, "Mora-san! Mora-san, my finger!" At first I thought he was joking, but the saw was still running, and his voice sounded hysterical. His hand was gushing blood. I put on a makeshift bandage and we ran to the road, his hand up in the air. I stopped a car and got him into the hospital. Everyone was staring. We must have looked a sight, both filthy and ragged, his T-shirt spattered with blood and me in my wellies. It was a very nasty cut, right through the bone. They patched him up. He still worked hard, helping me prepare for sesshin.

Yokogawa-san came. She was preoccupied, worried about how her dog would settle in. She slept in the shed with the dog so he wouldn't be upset. I had promised to help Mia-chan, a semi-paralyzed girl; the kitchen was understaffed; I had the official priestly serving duties, and I badly wanted to do dokusan. But so often I'd be nearly at the head of the line when I'd have a job to do. I got in about three times in all. At night I stayed up doing zazen, scarcely sleeping, and any free time seemed to be absorbed. Tessai-san wanted his clothes mended. Dom or Mia-chan needed a shoulder to cry on.

Dom fizzled out. She had some incredibly strong resistance in her. She had to phone her mother in London and talk for 45 minutes. Several times she ran away, became very vehement. Mia-chan, on the other hand, at first didn't seem to be putting herself into it, but by the end had gotten a lot out of it.

I was tired and still pushing myself. It was great having Galli-san as an ally. In the zendo he'd be doing *jonin [meal-server]*, walking slowly with dignity (and a plastered fist) round the hall, holding the kyosoku, me carrying the buppan. We'd catch one another's eyes and suppress smiles. At those times, it felt as if we were everyone's parents, taking care of them, helping them on this great thing. He said, "I can't be serious with you around." It was mutual. He went to dokusan, and Go Roshi said he should marry someone doing training, like Yokogawa-san. Galli-san said no, that he wanted to marry me. He told me, warning me that Go Roshi might mention it.

I was waiting in the dokusan line, frustrated because Tekkan-san wouldn't let Mia-chan cut in and she could never make it to dokusan. Galli-san was at the front of the line. Tetsugen-san wasn't there, so Galli told me to take his own place. I asked him to give it to Mia-chan. Chiba-san struggled up the stair slowly, like some dogged animal, with her on his back. Galli-san was helping. They bowed. That bow was so beautiful that tears involuntarily streamed down my face for 10 minutes. I listened to the mu's, felt their pain and their hope, a pain and hope of my own, a nostalgia and joy. Again I wept.

In this overly sensitized state, I went to dokusan. Go Roshi told me I was to marry Tetsugen-san on September 18th and stay in this temple. I said I didn't want to. He was pushing me, pushing hard. It was killing me to refuse him. I loved him so very, very much, and he was being so insistent, thinking of everything to induce me. I begged him not to ask, no, not that. Finally I broke down and told him something of Tetsugen's two characters and of my dreams for Ireland. He said he'd think it over. I went out in tears, became quite hysterical. Tachibana Sensei was upset and so

227

was Galli-san. They took me outside. I knew I was being ridiculous.

All along I realized my reaction was all out of proportion to the situation. We were walking back towards the zendo when my legs gave way. I fainted. Galli-san laid me down in the entrance to Busshari-To and shouted to Jakuda-san. I only wanted a cup of tea. They brought me inside. Everyone was fussing. I couldn't understand—just a cup of tea. I tried to calm them, tried to stand up, but collapsed twice. They were worried, massaging my feet, applying carbon, and discussing cures.

Something left me, some huge oppressive weight that I'd never even known was there and only recognized in its lifting. I felt so light. I was laughing and crying. Euphoria. They were alarmed. I assured them I'd never felt so wonderful in all my life. (Tetsugen-san had nothing to do with it any more; he was merely the trigger.) My breathing was a kind of panting, as if mounting to some emotional climax. Galli told me to breathe deeply, to do zazen. I tried. My breathing stopped. My mind never felt so clear or lucid. The voices were very far away. I was in a crystal paradise. Galli was screaming at me to breathe. From somewhere I heard my voice softly answering, "Hai." In the distance Tetsugen was calling the hospital. What an effort. But I'd have to show them I was okay. I snapped out of it, sat up, normal as hell. "You see, I kept telling you I was okay." They were relieved, but I only wanted to do zazen. I stayed up doing zazen, but I was too tired for it to be much good.

Next day, Go Roshi said "Until last night you were human trying to become God; now you're God. I'm Buddha." He shook my hand. "We must help the others."

He said it would be all right for me to go back to Ireland after three years.

I was looking forward to living with Yokogawa-san. She has a very quiet, strong, and beautiful nature. When she smiles, it's like the August sun in February, and even my toes have to smile back. At the end of sesshin, during the big party, I was pouring her some beer. She began to cry, threw her arms around me and said she was crying from happiness. I was confused. She didn't seem happy—maybe it was all the build-up and not getting kensho. I was very moved, though, to see her, a Japanese woman, openly displaying such a depth of emotion (though everyone else seemed to find it ridiculous). The next day she left to bring her dog home and never came back. Tetsurin-san (with whom she was apparently having an affair) phoned several times and said it was decided at shosan that I'd return to Tokyo and she'd stay at Kannonji.

For the first time, I really believed I'd return there, and I put my luggage in order, started to bid my good-byes. Tetsugen was freaking, asked me to refuse. I said that if Go Roshi told me to go to Toshoji, I'd go there; if he said Kannonji I'd stay there. He said he needed me. I was his Kannon sama. He mourned the garden that would fall into ruin, his health that would collapse. I was aloof to his protest and felt that life with just the two of us there was sucking at me like the whirling vortex of a drain dragging me down, to swallow and drown me. To have had three of us there, almost any three, to break the couple structure, would have been a relief.

But of course all this was only imaginings of my own construction. Yokogawa-san didn't come back and Tetsurin-san ran away from Toshoji, so I mentally sketch in a romantic elopement and feel happy for them—but stranded myself with a rising tide.

Sasaki-san was also very put out when we thought I might be transferred. It was understandable, what with all the bitching and back-biting that goes on, that it would be natural for her to want an ally here. As a result, when the politicking for a successor at Kannonji arose, Sasaki-san agreed to accept Tetsugen under the condition that for as long as I remain in Japan I'd be kept at Kannonji! And Go Roshi gave his consent.

Strange. . . . Yokogawa-san didn't even stay one day beyond sesshin, yet her presence brought me closer to leaving Kannonji and left me further from leaving than ever before. I had a sinking feeling, a trapped feeling. Tetsugen couldn't suppress a slightly smug smile. I refused to admit I was a bit disappointed, to acknowledge that in his pathetic way he'd won. But then, the stirring thing—whether the thought of losing me, the security of being given Kannonji, or whether something happened in sesshin, I have no idea, but he was a changed man. Still occasionally bossing me, but also actually treating me with respect. We became two equals cooperating in a partnership. His whole disposition is sunnier. I keep waiting for it to pass, for the depression to set in, but it doesn't seem imminent.

After sesshin came the massive job of cleaning up, of hauling out all the futons and covers, pillows to be aired (twice), washing all the sheets, *oryoki wrappers [eating bowl covers]*, futon covers in the tiny, not automatic washing machine. It took days, and before it was really finished I had to start cleaning in preparation for Go Roshi's return and *obon [summer remembrance festival]*.

Shimo-san arrived again. I have to laugh and admire his bull-dog tenacity and thick skin. Roshi permitted him to stay for obon and help us as rusu-ban with Abe-san. In Toyko everything had gone mad with everyone either being asked to leave or running away. No more priests.

I was busy. Some mornings we left as early as 5 or 6. I'd have to get up the buppan, fix the day's food for Abe-san and Shimo-san, offer ookyo, come back, start cooking, light the bath fire, do washing and mending, soji, etc., etc. I did the soji in Go Roshi's room as I waited in dokusan line. It was hectic but okay.

Roshi asked me how many hours I slept. He said that since the war there was no one my equal. I was Irish, he Japanese, but since the war I'm the only one who is his equal. Of course, I'm not. Not at all. But in a sense it gave me something to live up to. Since obon, my practice has improved. We eat earlier, so I have more time for zazen, each day four to five hours, once a week all night. (Well, last night I did doze a couple of hours.) I ram a desk up in front of me,

231

so I really do sleep sitting up and have stopped eating in the afternoon. I'm sleeping about five to five-and-a-half hours a night. Some days I feel as if I'm near some kind of awakening, because my consciousness is different, spontaneously, truly losing itself in menial tasks. Other days, more cynical days, like today, I think I'm closer to a "sleepening." That's only because I'm tired and too half awake for my mind to make the effort to run around; it's all I can do to guide my hand peeling the potatoes.

Of late I feel ridiculously happy. No reason. Just bursting with joy. I remember when I was young, deciding to commit suicide at 26. Once one hit 30 one was over the hill, so 26 was far enough to live. I reckoned that if I hadn't got done by then whatever there was to be done, I never would, so I might as well end it. Now I'm 26, and I feel as if I've lived my life. Strange sensation. Almost as if I'm close to death. Any desires, ambitions, hopes I may have had have either been fulfilled or spontaneously dissipated. I'm totally content. Of course, I want to get deeper, see clearer, but even if I could only have this paltry, shallow awakening, I'd be quite satisfied. Facing into a long, cold winter is not only fine, but I know I'll enjoy it. Everything seems wonderful. Even undesirable, painful conditions have a poignant beauty and exaltation. So in a sense I feel I have died; for myself there is nothing else to strive after, nothing more to make my life worthwhile or to justify it. At 26, a living corpse and such a life!

I'd be embarrassed to tell anyone, it sounds so wishy-washy, but now I have maybe 50 or 60 years (who knows?) of time, of a life, open, blank, ready to offer. I want to live it for other people. What else is there to do with it? Not that I expect to change the world or even a blade of grass, but it's as if to give myself is all I can do, as the flowers have no choice but to blossom. At the moment the best I can see to do is to give to people this freedom, this bliss, and how better than through zazen? So I must go deeper and deeper and work hard, no longer for me but for everyone I can help. And still I can't save anyone. They must work themselves, and not every one will. Thus I should also work politically, work to make people's surroundings that much more tolerable, work for a society that fosters more spiritual, more human, values. A society for people, not profits. What better way to instill the Bodhisattvic spirit in people? But they should work for each other, not for personal gain, and they shouldn't have to worry about economic muck.

Who knows but God-as-a-person may be tentative. We as people don't exist, nothing exists, yet for ease in conversation and life in general we use names and ascribe a tentative existence to ourselves and things around us. In such a way, perhaps, a personal God could be said to exist, but only in this labelling, not fundamental, degree, but existentially.

In a sense, though not his sense, Descartes was right—I think, therefore I am. It is the reflexive thinking that creates the isolated subject.

PART VIII

Mom's Visit

Dear Mum,

Great to hear from you and to know that you are still coming. Things have become a little complicated at this end, but being adaptable as you are, things should work themselves out.

Poor Go Roshi is really near the brink of death. He has lost a tremendous amount of weight from stomach cancer. His doctor says he's already a unique case in the medical history of Japan, to have lived this long. It's pure will power, but at the last sesshin he collapsed and said it might well be the last one he could give. But he doesn't stop pushing himself, keeping up a teaching and ceremonial schedule that would defy two young, healthy men to keep up between them. He told me that he's only extending his life to wrap up unfinished business. That's why I feel really infuriated at the ingratitude of the Toshoji priests who ran away. However, sorry, I got into a diversion. What I meant to explain is that there's no one to send up here. (He may get new monks but they would be very raw recruits.) So I won't be very free for touring. However, suppose I came down to Tokyo to meet you and we spend a couple of days doing Tokyo? (We could stay in Toshoji if you can stand the schedule.) Then we could come to Iwate. There are many day trips and local excursions we could make from here. . . . I'm wondering if you'll still be here October 1st to 5th. I had signed up for sesshin then (thinking your visit would be in September). Aside from the fact that with no priests I'll be needed, I also really want to do this one. I was so busy in the kitchen at the last one that I scarcely got to dokusan and, as I said, this may well be the last one. If you were still here at that time you could do it, too. It would be a unique "inside glimpse" for you. About a third to a half are first-timers, and it would also probably be very good for you. . . . I won't be coming back with you. I'd like to do one more takuhatsu (begging) before I go back, though if Go Roshi doesn't last that long, I might just return before then. At the moment we're right at the edge of a typhoon. Also, it would be a good idea to have a small stash of gifts for the people who will inevitably overwhelm you with kindness. How's your Japanese? During sesshin the TV people came out and did a stint, including me doing dokusan and a small interview. Not only did I have to make a fool of myself with my wretched Japanese, but they also had me translating for Galli-san. Wisely they added subtitles for his bit.

See you soon, M.

Dear Mum,

. . . Remember my casually mentioning that we were at the edge of a typhoon? Well, it hit. The worst one in 33 years. (They seldom come this far north.) I was enjoying the warm winds and feeling of excitement. We had to do a special sutra-chanting for about 60 people in Morioka, so we went into town. (I did Ino *[invocation reader] for the first time before such numbers.) On the way back, we were quite amused by the flying chimneys, downed signposts, and overturned bus shelters. It wasn't quite so amusing when we got back to Kannonji and in the pouring rain with pathetic hand saws had to saw our path in. Loads and loads of trees are down, my poor little garden quite leveled, branches and dirt every-where and all inside the building, too. What a sight! Me, enjoying the winds so much, had left my window wide open. It was so full of tree bits and leaves that you'd have trouble recognizing it as a room at all except for the soggy remnants of human habitation. We'll be ages cleaning up after it. Anyway, it's over and it was exciting. . . .*

Hurry over, etc, M.

Dear Nana,

. . . Mum left the day before yesterday and now I'm back in Kannonji. . . . She will fill you in on all the details of what we did. I freeloaded on all her entertainment and did more feasting and sightseeing in that time than I've probably done all told. Poor Mum started with a dose of culture shock but bounded back admirably so that even the Japanese were commenting on her adaptability. . . . Mum's last week was a wild whirl as we had a retreat in Tokyo. The kitchen was understaffed, but Mum jumped right in. She was a born turnip beveller, mushroom fanner, and even without a knowledge of Japanese, she would nip off on the bike (terrorizing the neighborhood) and pick me up the last minute bits as the meal approached count-down. I'm sure she'll have plenty of tales with which to regale you.

Love, Maura

Dear Mama-san Rootu,

When I got back the place was in a right mess. The "gnome" [Tetsugen] hadn't done any housework and had left up the same offerings, so even the tea was turning mouldy. A lot of the leaves are turning, and they're taking in the rice. Wish you could see it. The mornings, however, have been dipping down below freezing. I got my salvia and a few other things up and drying, the begonias inside, widened all the flower beds at the front of the house, put down a ton of bulbs, and now I'm trying to clean up the typhoon damage, so I'm out chopping wood every day. I got the log border made at the back. (Me and the wheelbarrow—very long logs. It was hilarious.) But it looks great, as if it always belonged there. We're going to try a sand garden in the square between zendo and hondo. So I'll make my mistakes here and do a perfect job at home. Tachibana Sensei (who sends his best) and I have started translating Go Roshi's book, so I seldom get to bed before 10:30 and he, poor man, a good 45 minutes later. It's very slow going, but my Japanese and his English are improving. I've started teaching English at the Yoshida's (remember the concert people?) It's great getting out once a week, and she's been teaching me a lot about traditional temple cookery. I never knew her that well before, but I find her stimulating, in fact, inspiring, company—extremely enjoyable and civilized evenings. . . .

Yomiuri Shinbun, one of the three major national newspapers, did a half page special interview with me. Actually I said almost nothing. The gnome prattled away, full of exaggerated praise. Now the TV people are pushing me to do an interview on a morning talk show, but I really don't want to. I'm sick of all this publicity nonsense—though there are some advantages. When I came back from Tokyo, I got a terrible craving for ramen [Chinese noodles] and searched all over the station for a ramen shop. Anyway, on the bus home, a neighborhood fellow who'd read about me in the local magazine came over to me. He owned a ramen shop and insisted on bringing me for a meal and then driving me home. It really quite took me aback.

I've started my novel, though I really don't know if I should. Remember at first I was stuck for themes? Now I find there are loads of things I really want to say, and the characters are taking on a life of their own. It's really strange. One feels almost like a medium, as some of them, based originally on people I know, are just spontaneously insisting on their own personalities. Even the heroine, who was originally based on me, now, although she has many of my experiences, has quite different reactions to them. It astounds me, for I wonder where they are coming from. Funny feeling. So all around the temple I have odd pages where I jot down notes as they occur to me. I've also started to write the thing itself, and this is why I say I don't know if I should. But now that there are things that I care about saying, and communicating properly, I find it disturbing that my English has turned so strange. As I read what I write, it has an awkwardness that is coming from having Japanese sentence patterns foremost in my mind. This seems inevitable as long as I'm here.

As for the poor old suitor [a priest heading a temple in Sendai], when I came back here from sesshin, I decided I'd had quite enough of this mooning business. So I wrote him an express letter making it quite clear that I wouldn't marry him. I didn't go so far as to point out the irreconcilable differences—like that I could never keep up with his laundry. But I was to-the-point, and the poor thing got such a shock that mysteriously the muscles of his Achilles tendon or something seized up, and he's been hospitalized for a month. He blames it entirely on his "great disappointment" but I'm relieved that he'll have a month to get over his "great disappointment" before I have to face him again. Anyway, m'dear, I've prattled on long enough, and I want to clean the hen house before the rain that's gathering . . . P.S. It seems you, too, may be in Go Roshi's next book. In one of his lectures he was criticizing the Japanese for only being religious for ceremonies and at their convenience, and he praised you for being determined to go to mass even when away from home, without the language, and at the risk of getting lost. . . .

Love, M.

Dear Mum,

Things certainly sound hectic at your end, and I imagine will stay busy right through Christmas. My book is slow, only about 4000 words to date, but really the hardest part is beginning. I still can't decide on whether to use the first or third person. I feel whichever one I choose will make it a different book. So far, I keep switching—1st person seems more vivid, but I actually enjoy writing more in the 3rd person. Strange. . . . I feel the lack of literature in my own background. While I always read, I preferred nonfiction as being somehow closer to "truth," "reality," etc. Of late I feel tremendously excited. I always thought that writing analytical books about Zen seemed so un-Zen. It set up structures, distinctions, and invited argument and speculation. The novel, on the other hand, requires the sympathetic understanding of the reader. If it's successful, he'll leave his own ego and "become" the character suggested, at least for the length of reading. This is much closer to a Zen understanding (intuition, even?). Really, Mum, I've seriously been considering studying English. That must seem funny to you.

T.C.D. [Trinity College, Dublin] sent me the standard boring forms about post-grad. At least in Sociology and Oriental Religions there's a deadline for applications. These are also formal

courses, a fact which has its advantages and disadvantages. I really
can't decide anything without talking to the professors involved and
being clearer myself about which is the discipline through which I can
best express my nondisciplinary ideas. . . . We got a nasty cold snap,
snow and the lot. Even the old-timers were surprised, and some of
them were caught without the rice in. I'm frantically chopping wood.
Tetsugen-san is very thoughtful about standing looking over my
shoulder and pointing out what I'm doing wrong. Still, his heart's in
the right place, and he shocked the life out of me yesterday by help-
ing me sweep. . . .

Love, M.

KANNONJI, IWATEKEN
DECEMBER 5,

Dear Mum,

. . . Try to do a bit of zazen every day, even if its just ten
minutes. You really sound great. When I first came to Toshoji and
the researchers tested me (remember?), they were surprised I'd only
been at it for three months and thought I had surely meant to say
three years. They concluded that I had a "natural" talent for it. I'd
say you do, too.. . .You asked about Go Roshi's health. Not good.
At the end of October they found 5 new lumps. They don't know

*whether they're benign or malignant but want to open him up
immediately. He says he's too busy. (He just had a sesshin in
Kyushu; now it's one in Toshoji and New Year's is the busiest time
for a temple.) So he won't go in until January. . . . This translation stuff is very slow. My own book is also slow, but I have an
appointed time each day, and whether the muse flows or not, I
write.. . .I've found a classical station on Ok'san's radio. This
morning I was making pickles, watching the snow fall and listening
to (believe it or not) the Boston Pops—heaven in my own dingy
kitchen. . . .*

Love, M

KANNONJI, IWATEKEN
DECEMBER

Dear Mum,

. . . *Thanks for the books. I'm half-way through* Zen and
the Art of Motorcycle Maintenance. *Rather than making me
all Zen-ized, I'd love to get a motorcycle—or at least have access to
one to repair it. The other books look as if they'll tide me across
many a pub-less evening.*

I really missed you and Paul during sesshin. Even that

246

strange old lady last October was another pair of hands. This time it was just me and Kondo-san, with larger numbers. Still it went off okay. One or two fiascos, like when I was using the carbon lamp to treat Go Roshi before dinner, but I didn't have the time to stay there, so he asked me to arrange newspapers to avoid a draught. Since it was chilly, I put on loads of them. Then the whole load went up in flames. Got the fire out, cleaned up the mess, but with only 5 minutes 'til dinner, I still had no soup made or meals on plates. What an exercise in concentration in the midst of chaos! But we made it in time. Afterwards I just lay down on the floor with a sack of rice as a pillow and fell asleep. Kondo-san (remember? always fixing you sandwiches) was marvellous, like an extension of my own arm, often anticipating what I needed done and totally responsible. A blessing.

The Deguchis came up from Nara for the occasion and send their best. Tetsumon-san and the little lady who gave you the fan send greetings, too.

Thanks to Tetsumon-san, who always sent me up to the top of the dokusan line, I got my share. Dokusan was also very stimulating, perhaps the best yet. I've gone on to a more difficult book of koans (and skipped one). Go Roshi is being quite severe about the koans but explains "A Roshi is like your mother, who comes half way round the world to make sure her grownup daughter is all right,

247

so no matter how good a student is, a Roshi will worry and push and push." (Although he always tells me in dokusan that I'm useless, apparently in one of his lectures he said that I'm the only successor to the Zen heart in Japan today!) He exaggerates, but it's nice. . . . A little old lady just came for a ceremony. Then another one came bringing me pickles. She's been out of sorts lately, and the bicycle trip with the pickles seems to have been too much for her. I told her to lie down for a while, and she's gone sound asleep.

When changing for the ceremony just now, I put on the leg warmers you sent. They're brilliant, make a world of difference. (My pickles lady just popped her head up and down. Life in Kannonji is as thrilling as ever.)

The greatest blessing you sent will be that can opener. During the sesshin I cursed a string of curses such as would put all Japanese tin openers out of action eternally. Right at a very busy time I had eventually to bash my tin open. . . .

I'd love to be with you at Christmas. In the supermarket in Tokyo they were playing "Jingle Bells," but there was no holly or tinsel or turkey or Christmas spirit. I know that dear Tachibana Sensei will play Santa Claus, but it's not the same. I suppose it won't do any good my brooding over it; still, I love Christmas. New Year will never take its place. Have fun and a good big feast and a peaceful family Christmas.

Love, M.

. . . *We're in the middle of a funeral. The procedures last for days. All morning yesterday was the bedside sutra, then at night 'til very late the mourners gathered in his home and more sutras. Today is the cremation—more sutras and tomorrow the funeral proper. The funeral and a big meal (I only found out last night!) are to be held here, so I'm up to my eyes in cleaning, sutras, New Year preparations, a mountain (no exaggeration) of beans that must be shelled, and I have to teach tonight. Never a dull moment. . . . Hope you all had a brilliant Christmas.*

Love, M.

Dear Nana,

. . . *Mum may have told you that I'm teaching English to a temple family that she met. While, to be honest, I wasn't crazy about the idea at first, but it has worked out wonderfully. The girls, three of them, are extremely intelligent and cooperative, a pleasure to teach (though the differences in levels is a challenge). It's not only an enjoyable evening with an exquisite dinner and a taxi home, but they have adopted us. They have an extremely wealthy temple and enjoy being bountiful; we're by far the poorest in the area. Since I started teaching, though, we haven't had to buy food. She loads me down with goodies that she searches out as not being sprayed, shot, or artificially anythinged (rare in Japan). She's really almost embarrassing. She heard I had a cold, so came all the way out on a snowy day, laden with presents, and she gave up her afternoon to wrap me in steaming ginger plasters. She knows all about old oriental medicine and has been teaching me that, along with cooking. (The ginger plasters really did seem to help.) Now she's trying to arrange that I study flower arranging with her teacher. He's an elderly master trained in Kyoto. She speaks very highly of him, and if her own arrangements are anything to go by, he really is a good teacher. It would be fun to learn. . . . I think of you often with very much love.*

M.

PART IX

Completion
1982

TAKUHATSU, FEBRUARY, 1982

Rescued this notebook from a fire. Tessai-san said I should keep a diary. I felt there wasn't time to write feelings and analyze reactions. He said feelings were *moso [something that can distract]*. I said they were not and he agreed, but said a busy person should just write events. Events will recall feelings. This seemed a fitting notebook to use.

The day I found it was in January. I got up at 3 o'clock, shovelled snow, did zazen, woke the others, made breakfast, cleaned up, went out to beg. We had lunch at Okawa-san's (tempura . . . she is kind, remembered that I love it). I came home, gave *Ojisan [uncle]* lunch, cleaned temple, lit fire for bath, made dinner, cleaned up, sorted *momi [chaff]* from rice, talked with Tessai-san (admire him profoundly), did zazen, and went to bed. Takuhatsu was a busy time.

KANNONJI, IWATEKEN
FEBRUARY, 1982

Dear Mum, Scott, and Beth,

*Phew! Finally I have a moment to slow down, catch my
breath, and write home. I'd been going at the same pace as sesshin
for a whole month. Tessai-san came up from Nagano to beg and
then stayed 'til the 31st. We walked [begged] every day, and then I
finished it after he left. Tetsugen-san walked on the days he wasn't
being drained [dialysis], and I hustled people who helped when they
could. Two gaijin came from Toshoji and walked four days.
Tachibana Sensei, after much initial reluctance ("but Mora-san, I'm
over 50"), led us during the winter school vacation and every day he
was free from school. He looked so comical squeezed into my robes,
his spectacles and grin under the huge straw hat and a polo neck
sticking out from under the layers of kimonos. Whenever we needed
a smile, we'd only have to shout "Sensei! Student, student," and
he'd duck, squirming, pulling the hat down over his face. "No, no,
where?"*

*Mum, you remember Megumi-san, my temple English stu-
dent? After we'd been walking a few days, I was bemoaning our lack
of numbers. She looked up instantly and said, "Well, maybe I'll
help." She's a marvel. The next day she was out on the streets looking more of a veteran than any of us, never seemed affected by the*

254

cold or the wind, just smiling and chanting. At the end I asked her if she'd do it again next year. This time there was no hesitation. She positively roared "of course." We're the only women who have ever walked in this area, and I suspect she's the youngest to have walked.

Tetsugen's case was close to miraculous. The first couple of days he was wrecked, but after that the walking did him good. Tessai-san also had a positive influence on him. He was shocked that I was literally doing everything while Tetsugen hovered over a stove crying "invalid." Tessai-san wouldn't put up with any self-coddling, and night after night he lectured him. Tetsugen was inspired on the days he was due for dialysis. He'd walk an hour to the hospital, even in storms before paths had been beaten in the snow. I was dumbfounded.

Last year the challenge had gone out of takuhatsu for me, so this year I decided to push myself further. We're allowed to wear socks with the straw sandals, so we usually wear several pairs plus plastic bags to keep out the wet. In the old days, though, the monks used just to go barefoot with the sandals through the snow. I wasn't sure if I could. When the snow melts and refreezes it's just like walking barefoot on crushed ice, but as Go Roshi says, if you just take one step at a time, you can do anything. And it's true. It was fine. The others, except Tessai-san, tried to discourage me; they said it would be too much. He only said if he wasn't so old he'd like to try it too. Then one night we were sitting up late by the woodstove, *drinking tea, with him telling me stories about Go Roshi when he was young. It was then a week before the end of takuhatsu and Tessai-san said, "You see, your limits are mostly in your mind." Then he gulped, as if only realizing for the first time what his words really meant. Then he said, "I've only a week to go, but I'll do it barefoot," and he did.*

So we all learned something and maybe got a little stronger. It was also a lot of fun, maybe the most enjoyable takuhatsu yet; all the walkers got on very well, and it was just plain good fun. Many people gave us meals; Megumi-san's parents did so four times. It was a help, especially for me. I'd be up most days at 3. Then if there was snow-shovelling to do, I'd get it done before zazen time, then sit at zazen, make breakfast, put the offerings in front of the statues, go out and walk, start lunch as soon as I'd walk in the door, get it all cleaned up, and start cleaning the temple, bring in the wood (give the chickens their hot water bottle), light the fire for the bath, take down the offerings, make dinner, clean up, wash the rice, prepare the next day's vegetables, do laundry, shell beans, take a lukewarm bath, and conk out for a few hours.

The climax was yesterday when all the temple supporters and Go Roshi came for a ceremony and dinner, but the day before was zenkai, so trying to keep the whole place in order and the new snow all shovelled out was near miraculous. But it's over, and today I'm just taking it easy. A Swiss friend is going back soon and is having a big "do" at the Grand Hotel—an 8000-yen-a-head affair. It seemed a bit extravagant to me, but Jim insisted on paying for me, so I'll go mad tonight.

Scott, it's a pity you couldn't have been here to walk, too. As it was, this year I got even more publicity than before (the radio once, papers twice, and local and national TV four times), but they would have loved Scott. The bit I enjoyed the most but hadn't looked forward to at all was a TV current-affairs interview spot. It was in the studio and a bit awesome with all the cameras and mikes and things, but we really had a great laugh—even in Japanese. Everywhere I go now, strangers point at me and run out to shake hands. It's weird.

One of the gaijin who came up for takuhatsu, a Scotswoman, Allison, had reached one of those "life turning points," tried everything but was not satisfied, etc., etc. After a couple of late-night heart-to-hearters, she decided she wanted to try being a monk, at least for a couple of years. When she went back to Toshoji, she had her initial ceremony. She's supposed to come up and help me here next summer. I presumed I'd just continue here "as is," but I'll probably go back to Tokyo after Tetsugen-san's ceremony proclaiming him the head of Kannonji temple, probably in September. Allison phoned from Tokyo frantic that Go Roshi, wanted her to come up immediately, and she wasn't sure if she wanted to be in such an isolated position. I still don't know her decision. However, apparently the monk who was translating for her didn't want to disappoint

Go Roshi so he made it sound as if she was more willing to come than she is. Anyway, Go Roshi came up here, full of plans for my remaining time. He wants me to do my remaining two ceremonies. (To do this I'd have to spend a period of time in Toshoji, so Allison's coming here would free me.) Then I'd be all official, registered at the head temple and qualified to head a temple, though not yet to teach.

Up to now we have our busy times here, then the calms while I recuperate. But Go Roshi wants me to help cover both temples and go back and forth between Toshoji and here as well as doing various ceremonies with him around the country. At the moment the schedule is March and early April in Toshoji, then back up to Kannonji, down to Kyushu in May, then maybe Nagano. Back to Tokyo for my ceremony in June, in July sesshin at Kannonji, then July obon [Buddhist All Saints Day Festival] in Toshoji, August obon at Kannonji, etc. He says he wants to bring me around Japan as an example to others, but I'm seriously wondering if I can keep up the pace of this 72-year-old cancer patient. Anyway, I'm game to try.

Up 'til now the only thing I've regretted about Kannonji was only being able to do dokusan once a month, but Go Roshi says that while we're together he'll do extra ones at noon and in the evening. It's very kind of him; it would be as often as sesshin. I'd certainly finish Hegikan Roku ["The Blue Cliff Record" book of koans] and maybe the next book. He says when I leave he wants it to be with a certificate to teach, but that usually takes 10 years. It's unprecedented to be given one after 3 years (as it is for him to do all those private dokusans). I feel very touched but very unworthy. He only sees me at my busy times, when I've no choice but to do my best. Anyway, it's very exciting but completely depends on Allison.

Mum, he seems to be taking his discussion with you seriously. He hasn't even jokingly suggested my staying on next year (even when one of the papers mistakenly printed that I'd stay 2 more years). I was wondering with all that activity how I'd work on my books. My novel is okay, as I've pretty much figured it out and it's just a matter of getting it down, which I could do when I get back, but the translation needs to be done here. We hadn't mentioned it to Go Roshi yet, so he stunned me when yesterday he announced to the supporters that all the contributions they'd made were going into an account he'll open in order to publish his books in English if I'd be good enough to translate them. So I've a busy few months ahead. Scott, I hope you won't be bored if you come over, because I won't be able to devote myself to you as totally as I'd like. Anyway, all of you take good care.

Very very much love, M.

WEDNESDAY, FEBRUARY 24

Overslept. Meditations not very good lately, but feel incredibly indefatigably happy. Still, should try to get more proficient in samadhi. Miko-san came and taught me about seika flower arranging. As always many presents. Dominique phoned; I will meet her tomorrow.

FEBRUARY 25

Morning meditation was good at the beginning and end. Even when not concentrating, I felt suffused by an incredible joy. It amazes me that such a physical thing—no supernatural gods interfering–as just sitting, maybe breathing a bit differently, can fill one with such elation. Did a million things at once and left early to meet Dominique. Talked in tiny, cozy, intimate cake shop. She worries so about nothing but has fantastic heart. Got her to agree to try zazen daily for 6 months. She always asks a million questions and explanations are useless. I spent a long time with Umezawa Sensei. He's deeply enlightened, sees everything as flowers. All existence in threes: shin, jin, tome/ past, present, future. He had that one koan but came to understand everything.

FEBRUARY 26

Tessai-san at hospital. No-one came; didn't get a ton done. Tessai has really changed, become much nicer.

Yesterday he actually did some cleaning. Today he brought me home a slice of cheesecake. Evening meditation drowsy.

FEBRUARY 27

Morning meditation awful, three quarters asleep. Must improve. How? Went to *Fukudo-ji [Happiness Hall Temple]* where Go Roshi was raised. His elder-brother-*deshi* [disciple] and family were there. The scenery was exquisite. Very cold. The stories of Go Roshi as a child clipclopping down the road in thin geta (no socks) through the wind and snow, crying from the pain, came alive. Of being awakened and beaten at 3 in the morning with snow on his futon. We also went to nearby Tendaiji, high on the mountain. Very remote and peaceful. Heavenly for training. Nice day. Night meditation good. Lately I always get sleepy about halfway through, so I took a break, had a cuppa and a bit of a read, then was able to continue well. I haven't solved the koan but had some samadhi. Around 11 o'clock, I heard strange laughing—howling like a woman's voice. Very eerie, but I presume it was owls or something.

FEBRUARY 28

Phew, time is flying. Morning meditation bad. Gion-chan was sleeping with me. In my semi-slumber I was loth to move her and got up late myself, 4:40. Got loads of work done. Fell asleep at 9.

MARCH 2

Morning meditation only okay. Allison came, it was nice to see her. We had a little celebration. Bad meditation.

MARCH 3

Go to dokusan but miss the bus, so we walked. It was a nice day; we did it in 80 minutes. Roshi says that in 30 years of training I'm the only one of his students who trains as if *"inochi o steru" ["to abandon my very life"]*. I messed up the koan a bit, but it was generally okay. Home very late.

MARCH 4

Gidaji, flower-arranging. Home late.

MARCH 5

I'm a bit tired but have to do ookyo at home of dead neighbor. The woman, still in *nemaki [nightgown]*, could have been asleep except for purple ears and hanky on her face. Disconcerting. Her child lay on his stomach in *kotatsu [a quilted warmer]* and stared at the corpse on its futon. Relatives kept wiping her lips with water; it shone on her dead mouth. A single tulip, a candle in line so the stem and the stalk coincided, the flame rising from the base of the tulip. She had a cold that didn't get better, so they operated on her throat in the hospital and killed her. Forty-three years old.

MARCH 6

Met Reiko-san and had a sumptuous lunch, then went to a magnificent flower-arranging exhibition.

It seems to me the difference between life and death is consciousness (even plants are conscious), and the difference between human and other life is self-consciousness. In Zen, the narrow subjectivity of consciousness is transcended, becomes pure subjectivity rather than relative subjectivity.

Allison is sick.

SUNDAY, MARCH 7

Morning meditation mostly drowsing, but I solved the koan that had been annoying me. Go Roshi pulled a great one. When Kondo-san's people came looking for him, Go Roshi first tried to persuade them not to pursue him, then he pretended to give up, hid Kondo-san in the pre-fab, and had one of the monks pretend he'd run away from Toshoji. They then gave up but threatened that they'd be back in touch. Then someone stole Jean's money, and Go Roshi, suspecting Atchan, went prowling around in the dark to check on him. He fell and hurt his leg. He's sleepless with concern over the theft.

MARCH 8

Allison is still quite sick. She went into hospital. They

say it's enteritis and give her pills that only make it worse. She's brave.

Toshoji, Tokyo
March 18, 1982

Dear Mum,

A huge package of books arrived from you the other day. This is the first moment I've had to write and thank you. I'm dying to launch into them. The Kadowaki one, "Zen and the Bible" looks particularly fascinating. Just leafing through it, the man seems very illumined and obviously has grasped and lived both worlds. I was extremely impressed with just the little I've read.

It seems to me that every day something happens and I say "Oh, I must tell Mum that," but now I don't know where to start.

My ceremony has been moved from June to April 25th. Go Roshi says he's not sure if he'll be alive in June, so he wants to do the ceremony as soon as possible. I'm going bats trying to learn all the stuff. It's old Japanese and has completely different tonality and pronunciation from regular conversational Japanese.

For a week I was doing ookyo at the different people's houses (just by myself I did about 70 houses). It was fascinating. The people around Morioka are really pretty much all of one type, but here (in the Shingawa section of Tokyo] I got much more of a cross-section, from modern, luxurious, western-style concrete, with plate glass and a dining-room table, to tiny, dark, second floor hovels. Some were weensy little garrets where, after stepping over boxes and up a two foot wide staircase, there would be a single room where a whole family lives in oriental harmony. The people were very good to me, and I was amazed at how broadminded they were. (How would you react if a young girl from Bombay dressed as a priest walked into St. Joseph's Church to offer Mass?) Quite apart from my being gaijin, most had never even seen a woman read ookyo before. It was, however, exhausting. I did a house an hour.

I got around by bicycle and have become adept at misreading Japanese maps. No one can come up with more original ways to get lost. Meanwhile Go Roshi was bombing around on his bike—you know, like the big, black, 2-wheeled armored tanks that the Irish police, down the bogs, use. Other mornings he'd be out at 5 o'clock when he had to catch the subway to a distant house. That part wouldn't be so bad, except that he's doing it on a sprained ankle which has now become extremely painful and swollen.

He got the sprained ankle while checking up on a young *"delinquent"* we had here who used to borrow money and get jarred over in the prefab every night (the little house where we stayed when you were here). But it is because of another fellow that we are in bad odour with the police here. The guy was from Morioka and had committed offenses that I'm sure any American policeman would smile at, but they were real shockers in Morioka. His mother was a wreck (her only beautiful boy—and he is gorgeous), so she begged Go Roshi to take him. She didn't mention that he was on parole and not allowed out of Morioka. The police caught up with him just after they found out about Kondo-san. (Remember the sweetheart of a monk who was always fixing you sandwiches?)

Anyway, the young man was a friend of Reiko-san (the temple, mum, where I teach English), and his father was a monk, who re-married after Kondo-san's mother died. It was a classic Cinderella tale. The stepmother hated him, favoured her own son, whom she wanted to inherit the temple, rather than Kondo-san who, as eldest son, was in line for it. So she succeeded in making life miserable for him and in promoting her own son in the father's favour. Kondo-san, from young childhood, had to do most of the cooking and cleaning in the temple and sell newspapers after school. On the one afternoon a week he had free, he worked with handicapped kids. Well, after 20 years and no sign that things would improve, even Kondo-san was starting to get discouraged. Reiko-san stepped in and helped him to run away. (Imagine, 28 years old and having to run away *from home, but such is temple life in Japan). It was summer. Bit by bit he smuggled out boxes of clothes, mostly winter ones, so that it would look as if he was going to Hokkaido. Reiko-san, as wife in a very prominent temple, was putting her neck on the block. They got him to Toshoji.*

For a month the police didn't get wind of him. Then one of the dormitory students got stopped for drunken bicycling, and Kondo-san went to bail him out. They asked his name and birthplace. Not having a sly bone in his body, he 'fessed up. Explosion! His people came down for him (after many intense phone calls). Finally Go Roshi hid him in a cupboard and had another monk let on that he had run away from here, too. I don't know what will happen next, but the police have black-listed Toshoji. There's certainly never a dull minute here.

I've kind of adopted that poor mutt Guru (remember the one with the unearthly howls?). I never thought of myself as a dog person, but dogs are really great. They give you so much more of a reaction than cats.

I'm blasting through koans these days. I can scarcely keep up and seldom have time to prepare them properly, but Go Roshi figures that if he at least gives me the key to them, then I can digest them later. Phew! My head is spinning a bit.

A couple of days later . . . I'm very excited about the news that Scott is coming. I only wish he could have been here in time for my ceremony. We're busy preparing for sesshin. Right now I'm up

267

on the roof mending futons. It's a beautiful sunny day, a change from the weather of late. It's so very pleasant sitting up here in the sun and wind, sewing, listening to the children playing in the streets below.

Today a woman from some Tokyo magazine came for an interview, and before I left Morioka, I did a long radio thing that was to be played in installments for a week. I wouldn't be surprised if Scott ends up on radio or TV or in some magazine. I haven't worked on my novel for weeks, but it's in the works. How's about Christmas in dear old dirty Dublin?

Much love, M.

Toshoji, Tokyo
April, 1982

Dear Mum,

Happy Easter! It's a glorious Easter Sunday here but without a bonnet in sight (in fact, only conspicuously bald heads). They'd give anything for Easter weather like this in Ireland—seems a shame to waste it on infidels.

Sesshin is over, and practice for my ceremony is in full swing. I'm going over, and over again, the same meaningless syllables *(ancient Japanese that even the Japanese don't understand). I have to do all the tonality and pronunciation in a peculiar oratorical style resembling the Kabuki narrators. It's going to be unusual anyway. . . .*

Scott, I'm as excited as can be that you're coming. For clothes, the young Japanese casual uniform is a track suit, though that may be hot in a Tokyo summer. You may want to ship back most of your baggage ahead, as we'll travel light in Thailand and India. My ideal is one of those weekender packs, a sleeping bag and rain poncho that can open into a ground sheet, a set of clothes on one's back, a set in the pack, and a light jumper or cardigan (maybe not necessary; I must check the likely weather.) I don't believe in money belts. Everyone knows about them, and the pros all know how to relieve you of them. Get both large ($50.00) and small travellers' checks so you don't need to carry too many. Bring a nailbrush. Where do you want to go? Flights within southeast Asia are cheapest from Hong Kong, so we should start there, and flights back are cheapest from Thailand. Also, bring Lomotil in case of tummy problems. So start researching and dreaming, and let's have some fun.

Love, M.

MARCH 30

Put out futons to air. Dug garden. Made oryoki. Six hours zazen. Nakamura read me koans on the floor by flashlight. First hint of any interest in me.

MARCH 31

Changed address at *Yakuba [ward office]*. Preparing for sesshin. I feel an incredible joy, incredible energy. The koans are still hopeless.

> *Somewhere a door creaks*
> *I crane for a*
> *certain footstep.*

APRIL 1-5

Sesshin. Kitchen great, I wasn't tired, it became the heart of the temple. Everyone streeled in in dribs and drabs if they needed a chat or a cry, an ookyo book, rice balls, a cup of tea, if their legs hurt or they had a headache or cold, if their kimono needed sewing or their rakusu, if their dokusan needed translation or if their address book had to be fished out of the toilet; they all came to the kitchen. Me and Kondo-san were the mother, Go Roshi the stern but beloved father. During their meals I'd lie down on the kitchen floor with my head on a rice sack, and a smile would creep across my face. We were very happy, worked very hard, and laughed very hard. My koans weren't great, I had scarcely time to prepare them. Still, Go Roshi says that of all his disciples I stand alone. Politically, we could never agree. I appreciate his points, and if everyone felt like him, as apparently they used to, it would be great. I doubt he'd ever appreciate my point.

APRIL 1

Allison and Mike got kensho. It was very beautiful to be with her then, but later she was disillusioned and depressed. She still doesn't really know she's Buddha. Mike had no expectations or disappointments.

APRIL 2

Kiguchi-obasan from Morioka had kensho. In zendo she could hear my voice doing ookyo (but I wasn't); then she was crying and got into the dokusan line. I was watching Namura suffering and failing dokusan, and Kiguchi was crying beside me. It became too much. I began to cry, too. She was deeply moved and had kensho. I ran downstairs, collapsed in a heap in the corner by my rice bag, sobbing uncontrollably. They were all suffering so. Stuart came in, was shocked and comforting. I left meals outside Namura-san's door. He wasn't getting kensho, and I was afraid it might bother him to think I was watching. He tried with his heart and soul, and mine, but he didn't get kensho. Even in the kitchen I'd call "Mu, mu," to him, but my concentration was bad. He seems sad these days, hasn't been doing zazen.

I'd like to reach out to him, but he often seems strained in my presence.

Go Roshi was an inspiration. His leg is still dreadful, but he struggled to sit on it. I begged him to use a chair but he refused. The leg has swollen to twice its size. In dokusan, he was continually shifting because of the pain of sitting long hours on it. This sesshin I was right weepy. Tears just streamed down my face, touched that he'd do this for us, pained to see him. He says I'm not to go back to Kannonji.

APRIL 7

Roshi went to Morioka, Yamaguchi goes home for a couple of days. Drizzle day, mostly sewing.

APRIL 8

Count Basie concert with Yuriko and Hiroshi. Roshi still in Morioka. I knocked down an old shed. Went for a drive with Izaki-san. It was pathetic. Surrounded by concrete warehouses, a towering official with a walkie-talkie, Izaki-san looked up at him and said, "We just want to see the sea." A gull circled overhead. "Impossible." We drove for ages and finally saw a bit of the sea by the airport. I talked to Namura a bit, but he seems very cold. He hasn't seemed well since sesshin. In torrential rains in the afternoon, met Roshi at the station. Yen phoned, Allison frantic that I won't be returning to Kannonji.

April 10

I chopped up the shed and put the wood away. Put ashes on the garden. My practice for *Hossenshiki [koan graduation ceremony]* not very good. I'm sleeping four and a half hours with no problems. Feel good.

April 13

I decided to approach Namura. He looked so mopish and depressed. He hadn't been doing zazen in zendo. But I came on like a bulldozer. He didn't know how to react. I asked if he was okay, and he said he didn't seem right. Then, Japanese style, he started apologizing. I ranted and raved about the Japanese repressing their feelings, etc.

A new American woman, Jocelyn Ford, entered. Seems she may be serious.

Izaki brings me cheesecake.

April 15

I put mondo to Go Roshi.

"The stone that is now preaching the Dharma, is it living or dead?"

He said "*Isshi, konna ishi?*" ["*Stone, this stone?*"], indicating.

I said "Hai."

He said "I don't know," then laughing, "ask the stone."

I said, "I am asking the stone." We were both laughing.

He said, "I'm not a stone. I'm Ban Tetsugyu" and we both dissolved into laughter.

Jiko-san came, back from India.

Bad zazen, very sleepy, disorganized. Couldn't do dokusan in the morning. Pouring rain.

April 17

Abe says he'll help, and I have written to various people asking them to visit Allison.

Actually had a five minute conversation with Namura. Since my outburst, he seems in much better humour. I don't know if there's a connection.

In the evening went to zenkai with Go Roshi. Maezumi Roshi was there. Seems good. The whole thing was great fun. Roshi was in a very good humor. We went by subway with Maezumi Roshi asking Go Roshi, "Where's your car?" Go Roshi wouldn't let either of us carry his bag, so Maezumi shared it with him. They fought like little boys going down the street in the dark, and finally both carried the minuscule briefcase. I walked behind in undignified convulsions of laughter. Roshis!

April 18

It was Go Roshi's grandchild's birthday. They invited me over. I was very touched.

Allison phoned, she's not getting on with Tetsugen.

I went to see Kiguchi-san. His mother was returning in the morning, and I wanted to stay and give her an obento. Turned out it was Kiguchi's birthday too, and Namura was there. I left to phone Allison, planning to come right back. He left.

Allison was asleep, but I asked Tetsugen to give her free time each week. He didn't seem to mind. Sounded good.

I felt disappointed that Namura was gone and annoyed with myself for being disappointed. Zazen was bad, so I went up on the roof. It was getting late, and Namura's laundry was out, so I was putting it away just as he came for it. We talked for a long while. It was nice, but when Izaki and Kiguchi appeared, Namura scarpered.

Kondo is a sweetheart, brought me an eclair.

APRIL 19

I decided to try three hours sleep. I was exhausted. I tried reading the paper, next thing I remember it was 4 o'clock and Go Roshi was knocking on the door, calling me to dokusan. Things went wrong all day. Really seemed jinxed. I suggested to Roshi that Gen go to Nagano, Mio to Toshoji, and Allison to Kannonji. He said he wanted me to marry a Japanese man and run one of the temples. He's given that a rest for a while. Another goof: I tried to give Kiguchi a late birthday present, poised it atop his window ledge, and it fell. Highly breakable. It was Roshi's 33rd wedding anniversary.

APRIL 20

Go Roshi stunned me in dokusan. I'd been thinking about Namura being seven years younger than me, and that really this attraction is absurd, when Go Roshi told me the story of the woman who jumped into the toilet to save the cat. From all the priests she had picked out the best one, the one most serious about training, as she herself had been. The one she chose was seven years younger than herself. Roshi looked at me meaningfully. "I want you to follow her, that is, choose for yourself."

My Hossenshiki *renshu* [*practice*] is 120 percent thanks to Abe-san, who drills me very kindly.

The funny, drunken former tenzo came back again. He sat with his sandals outside the gate, heaving big sighs. He became a bit violent.

APRIL 21

Go Roshi is pushing me hard to stay in Japan and become his successor. I feel disoriented. All my previous principles, goals, opinions seem totally changed. Whether I'm here or in Ireland, married or not, none of it seems a big deal. It seems I should assent and truly throw my life away for training. Mum would be upset. In the real world, Roshi's and my ideas are so different. But it seems I have no criteria left by which to make a decision. Anything is okay. It's a strange feeling, not a problem, but definitely disorientating.

I did *insatsu* [*printing*] in the evening, with the rain falling.

Roshi said my interpretation of the koan was deeper than the koan. Then he thanked me. I was touched.

Allison phoned again; it's hard for her.

APRIL 22

I planted flowers, weeded, did insatsu, sewed. I love all the people in Toshoji, each and every one of them. They're all excellent, not a bad apple in the bunch.

APRIL 25

My ceremony.

I practiced too hard the day before so my voice was not at its best but was okay. Wonderful day. I had prepared a good speech, but when asked to speak, could only burst out crying. I got very emotional and kept bowing and thanking people. (I spent all my money in a frenzy of gratitude, buying things for everyone.) Many beautiful gifts to me; I was extremely moved.

In the evening we had my party. Kondo-san hurt his back, so I had to do all the cooking. Tired. Up at 2:30, great energy in hossenshiki, then no break. Cook and clean.

They all dedicated songs to me. Yamaguchi was roaring, looked as if his blood vessels would pop, thumping his leg. Izaki, swaying, romantic, asked Namura for a song, but Namura said he couldn't sing. Later he stood up shouting, "Everyone's done a song for Mora; only I haven't because I can't sing." So he did a wild, impassioned, cheerleading type of thing, punching the air, creating dazzlers, screaming my name. I wanted to run to him.

Later I couldn't meditate for thinking of him, so I went to the roof. Kondo-san was lying on his back, drunk, singing powerfully to the stars. He then calls into the night: "Mora-san, I made a mistake (in the ceremony). Sorry." He's so pure, beautiful. I sat on the steps. I was a bit worried about Kiguchi, so I headed that way with the dog, met Izaki, Namura, and friends going to the baths. I asked directions to the park; Namura didn't show me the way.

APRIL 26

Poor Kondo-san, still maimed. Abe-san is doing massages and needles. I am doing the kitchen.

APRIL 27

Namura is definitely not interested, so to hell with it. I'll just forget about him.

I spent hours getting Roshi's *tabi* [*socks*] dry by the morning, then he didn't wear them.

There is nothing dead. Everything alive is in movement, if only in time.

MAY 1-5

Did sesshin in traditional temple in Kyushu. Allison

shaved her head. Go Roshi was happy. Her poor legs gave her agony. We ate and slept in zendo. I made many mistakes in protocol, but Tetsumon-san helped me.

It was the best sesshin I'd ever experienced. I had two minor awakenings. On the second day, in dokusan line, I realized–really experienced–*"ten ni mo chi ni mo tada ware hitori."* [*"In heaven and earth, there is but I, myself."*] That "ware hitori" includes everything.

Later, during teisho, I felt such intense gratitude toward Go Roshi, I could only cry. I cried for about an hour and a half.

On the fourth day, my awakening began in the corridor and became intense while I was eating. Everything is perfect. Everything is enlightening, just as it is by virtue of being. As it is, it is *narikiteru* [*totally being*], even *bonpu* [*the mundane unenlightened state*] is narikiteru bonpu. It was revelation, the perfection within the imperfection. Many times Go Roshi's words of remonstrance penetrated to my very core. "Is there even one of you truly narikiteru?" I'm not.

At the end, Hukokuji's Roshi made a speech and referred to the fact that, like Dogen Zenji, I hadn't slept lying down for a thousand days. I was so ashamed and also inspired to do better during the final *Shiku Seigan Mon* [*Four Vows*]. I was weeping again, intensely grateful to have the opportunity to experience this sesshin.

I forgot about Namura. I must just do good training, no distractions.

Tetsumon-san made a weird speech. He likes me (loves me, he says) but is justifiably put out by Roshi's exaggerations of my worth and his condemnation of the Japanese. I wish Roshi wouldn't do it.

Allison is to come to Toshoji in July; I wonder how Namura will feel. People have started doing zazen. At first it was only me, now there are five of us in the evenings.

I feel ecstatically happy. It's a gorgeous May, warm and breezy. I love the world.

May 14

Last night I stayed up late talking with Namura—very good, very open, spontaneous, and relaxed. I realized many things. I grew to like him more, and I feel closer to him, but am put off him as a man. He's still too young. I'd hate to either dominate or mother him, as would be inevitable. That leaves me freer to concentrate on training. But he's a wonderful person.

Go Roshi returned. He seemed tired but strong.

May 15

Reiko-san and Megumi came to visit. I was very happy. Megumi is unsure about her future. (A Morioka woman who was apparently moved to tears to see me in takuhatsu, wants me to help her son tread the right road, return to school, etc. These are strange cases. I feel wilder than the kids.)

I have started cleaning the toilets again at 3 o'clock in the morning. Three hours' sleep. I am pretty much asleep sitting up, but still bad.

The weather threatens rain, but it is beautiful.

TOSHOJI, TOKYO
MAY 17, 1982

Dear Kate,

. . . Just had a phone call from Jane. Nearly dropped. It's May 17, I wished her happy birthday, she said it wasn't her birthday. Beginning to wonder if I had 2 sister Janes or was going soft in the head. It's still yesterday there (and Go Roshi always says the past doesn't exist).

It's sunny. I'm watching the beans grow. It's a happy, peaceful day, neighborhood. People all doing Oriental neighborhoodsy things, and the kids are feeding shoes to our dog, who is called Guru, and kept on a chain. This morning we did a funeral for a cat. I became an official female priest on Ruth's birthday. I'm Soshin osho now.

The funeral people brought us a big feed of sashimi in thanks. Seems appropriate to get raw fish for burying a cat.

I'm sitting in May sunshine and winds overlooking Tokyo. If it was a clear day, I could see Mt. Fuji, but it's not, so I can't. I've been sitting up here mending Go Roshi's patches. He's been wearing this robe for 50 years, so I'm putting patches on the patches, and it's all fraying in my hands and these heavenly May winds. So I'm taking a break and writing to you, without much to say.

Days fly past, cleaning and sitting and having a laugh. It's nice living with people again. All good people, but like any bunch living in a small space, many undercurrents. The Japanese aren't big on face-to-face encounters, etc., yet everyone just seems to know what's afoot. I've shocked more than one by saying the unsaid, out.

Go Roshi is good. Had planned to die this year. It's the year of the dog; he was born in the year of the dog, so he wanted to have a big bash and pass on. But his book's been delayed, and half the text has gone amissing, so he's putting off his retirement.

*

Another day. It's three in the morning. I've just finished washing all the toilets, pulled up the poles, and opened the gates, put out the offertory box and the outside offerings. Some drunks are staggering home, and I still don't feel quite coherent but reckon you've been waiting quite a while for an answer.

I guess the most exciting thing that's happened to me lately is the sesshin in Kyushu. Kate, it was great. I got to just be a participant. No cooking, serving or patrolling, but loads of zazen. Anyway had a couple of real breakthroughs. Very overwhelming, tears and laughter and a long sit in a pebble garden. Now they seem tenuous. Old habits die hard but the experiences are there, I now really know what I had theretofore assented to as being true. Anyway excellent, though as excitement it probably seems boring in the context of what you're doing. (Well, to hell with contexts.) . . . Kate, I have to go. Write again.

Take care, M.

MAY 18

The clock stopped, and the dog broke a bag of garbage. I saw both and took care of neither. Funbetsu—I'll do it later. I haven't the responsibility here.

MAY 19

I'm making myself do jobs when I'm willing to turn a blind eye. Made juice, sewed clothes on the roof. I began work on the *Mumonkan* [*"Gateless Gate" a book of koans,*] translation again.

MAY 21

I had an incredibly wonderful walk with the dog through the streets. They were playing music; I wanted to dance. A mother watched her child eat pink ice cream. The summer plastic festoons have gone up, silver and blue. The streets seemed to be in festival. Smells of soba. Vegetable stalls. Old man on a bicycle. Young lovers not holding hands.

Ichigawa-san was afraid to sleep in her room, so we traded. Had a laugh. I heard funny noises and thought Namura was playing tricks on me. He'll be a fine man, but not right for me. Nice to really know it and nice that he's relaxed with me. The dormitory students have been coming down with things. I like mothering them. Everyone takes care of me in so many ways—fixing me treats, giving me papers, helping me with my koans, shaving my head. They're all patient, kind. We love one another beyond nationality or sex.

I have been tired for the last couple of days, almost no sleep. I am ashamed, though, of my shoddy efforts. I read about the old masters, bow to the living Buddha before me in dokusan, and try, but I am still very far from *risshin* [*success*], from narikiteru.

It was a rainy day, very nice. Greens intense, pink roses.

MAY 23

Jim and Dominique are in town. I stood bald under the *Star Wars* sign in Ueno Park. Many stares in the razzle-dazzle of the night. I met Jim's mum, her birthday is the same as mine.

MAY 24

My birthday. Paul sends instant birthday kit from Dublin: Guinness, cake, and tapes. We have a hell of a party, dancing on the roof. Lovely gifts. Crazy night. Tired next day.

MAY 26

In the morning I felt exhausted to my bones. I feel I will surely collapse, I have reached some kind of limit, breaking point. I wanted to sleep 24 hours. I will surely collapse in sesshin. The tiredness has accumulated. Sleep after breakfast for an hour. During the morning the tiredness falls away. I can scarcely believe it. At lunch I feel alert enough to write letters. Really strange. My shoulders feel tight, but my body no longer seems tired either. (Izaki-san, so funny, doing zazen he feels strength he says came from me, sitting opposite.)

June 6

We had sesshin from June 1-5. Time flew. Allison and I in the kitchen. She's moody but a very big help. Kondo-san has kensho. I'm delighted. Also Ichigawa-san and a German, Helmut. I was translating for four people. Very busy, often began at 3:00-3:30, clean toilets, work all day.

June 8

We went to the park, danced barefoot. Kikuchi and Izaki-san played the guitar and sang. In the distance we could hear a baritone and flute player. We raced bikes home. I fell asleep in zendo.

June 10

Namura's folks came, worried about him. Made us promise not to tell.

June 12

Galli-san phones, trying to come to sesshin. No expectations or anxiety. I can't imagine. His voice was good. I am working on *Tetsugyushi* [*Go Roshi's book*] and Mumonkan. In the evening I met Namura on the roof. The air was heavenly. We had a good chat, open. I told him some of the problems I had at the age of 20; he seemed eased.

JUNE 13

Izaki-san came back, did some Mumonkon. I was starving. Kondo-san is doing the wedding arrangements. I cook for two ceremonies. Did a fantastic zazen on the rooftop.

JUNE 14

For the first time since he was sick, Namura did ookyo the energetic way he used to. I'm delighted.

JUNE 18

I begin *Denpo-shiki* [*transmission ceremony*]. Three thousand full bows. Have one week to do it in. For the first ten minutes or so it felt good. Breathing deep from the hara, "*Namu san ze sho bu(tsu)*" ["*Homage to all the buddhas of the Three Worlds*"] again and again. Up and down, head bowing, blood rushing to the head, hyperventilating. Then I began to feel dreadful. Everything hurt, breathing, legs, stomach, dizzy. Kondo and Izaki gave me treats. I continued, barely took breaks. Was drenched in sweat. I began to lose awareness, felt there was a noise, a movement, vague sustained awareness of heat, but no "I." If I stopped, the pain in my legs was excruciating, but doing it again, I became unaware of them. Fifty wooden chopsticks from side to side. I finished 3036 the second day. Everyone was incredulous. Do banka, then straight out to zenkai. I was falling asleep there. The stairs were hell.

JUNE 20

Father's Day.

Up early. Legs dreadful.

I have my Denpo-shiki. Very moving. Early in the morning, 50 bows. I do *doshi* [*officiate*]. Hardly notice my legs. I have to concentrate. I can scarcely do all the bows. We bow together. Abe-san attends. Go Roshi removes my *okesa* [*outermost robe of the fully ordained*] and gives me a gorgeous okesa. When it finishes, I cry more.

I sneak into his room and leave pens, goodies, a card, and roses.

JUNE 22

Usha, an Indian Hindu, comes for the night. She's a very wonderful, intelligent, unusual woman. I'll visit her again.

JUNE 24

I spent the day getting photocopies. I lost and found my dokusan notebook. Izaki was incredibly kind to me.

JUNE 25

I returned a book to the Zenkai temple. There was a

letter from home. I phoned Scott's host family to let them know when he would arrive.

Dear Mum,

. . . Hope Scott comes soon, as the 10th of July until the 6th of August will be hectic for me with the summer equinox sutras. I have to do 80 houses in 5 days, then race up to Kannonji and get the place ready for sesshin, then do sesshin, rush back here to prepare for the August sesshin, cater that (sweltering Tokyo in August). So anyway, I hope he comes soon. Did you get my letter telling you how Paul, from Ireland, managed to give me a brilliant birthday party? On Go Roshi's birthday he phoned from London. He said he had a great time in Dublin. . . . I've been working every day on translating Go Roshi's book. It's very hard. When I go back to Ireland, I want to study Japanese seriously. In order for proper Zen (not "pop Zen") to take root in the West, there are a lot of vital

texts that simply must be translated. All present translations are really inadequate. I'll explain another time. I'm not crazy about translation work, but it has to be done, so . . .

Koan study is proceeding at a dizzying pace. Quite a few foreigners are coming these days, so I translate all their dokusans. This is a great opportunity for me because I see again and again how to deal with beginners and to adapt one's approach and one's answer to the needs of the person. So I'm thriving, but by October will be ready for a break. . . .

Love, M.

TOSHOJI, TOKYO
JULY 4, 1982

Dear Okachan [Mum],

Well, your son has safely arrived and quickly acclimatized. There was an accident on the runway, so his plane had to circle overhead for ages. I was there at 3:30. He finally arrived at 8:10. It gave me plenty of time to talk with his host family. When he arrived, they recognized him; I didn't. I insisted that grown-up young man wasn't Scott. Like Peter, I denied him three times before it finally hit me that it might indeed be my brother. He's much changed, very likeable. The poor kid had been awake for 28 hours but managed in a foreign culture to be very gracious, helpful, attentive, and extremely positive. Really he was delighted by everything. He tucked right into the raw fish with relish, likes his family very much, and when he finally got to go to bed, he wanted to unpack and put away everything from his suitcase first, so as not to be messy! Really, I was very impressed with the way he only saw the good side of everything and made a real effort (though it seemed effortless). But I can't get over how very American he seems.

His family let me spend the night there. They are lovely. The father is gentle, with smiling eyes, very intrigued by Scott. He only knows how to say "thank you" in English.

Scott took to the whole thing like a fish to water. No awkwardness, as if he'd been in Japan for years. He seemed to know all the right things to do, how to hold his glass, to pour for others, how to sit politely, etc.

The mother is delightful—one of those super duper Japanese housewife types. She had worried awfully about Scott coming, afraid he'd be too tall for the futons, etc. She actually lost weight worrying. The older son is 24, has spent over a year in the States, so speaks fluent English and understands how it is to be away from home and in a strange culture. The girl's English is good, though slow. She's outgoing and fun. They've arranged for Scott to attend her school. All the girls there are dying to meet him. In short, things got off to a very nice start.

*Scott wants to give sesshin a try, though he'll miss the
Kannonji one on account of school. It's a pity. I wanted him to meet
all the folks up there. We were both dismayed by our mutual dates.
The very earliest I can leave (doing all my packing, buying, goodbyes
before sesshin) would be October 7th. Scott feels he must be back at
school by mid-October.*

*A wonderful Indian woman came to stay here recently. She's
50, single, a lecturer in psychology, and the student of an Indian
guru. She has a house and servants on the Ganges. We got on
extraordinarily well, and she invited me to come and stay as long as
I wanted. In October there's a festival of lights and one of good and
evil that she wants to show me. She says that October is most pleasant and she'll take me to various places of Buddhist interest as well
as a visit to her ashram in the mountains. I wish there were some
way that Scott could work things to come with me. I think I'd really
enjoy his company.*

Love, M.

TOSHOJI, TOKYO
JULY 16,1982

Dear Mum,

*. . . We are into obon now and suddenly two 69-year old
parishioners passed away. Remember, that involves wake, service at*

home, one at temple, one at crematorium, and one at the grave.
We're going bonky. One of the dormitory students who has been
growing out his hair came home last night after a few drinks, merry,
singing, and rubbing his new hair, only to be told that we're desper-
ately short of priests. Would he mind shaving? God love him. Not a
grumble, just where are the clippers? Today I do ookyo from 8 in the
morning til 7 at night, then out to the wake. I hope someone feeds
me. Will write when there's more time. . . .

Love, M.

SEPTEMBER, 1982

Dear Mum,

. . . We can't get info here in Tokyo on flights back to the
States from Thailand (the bargain ones) for Scott, so we'll wait till
we get to Thailand and then see what the story is there.

[Later] I've been having terrible trouble cashing our dollar
checks. Don't know how the Japanese handle international banking
at all. It's unfortunate that all this coincides with ohigan. I'm unbe-
lievably busy. (It's now 3:37 in the morning, and I'm stealing time
between jobs to write this.) It looks, however, as if the checks will
pass through by Monday.

I tried to contact Sr. Ruth Sheils, but our schedules didn't fit
well enough so we could meet, but we had a very nice long phone

chat. She's a very interesting and intelligent woman and will look me up in Ireland next summer. She told me a lot about Sacred Heart, Tokyo, and it sounds excellent.

Days and days later: We've had ohigan, then a sesshin, in between my trying to organize packing, posting, visas, shopping, money, goodbyes—am totally exhausted, but it's almost over. The reason this took so infernally long was that I was waiting for definite news on our travel funds. It was hell. Anyway, I must post this NOW or not at all.

Sorry! You can't imagine how busy things are. Will write.

Love, M.

EPILOGUE

In October of 1982, Maura finally set out to return to the West. Before going to Ireland, however, she planned to tour for two months in southeast Asia, then spend Christmas with her family in Maine. The temple people didn't want her to leave, but the fact that I was due back in school by mid-October gave a good reason for our early October departure from Japan.

On the flight from Tokyo to Bangkok, we met a charming Hong Kong woman who invited us to stay in her apartment in that city for a few days. So we explored Hong Kong and then took an overnight trip to Macao. Hotel rooms were too expensive there, so we spent the night on a huge rock that jutted out from a wall in Macao. We caught up on our sleep next day on a bus trip through the Chinese countryside, then back to Hong Kong.

Next we flew to Bangkok where we stayed several days at a guest house owned by the Devahastin family, Thai friends whom we had known in Dublin. Here Maura arranged the itinerary for her Asian journey, which was to start with a bus trip to the ancient capital of Thailand in the north, Chiang Mai. She was one of the last passengers to board the bus for the overnight trip so she sat at the front near the driver. When he fell asleep near dawn the bus went off the road killing Maura, the driver, and two other passengers. Although her passport and journal were stolen with her luggage, the police were able to identify her by means of a ticket stub they found in the pocket-like sleeve of her monk's robe. On October 23rd, I received the phone call from the U.S. State Department informing us of the accident. The consul at Chiang Mai arranged for the return of her remains after the cremation at Lapsang.

Maura's ashes are interred beside her father's in Mt. Hope cemetery in Lewiston, Maine.

—Scott O'Halloran

[A letter of condolence from Tetsugyu Ban to
the O'Halloran family]

 On December 8th, 1979, Maura O'Halloran
joined Toshoji Doairyo, and we had a Tokudo
Ceremony on December 10th. Her Tokudo
name was Daigo Soshin Hikyuni. She began her
vigorous training from that day.

On January 5th, 1980, at 6:30 A.M., she left Ueno
Station to the Kannonji in Yahabacho, Iwate-ken, with Sato
Jiko and Dote Tessen. For thirty days, from January 6th, she
trained in strict "Kan-Shugyo" (training in the freezing
cold). It was -20°C weather in Morioka where she had her
training. She returned to Toshoji on February 6th.

When I was ten, I had my Tokudo Ceremony at
Fukuzo-ji in Johoji, Iwateken. My master Fuchizawa Chiaki
said, "Zen monks must work 20 hours, and 3 hours for sleep
every day." Maura did exactly that.

Our grand master Dogen went to China and to the
Tendo mountain for one thousand days, working hard all day,
he sat for meditation at night. He slept two or three hours in
the sitting position. Maura did the same. She was the modern Dogen.

There was a spring training at Kannonji from May 2nd
for five days. Maura reached her enlightenment on the first
day. She went in for meditations twice, three times a day, and
solved all three thousand koans. We had her Hishinsai (graduation ceremony) on August 7th, 1982.

She requested to become a Tenzo for the fall training, starting from October 1st. Her wish was granted. She completed her circle and left Narita airport on October 9th.

I received an international telegram on October 25th, 8:00 P.M., which said Maura had died of accidents in Thailand on 24th. . . .

She had achieved what took the Shakuson [Shakyamuni Buddha] 80 years in twenty-seven years. She was able to graduate Dogen's thousand-day training. Then she left this life immediately to start the salvation of the masses in the next life! Has anyone known such a courageously hard working Buddha as Maura? I cannot possibly express my astonishment.

—Ban Tetsugyu
October 27, 11:00 P.M. as
I watch the eleventh day moon.

Maura Kannon (A brief history)

Miss Maura O'Halloran from Ireland.

On the 10th of October in the 54th year of Showa [1979], at Toshoji Temple she became a nun and completed 1,000 days of continuous Zen practice at Toshoji and Kannonji Temples. Her daily practice included three hours of sleeping in the zazen position and twenty hours of devotion to her studies in order to attain salvation not only for herself but also for all people.

On the 7th of August in the 57th year of Showa [1982], she was conferred an authorized certificate of "Enlightenment Achieved."

On the 22nd of October, on her way back to Ireland, at Chiang Mai, Thailand, by some traffic accident her life ended at the age of twenty-seven.

She is given the posthumous name of "Great Enlightened Lady, of the same heart and mind as the Great Teacher Buddha." Miss Maura has been a real incarnation of Kannon Bosatsu to be loved and respected forever.

We dedicate the Maura Kannon Statue here to her extraordinary memory.

Nirvana Day [February 15th] in the 58th year of Showa [1983], by Tetsu-gyu So-in, founder of Kannonji Temple.

—translated by Shiro Tachibana

AFTERWORD

The life and death of Maura "Soshin" O'Halloran became known to me one late spring afternoon in 1987, during a tea break at a Soto Zen monastery in western Japan. I had recently been sent from our women's monastery on the Pacific side to be, as it turned out, the one American female monk among 28 Japanese male monks for four years of teachers' training. On a day after I had been there several weeks, Tessai-san, a senior monk, quietly related the story of his Irish-American Dharma sister, "Maura-san." Deeply touched to hear of her selfless practice, I asked him for a photograph of her. Although she had not been in my lineage, I wished to honor, with a daily offering of incense, the memory of an American sister in the Dharma, whose understanding would have been of so much help to others. Although there is a growing number of western female monks who have become fully transmitted Dharma teachers and did all or most of their Soto Zen training in Japan, at the time of Maura's transmission only two had preceded her.

Shortly after I returned to America, an article came to my attention from the *Commonweal* magazine, written by Ruth O'Halloran, containing excerpts from her daughter Maura's journals. When I read for myself the depth of Maura's realization, I began a correspondence with her mother. Before long, I received a copy of the full manuscript for a book that Mrs. O'Halloran had built around the journals that Maura had sent back home before her departure. Through the work of Mrs. O'Halloran, and through this "record of a pure heart" (one variation of a translation for "Soshin," her daughter's Dharma name), Maura's realization and practice are available to others as her teaching.

The structure of Maura's monastic Zen practice supported a "waking up" or enlightenment through intense meditation, known as zazen, for long hours in natural temperatures, full-voice chanting, sustaining oneself on the minimum necessary sleep and food, and working single-mindedly under the guidance of a master, or Roshi. Maura says here Roshi is delighted that she is not used to the cold, for it is better training—"When we sing, we see our breath." Getting up early is hard for her, so she gets up earlier yet—there is "the time of lucidity that comes after the tiredness"; "tiredness drains the discerning mind."

There are other rigors of monastic life, cooking, cleaning, sweeping, and cleaning some more. At first, Maura doesn't "get" it. Early on, she mentions the "stupid" menial cleaning and with no enlightenment. Later she can say, "The cleaning will be fine, Takuhatsu will be fine." One by one, the things she fears and dreads become acceptable.

In the early stages of training, nearly everyone comes down with one form or another of malnutrition, to which the body eventually adopts. It is often then that a better balance between body and spirit takes place. While Zen cooking contains many elements of the macrobiotic diet, it is not based on the idea of "health food" alone; it is "pure food," food donated and prepared with a pure spirit, but not necessarily nutritionally complete.

When Buddhism was brought to cold countries, famine often meant that much of the populace had nothing to eat themselves, much less to donate, and Zen monks could not be expected to live solely on alms. Zen practice was therefore speeded up in order for the monks to fit in the hours necessary to cultivate the fields and grow their own food. Consequently, not a morsel of food, a grain of rice, is ever wasted. Although the Tenzo monk, or cook, will often cut carrots and other vegetables into attractive designs for the noon meal (as Maura's assistant was doing), all leftovers, anything edible remaining from lunch, including the rims and tips of the carrots, are chopped up finely and made into a leftover rice and vegetable porridge for the evening's "nonmeal. Maura is cautioned by her Roshi not to be different from the others, ". . . I eat fish for lunch because I eat what's given me."

Maura was assigned the role of Tenzo monk, which in the Soto Zen tradition is second only to that of the head of the temple because the Tenzo maintains the health of everyone else. Closely following in importance is the role of the Enju, or garden caretaker, which Maura also performed. His or her boss is Providence, and it is the fruits of the gardener's labors that, outside of alms and donations from the parishioners, supply the Tenzo. Maura planted vegetables, built compost retainers, made new beds, even hauled logs for borders alone on a wheelbarrow, and felt "at peace with dirt and wriggling things worth not more nor less than I." Maura carried out both these duties with full body and mind.

The ceaseless hard work, the spending of oneself, was not something outside of Maura. Doing what needs to be done, selflessly and singlemindedly, can be called a polishing of the heart, and it is from this that solid Zen practitioners appear to shine. Maura speaks of the radiant light that emanates from her Roshi, but is she who shines and begins to take on a new appearance, seeming younger and more vibrant as her practice grows. And as her practice grows, her deep understanding becomes more and more apparent. She writes, "I want to live [my life] for other people. What else is there to do with it? . . . It's as if to give myself is all I can do as the flower has no choice but to blossom. . . . So I must go deeper and deeper and work hard, no longer for me, but for everyone I can help." Maura-san has come to understand that practice itself is enlightenment.

A central element of Maura's Zen training is takuhatsu, or begging. The important spiritual practice of this going out to receive alms food once pervaded all Buddhist countries. Today in some Theravadin countries, monks still make the alms rounds with their begging bowls to the homes of lay followers in their area for the monks' once-a-day meal. In Mahayana countries such as Japan, offerings of uncooked rice and vegetables are more often the rule, especially at harvest time. Both male and female monks carry tubular cloth for holding rice and go from house to house to receive the offering. The rice is poured into one end of the cloth, which is tied shut, balanced on the shoulders, and carried on to the next house. Full, the sack can weigh 40 pounds. Most of the year, however, offerings are monetary. Kangyo, the practice of begging in the cold, further deepened Maura's practice by making her experience the direst circumstances. The monks walk with bare fingers, holding a Buddha bowl in one hand, and a bell with a cloth-wrapped handle (so the fingers don't freeze to the metal) in the other. The only time the arms are lowered below elbow level is when receiving an offering. In summer, monks try not to prance in place as the heat of the asphalt pierces their straw sandals. In winter, straw sandals are soaked in the first steps to the monastery gate, and it is the continuous pace and the deep breathing for the chanting that warm our bodies.

The first winter, Maura follows the other monks light-heartedly, comparing the chanting on the way to "Christmas caroling every day." She cannot notice then that the mood of her Dharma brothers is that of preparation for the annual challenge, even when they solemnly bring her bandages for her symbolic "wounds." The second year, she is actually looking forward to it, "Sometimes you could actually feel an energy of givingness and purity from the people and I'd feed off it, it surging through me, my voice becoming loud and untiring." Going deeply into the practice of alms rounds in the snow, monks like Maura have no "me." It is the chanting that chants.

In the first winter, Maura speaks of the blessing she cannot give after each donation is made. Perhaps she had not yet been able to memorize the gatha in Japanese meaning, "Two offerings of materials and teachings. Virtue is boundless. Offering Wisdom—Dana Paramitsu is perfectly achieved." Takuhatsu is a mutual exchange, face to face, of spiritual and material. The sight of monks, heads down, the umbrella-like straw hat aimed against the driving snow, is an inspiration to their donors to persevere likewise with the problem in their own daily lives. And for monks, going each day is the lesson of humility that, without donors, a monk cannot exist. It is itself significant that by her third year, the local villagers considered it an honor to donate alms to Maura during takuhatsu.

O-Higan and O-Bon are two of the most important and busiest Buddhist events on the calendar. The word "higan" means "the other shore," or "Nirvana," the opposite of "shigan" or "this shore of life and death." The O-Higan E is a week of Buddhist services and sutra reading for the deceased in parishioners' families, the middle day of which is the equinox, either vernal or autumnal. O-Bon is the Japanese word for the Sanskrit term "Ullambana," which means "rescue from the torment of hanging upside down in hell." It is observed on the 15th day of the seventh month. In metropolises like Tokyo, it occurs in July, following the Julian calendar; in the countryside, the lunar calendar is followed, making O-Bon one month later. Sutras are recited by a monk in parishioners' homes, in front of the Butsudan, or family Buddhist altar, in order to soothe the torments of the deceased in the lower realms of existence. The story behind this practice is that the Buddha's disciple, Maudgalyayana, saw with his "divine eye" that his mother had been reborn as a hungry ghost and wanted to save her. The Buddha said that only the combined efforts of all Buddhist monks could ease the sufferings of the tormented; thus, sutras were recited and offerings were made to liberate them. The story teaches the importance of caring for our ancestors and family members, and the transference of merit to those we love.

The sutra recitations of O-Bon and O-Higan are not only for the repose of the deceased, but for the spiritual benefit of the entire family. Alms and parishioner dues, as well as the income from sutra recitation, make it possible to train and feed monks gratis. And because others make the "awakened way" financially possible, a deep understanding of interdependency and gratitude fuels the monks' practice—a practice that does not end with oneself, but affects and includes those who have made one's very practice possible.

Outside of the Asian Buddhist population in the United States, a devotional sense, or a Bodhisattva Way of Zen practice as lived by Maura, has not been considered vital to Zen training until recently. In the early years, we were very enthusiastic about zazen, meditation. We couldn't conceive of real Zen practice as being anything else. Religious ceremonies and daily rituals weren't fully understood. But in actuality, at least half of a Zen teacher's life is devoted to the Bodhisattva Way.

Maura's practice was formed from both these halves—of zazen and the Bodhisattva Way, meditation and sacrifice. Her journals are a poignant record of this practice and will make Maura's unique understanding available for the benefit of others. The Buddhadarma as lived by an Irish-American female monk is now a part of modern Zen history.

Once renunciation and the awakened mind have been fully realized, the way to Buddhahood is clear. Liberation is complete and such liberated beings are then bodhisattvas and buddhas: "enlightened ones," or "empty dwellers." Their usefulness to others both before and after their physical death, is impossible to conceive. They are nothing but useful energy leading to liberation for all beings still caught in conditioned existence.

—from a tattered, anonymous page of copy
kept long years ago, when any Dharma
in English was rare and precious.

—Patricia Dai-En Bennage

Photograph taken in April, 1980

Creaking to the post office
on my rusty bike
I saw one purple iris
wild in the wet green
of the rice field.
I wanted to send it to you.
I can only tell you
it was there.

—Maura O'Halloran

Now and Then

EMILY KIMBROUGH

Now and Then

Drawings by Mircea Vasiliu

HARPER & ROW, PUBLISHERS
New York, Evanston, San Francisco, London

NOW AND THEN. Copyright © 1972 by Emily Kimbrough. All rights reserved. Printed in the United States of America. No part of this book may be used or reproduced in any manner whatsoever without written permission except in the case of brief quotations embodied in critical articles and reviews. For information address Harper & Row, Publishers, Inc., 10 East 53rd Street, New York, N.Y. 10022. Published simultaneously in Canada by Fitzhenry & Whiteside Limited, Toronto.

FIRST EDITION

STANDARD BOOK NUMBER: 06-012366-4

LIBRARY OF CONGRESS CATALOG CARD NUMBER: 72-79678

Designed by Pat Dunbar

To Alis (A.) and Margaret (B.)
with love

Contents

Now and Then

I

Double Image

Agatha Christie's astute spinster Jane Marple solved mysteries Scotland Yard's best could not penetrate, by linking each one to an incident in the village in which she lived. The village incident was too unimportant for even the notice of the local constabulary but Miss Marple, like a good cook tasting a new dish, could identify the basic ingredients and prove them to be identical in a simple village incident and a very fancy crime.

Of course Miss Marple's pattern of association had nothing to do with having twins. I apologize for even mentioning such an indelicate impossibility, but I have wondered if somewhere between the spinster, for whom the life of her community supplants a family, and a mother of twins there is a common denominator.

A mother of twins sees and thinks in double images; this stems from the necessity of double dealing. She sees two cribs, proffers two bottles, holds two babies. (In order to keep a hand free and useful, I learned to carry twins single file down and over one arm.) I think I am speaking for all such mothers when I make these assertions of division and multiplication though I have not done any research. In a library I would not know under what category to look for such data and I cannot compare my own findings with other mothers of twins, because I do not know any. My friends have had and brought up their children one at a time. Paradoxically, I have met, I think without exaggeration, hundreds of mothers in my category, but always under particular circumstances that make our meeting a brief encounter.

Twice a year I hit the creamed-chicken trail of speaking engagements. My topics vary, but invariably, for all my determination against it, I insert some mention of, or anecdote about, my twin daughters. If I were to ask urgently if there was a doctor in the audience, I could scarcely have a more immediate response. The only difference is the time lag. A doctor would stand up at once; a mother of twins—and sometimes there is a handful of them—is at my side as I leave the platform. I recognize them at once. We shake hands conventionally, but strong as a fraternity grip, there is an unexpressed wink of the eye and nudge in the ribs. We are "sports." If having twins is not sufficient mutation for us to qualify biologically as such, we are "different," and certainly qualify for synonyms of the other kind of sport—"showy," even "raffish."

We have time only for a quick exchange. The opening is usually:

"How do you feel when other women, outsiders, say, 'I envy your having twins. It must be so much easier.'?"

We smile understandingly at each other, and she moves on. I know her answer to this silly question would agree with mine, less violently expressed probably, and perhaps not accompanied by an impulse to do bodily harm to the nincompoop who has said such a silly thing.

There's nothing "easier" about having twins, from the burgeoning period straight on.

If my sisters in the sorority of mothers of twins look about my age, I know our bond is extra strong. Our pairs were born in the era of rigid schedules. If one baby woke fifteen minutes before bottle time the awakening was clarioned. This promptly roused the other to matching decibels and both screamed until the clock permitted them to be picked up, changed and fed—simultaneously. One compensation this era allowed was a nurse. Mine, young, warm, loving with babies, was German, trained in a children's hospital at Stuttgart. What a doctor said must be followed with scrupulous precision, and no lag. Therefore she "did" one baby, I the other; when the first was bottled she was handed to me to dress and put in her crib. While I dressed the second, Alma heated the bottles. With not a second between, each open mouth held a nipple, or a sodden glob of spinach. Services had not caught up with system. We had no Didee Wash— let alone Throwaways; between fifty and sixty pennants waved on the line every day. The special foods were prepared by Alma, with strainers and mashers for vegetables and pressers for extracting meat juices.

Given more time than our brief encounters allowed, we contemporaries would have asked one another why we allowed ourselves to be so persecuted by a system. We were fools, of course, but we were young and scared. We put ourselves and our frail little bundles under the care of a pediatrician. We had neither knowledge nor courage to gainsay him. Babies are tough. They grow up. How parents survive is the miracle, but they had grown up by the time we caught on to that. For three nights or more in a row, wrapped in a comforter I have sat in a room where a croup kettle steamed and listened to breathing that sounded like rusty

4

gate latches opening. Alma and I would take turns of perhaps two hours, allowing each other that much sleep. There always came a morning, thank God, when one could rouse the other with:

"The babies are fine. They've had a big breakfast. They want to get out of their cribs, and play."

We would have been happy to stay in our beds for a week, and sleep.

Every mother has known those nights and days, but every mother has not known double double toil and trouble.

That stage passed, we came to the phase—and it was not a passing one—of separate but equal. How it simplifies shopping and choosing to buy duplicate Christmas or birthday presents for twins. How twins hate it. Unless they count together, "One, two, three, *open*," one has no surprise from a package. My twins demanded birthday guests separately chosen—sometimes by drawing from names on slips of paper in my hand—two tables, the favors and decorations on each different from the other, and birthday cakes of individual shape and color, but certainly exactly the same size.

Did those women who tell us twins are "easier" consider the economic "ease," we special mothers ask ourselves. A twin does not fall heir to the outgrown clothes or possessions of the other. Two bicycles are purchased simultaneously, sleds, writing desks. The list is heavy; so are the expenditures.

We would not change our double standard for any gold, but it is *not* "easy" to maintain. To keep an even balance makes the tightrope walker in a circus, by comparison, a bumbling amateur.

Those are the things I know I share with the women who identify themselves as gemini bearers, clasp my hand with understanding pressure and move on. These are the things I wish there were time to ask:

5

Do they pair off instantly in their minds one incident with another, different but similar? I know a universal trait is expressed by "That reminds me," but do the reminder and the incident occur simultaneously? They do for me. I think the reason is my conditioning that began at the double birth and will last my life. I never telephone one of my daughters, I always call each of them. Is this perhaps why, weekly, I talk to my stepmother in California and my brother in Chicago, one immediately following the other? It occurs to me, as I review these idiosyncrasies, I invariably read two books simultaneously, though not literally one in each hand. Reading, hearing or telling, I like balancing one story with another.

When my twins were three years old, I took them one day in December to a Christmas play at a nearby school. It was the first play they had seen, and they sat wide-eyed, remarkably still. The following afternoon I was called urgently to the playroom. One child sat on a low stool beside a doll's bed. Over her shoulders was draped a blue dressing gown of mine that lay in folds, like a robe, around her feet. On her head she wore a towel that hung down on either side of her face. She held upright in hand a stick from a drum, evidently a candle. Leaning toward the bed tenderly, she sat motionless. Lying on the bed, side by side, were two stuffed animals.

The other participant seemed to be the impresario and interpreter. Pointing to the tableau, she announced with measured solemnity, as she had heard the day before:

"Here is Mary with the little Lord Jesus—and his twin," she added.

For these two spectators there had been two babes in the manger at the play. They had actually not seen only one.

They have taught me to see and hear by twos.

II

Cases of Detection

One Sunday recently my two daughters and I watched on television the World Ice Skating Championship. My twin daughters are deeply involved in the sport. One is a teacher; the other, who did not turn professional, is now a national judge. All the years they were growing up I was an ice skating mother. A skating mother I venture to say is unique in the world of sport: at least I have never heard of tennis or golf mothers. Our not so happy breed wears stadium boots, heavy coats with sweaters underneath, a scarf over the head and warm gloves whether it is July at Lake Placid or mid-winter at the home club. Hunched with cold we sit on a bench or a camp stool as close as permitted to that section of the vast field of ice before us known as a "patch." It has been reserved for the offspring who is having a lesson or is engaged in what is called a practice session. At these sessions, because we have followed the lessons we call out expert advice: "Keep your right shoulder down, bring that left hip in a little."

With few exceptions not one of us, if we were to put on

skates with double runners, could stand, let alone take a step, unsupported on the ice.

Dick Button was a commentator for this event. I am reasonably sure he was christened Richard, but I have never known him to be introduced as other than Dick. When we first knew him he was ten years old and called Dickie. Among his qualifications as a commentator are the statistics that he was twice a gold medalist in the Olympic Championships, won the National Championship in ice skating six years in a row, and chalked up the same consecutive record in the World Championships. As he finished explaining to the viewers points of technique in the event at the moment completed, B, one of my daughters, said:

"Do you remember when I got the mumps?"

She was looking at me, and I nodded. We shared a secret. She turned back to the screen.

Like Dick Button, B has a christening name that is never used. It happens to be Margaret. She is called B because she is a twin and her twin sister is called A. I vouchsafe an explanation of this even without being asked because I wince at a possible implication of "cuteness" or "whimsy." The reason for the abbreviated and particular nomenclature was both practical and unself-conscious.

The announcement that I had been delivered of twins came as a great surprise to their father and me. We had not prepared ourselves with names for two. As I daresay is still the custom, a bracelet was put on each infant. The bracelet was composed of beads each imprinted with a letter to spell, as identification, the last name. Since in this double situation the last name was insufficient, the letter A was added to one and B to the other. With a special precision of data, it was pointed out to me afterward, B also stood for the earlier arrival by ten minutes and therefore could be interpreted as before A; B has always insisted on a recognition of this seniority. Today these souvenirs would be discarded and dismembered, I suppose, within forty-eight hours, when the mother left the hospital. In those far-off and, to me, happy times, a mother stayed in the hospital for at least two weeks, was cosseted by her own trained nurse, and took the nurse home. Mine had the most beautiful fit of name to personality I have ever known. She was Mrs. Devine. In her many years of nursing experience these were her first twins. Afraid she might bring the same one in twice for a feeding, though I knew them apart from the moment they were presented to me, she paid exaggerated attention to the charts. Each time, arriving at my room from the hospital nursery, she would look at the bracelet before saying:

"I've brought you A" or "I've brought you B."

Mrs. Devine stayed with us for eight weeks. In the meantime there had been a christening in which A had become Alis and B, Margaret, but when Mrs. Devine left, the bracelet names were indelibly stamped on our tongues. They are B and A to this day. To each other's children they are Aunt B and Aunt A. Though each has black hair and blue eyes, their children have never confused their identities any more than their mother ever confused them.

For B to ask if I remembered when she had the mumps was as rhetorical a question as if she had asked me to remember when she and her twin were born.

It was a night in April when B's mumps began. The twins were twelve years old and we were on a train traveling from Muncie, Indiana, home to Philadelphia. The trip had been my proposal, a sentimental journey. I had been on a speaking tour and my final engagement was in Muncie, the town in which I was born. The sight of this on my itinerary prompted what seemed to me at the time a lovely idea and before I left home I made all the preparations to have it carried out. The twins were to be excused from school on Friday, and put on a train Thursday night. I would meet them in Muncie the day of my speaking engagement; they would be excused from that on their own request. We would then have the weekend, when they would come to know my roots and theirs. They had visited Muncie when they were a year and half old and again at five but had not been back since then. The memory of a five-year-old is quixotic. Theirs ranged from strawberry shortcake made of pie crust, which is the way we do it in Indiana, to a candy Mr. Roller made that merited national fame. It was called a Dark Secret. So was the twins' memory between it and the strawberry shortcake.

My plan unrolled as smoothly as a wedding carpet down the aisle of a church. Why I did not accept this tranquillity with foreboding I do not know. I should have recognized the stillness before a storm and braced myself, because in my pattern of living I have only to originate a scheme, work out in advance every detail toward its accomplishment, to have it blow up at the moment of execution. My well-laid plans do not gang a-gley; they explode. This one had gone from idea to accomplishment without a hitch and I had enjoyed it without misgiving; I must have been stultified by the rich food we ate.

My girls had a wonderful time. They fell in with their contemporaries and their contemporaries took to them, a remarkable occurrence, I think, because usually the children of friends hate one another on sight or even before. The only complaint voiced by mine, not so much a complaint as a request for praise of their docile acceptance, was that they had never been kissed so much and by so many people in all their lives; and certainly, born and brought up in Philadelphia, had not been told once, let alone numerous times a day, how much they resembled in one way or another their Muncie grandparents and great-grandparents.

A sizable crowd came to the station to see us off; not so large as waves to departing royalty, but gratifying and truly heartwarming. There was of course another round of kissing before we boarded the train.

Sometime in the night B woke her sister and me; we were sharing a compartment. The braces on her teeth had slipped, she told us, and were giving her terrible pain. I filled the hot water bottle I always carry with me, applied it to her face, and she went back to sleep but not for long. Throughout the rest of the night she was up with me or across with A. I rubbed her back and refilled the hot water bottle. When we came into Paoli station at about half past seven the next morning A and I were groggy from want of sleep and B was still in pain. I told them I would telephone the school as soon as we got home to have them excused for another day. Instead of leaving the house again once we had reached it, we would do better to stop off at Dr. Sturgis's office since this was the day they were due for a shot, what kind of shot I do not now remember. I do remember vividly, however, that as part of my well-organized plan I had, before leaving on the tour, engaged Roy Johnson, our local Bryn Mawr taxi man, to meet this train; he had first met me at trains when I was in boarding school in Bryn Mawr. He wanted to know if the children had enjoyed their trip to their mother's hometown. A was volubly enthusiastic but B sat miserably quiet. I explained to Roy her braces had slipped and that her mouth hurt badly. Roy was sympathetic and helpful. Why didn't he drive us home after a stop at Dr. Sturgis's, drop off A and then take B and me straight into town to the "brace man"? We probably would only be a few minutes there. Just a little screwing and unscrewing—B groaned—and then he'd bring us right back home, where we could settle for a good rest. I endorsed the suggestion.

The doctor's nurse gave the required shot, but as we were leaving Dr. Sturgis came from his inner office to ask how the twins had liked Muncie, surmising, he said, they must have met everybody in the town.

"Not the whole town maybe," A told him, "but everybody we did meet kissed us." She shuddered extravagantly. "It was fun though," she added.

Again I explained B's silence, adding we were on our way now to get the brace put back in place, Roy Johnson was waiting. Dr. Sturgis said he was glad it was nothing more than a slipped brace and stopped abruptly.

"Hold on a moment," he said. He had been shaking hands with B and patting her commiseratingly on the shoulder. A and I were already out the door and he called us back. He led B to a light on the nurse's desk, tilted the lamp up toward her face, turned her head from side to side, felt gently under the line of her jaw; she winced. He looked across her at me.

"Don't bother to go in town," he said. "Just get this child home and to bed; I'll be over later. She's got a double case of mumps, both sides."

If I said anything I have forgotten it, but I can almost still feel the shock and the numbness that followed his news. Probably it was stupid of me not to have thought of such a possibility, but B had said her braces slipped, that was where it hurt, and I had accepted it; furthermore, neither of the children had reported any case of mumps at school. I do not suppose I thought of these things at the moment. I stood like a pillar of salt in the corridor outside Dr. Sturgis's office. Though it seems unlikely, considering the nature of the child, I do not remember that even A said anything. B was crying a little and I think I had my arm around her. I have every reason to remember, however, what Dr. Sturgis called after us as we reached the door. He was a jovial man.

"Nice to know you kissed nearly everybody in Muncie."

A's response has stayed in my memory because it seems now as adequate an appraisal of the situation as could have been offered.

"Golly gee." I had nothing to add.

Roy's comment on the change of plan and the reason for it was a long whistle on a descending scale. That too seemed a good summing up of everything involved.

B's was a light case. In a few days she was out of bed, and a week after the swelling was gone, by Board of Health rules, she was back at school. By the same rules, from the fourteenth to the twenty-first day, A had to leave school and with me be put in quarantine. I wrote all the people in Muncie who had been so kind to us, miserably giving them the news of how we were repaying their hospitality. By the time we were out of quarantine I had had a good many answers admitting that the memory of our stay was vivid, widespread and never to be forgotten.

On the twenty-first day, the period of incubation ended; A and I were released. The date of A's and my return to the outside world coincided with Parents' Day at the school. The children and I went together that morning. I visited each of their classes, talked to every teacher. It was a happy day. After school we went to Best's store in Ardmore, the suburb next to Haverford, where we lived. Summer was adjacent too, and the twins needed clothes for it. Evidently a great many children on the Main Line had the same need; the shop was crowded with them and their mothers, most of whom we knew and chatted with.

That night I went to the theater in Philadelphia. Friends were making this a party of theater and supper afterward to celebrate my return from the cloister of sickroom and quarantine. We were eight so we drove in two cars, one of them mine. I do not remember the play but I know I was enjoying it thoroughly when shortly after the intermission, which had given me an opportunity to see and talk with other friends there that night, I suddenly experienced how it must feel to be "socked in the jaw." Astonished at so unlikely an occurrence in a theater, and certainly with no visible assailant, I instinctively put my hand to the spot that had been assaulted. An unmistakable swelling burgeoned under my hand. I knew what, not who, had attacked me, and I echoed to myself A's summary "Golly gee."

After my whispered announcement to my neighbor and a vehement injunction not to come with me, I managed to get away unaccompanied. I think the others were not so much cowed by my vehemence as by the indignant hissing from other audience members in front of and behind us. On the way home, somewhere in Fairmont Park, I was clouted again on the other side and I remember vividly the eerie experience of feeling another swelling grow underneath my hand. Except for my aching jaws I had no feeling of illness, fever, chills, headache. I would have welcomed any of these distractions from the appalling realization of the second round of letters I must write, this time to the school, to the friends with whom I had talked during the afternoon at Best's, others in the lobby of the theater. And what to say to the friends who had given the theater party? I was still making and discarding phrases while I put the car in the garage, walked back down the driveway and let myself into the house. A provided an immediate distraction as I closed the front door behind me. Her room was on the third floor; she was leaning over the stairs. She called down.

"Mommy, is that you? I'm sick."

"We both are," I told her. "I'm coming right up."

Once, in Paris, I fell down a flight of stone steps and suffered a concussion that wiped out all memory of what had preceded and what followed as well as the occurrence itself. No such benevolent oblivion accompanied my encounter with mumps. Mine was the most severe case he had ever encountered, Dr. Sturgis told me, adding that he had seen plenty. In the First World War at the hospital in which he served there had been under his care an epidemic of the disease, with two wards filled to more than capacity. Not one of them matched mine in circumference.

Apart from the acute pain it brings, mumps is a humiliating, ignominious affliction. Instead of lying wan and frail, whispering brave words of encouragement to my dear ones, whose faces were pinched with anxiety as they bent over me, I sat upright in bed day and night because it hurt more to lean against a pillow. I wore a scarf folded under my chin, the ends tied on top of my head, because, I reasoned, since old engravings invariably identified similar sufferers by a sling of this kind, there must have been a reason for it. There was, and I found it a good one. The sling bolstered up and relieved the pressure of the drooping jowls. Dear ones came to the bedside, but their faces were not pinched with anxiety; they were contorted by an effort to conceal and stifle coarse laughter.

A's case was as light as B's had been. The epidemic we provoked, though not so widespread as the one B had kindled in Muncie, penetrated more deeply into the events it influenced. The graduation at the school had to be postponed because the school was in quarantine. A sizable number of parents of seniors were taking their girls abroad as a graduation present; they were unable to change the sailing dates; the trips had to be canceled. The harvest of our sowing was more widespread geographically, too, than the one in Muncie because the twins' was both a boarding and a day school for girls. Relatives of the seniors were coming to the graduation from all parts of the country and could not accommodate to the change of calendar. Even as I write it so long after the memory of what we wreaked, I wince with shame and move on rapidly to Dr. Sturgis.

From the day he had first come to see B, not more than an hour after we had left his office, he had begun to question her about places she had been and friends she had seen. In the intervening hours he had checked with the Health Department and found no cases of mumps reported in the township nor over a considerable area beyond. She must have caught it somewhere beyond this vicinity, yet not in Muncie because the visit there was too short and the time of her coming down with the disease of too immediate sequence.

From the first questioning B insisted she had gone nowhere outside Philadelphia except to Muncie and I could verify it. Dr. Sturgis accepted this with reservations. He was a persistent and perceptive man and he had known the children from birth. The children loved him; he was my mainstay and counselor. After the second or third visit to B, when he had asked the same questions as he went over her, he had indicated he wanted to speak to me. I went downstairs with him and we talked, while B could hear us, of details of treatment and diet. At the front door, when we were out of earshot, he looked at me quizzically.

"I think B is holding out on us," he said. "There's something she doesn't want to tell."

He was more perceptive than I, or perhaps, in justification, I was too preoccupied with her misery and how to make her more comfortable.

When she had bounced back to health, as children do almost overnight, I thought I detected in her an evasiveness and a discomfort that was not physical, though I was not sure my suspicions were genuine and not implanted by Dr. Sturgis. In the interim between B's recovery and my succumbing, his visits and the questioning stopped, but both were resumed when A and I inaugurated the second round. This time there was no doubt about B's evasiveness and her unhappiness. The severity of my attack required the services of a nurse at Dr. Sturgis's order. B's insistence on helping did not make it easier for Miss Smith to render these services. B trailed her, asking at intervals of minutes if she thought I was feeling any better. She begged to be allowed to help in whatever Miss Smith was doing and to stay in the room, except when she heard Dr. Sturgis's step and voice announcing his approach. Then she would shoot out, pounding up the stairs to her room on the third floor. Miss Smith would mercifully be unattended until B was sure the doctor had gone. She gave A solicitous attention too but since A's case, like her own, was short-lived, and A out of bed in a few days, I was the victim of her devotion.

The first day A was well enough to come down to see me, she stared for an instant and then shouted joyous laughter at the sight. B kicked her in the shins. B's devotion was touch-

ing and wearisome, but I was too sick to be stern in my request that she go away. As I emerged from my self-preoccupation enough to care about anyone else, I realized B did not look well; that A, more recently recovered from mumps, looked better than she. At Dr. Sturgis's next visit I asked if he would take a look at her.

"Her behavior is touching but unnatural," I told him, "and I don't like the way she looks."

Dr. Sturgis with satisfaction nodded agreement.

"She's got something on her mind she's hiding, and it's something to do with the mumps. Let's get her down here and talk to her if you feel up to it."

Miss Smith was sent to fetch her and returned with the message B was sorry, she was very busy and could not come. At that moment I knew I was better and was going to get well soon. I lifted my voice to the third floor in a tone that brought B down. Miss Smith was sent on an errand. A was outside.

Dr. Sturgis placed a chair between the one he was occupying and my bed, B was invited to sit between her two inquisitors. She hesitated a moment but catching my eye, sat down. Her eyes were big; she looked at me pleadingly and then defiantly, her body stiffening. My feelings were as divided as her expression. I wanted to take her on the bed beside me and put my arms around her; at the same time I felt respect for her fortitude. Evidently Dr. Sturgis shared something of this; his voice was gentle. He said, I remember, something like this:

"B, we know there's something you haven't told your mother and me and we know it's bothering you. We're pretty sure it has something to do with your getting the mumps. If it has, I really need to know about it, because,

21

you see, if you had told us in the beginning that you'd been exposed—and something tells me you knew you had been" —he waited; B made no answer—"then I would have kept you at home for the time when you might have come down with it." He smiled at her. She was looking directly at him. "Maybe you knew that would happen and didn't want to miss the Muncie trip?"

B shook her head with positive denial.

"But you see," Dr. Sturgis continued, "you gave it to a lot of other people and I'm sure you haven't been happy about that. It's really why Mother and I are asking you to tell us about it. I would like to report it to the Board of Health to make the record complete, but I truly care much more about your being happy again. Then you'll be really all well and we'll forget the whole thing."

B turned to look at me and I nodded.

The silence was broken by a wail that rivaled commendably the siren on an ambulance. I am sure Dr. Sturgis jumped. I, leaning tenderly over my child, very nearly fell out of bed into her lap. While I was recovering my balance she buried her head in the comforter, sobbing and talking at the same time. It was not easy to distinguish the words but I remember them.

"Any other girl could kiss a boy for the first time and not have it spread all over the country. Lots of girls kiss boys and they don't have to tell it to the Board of Health, and he lives in New Jersey anyway. But I didn't want you to be sick, Mommy, or A or all those other people and have it be all my fault. Oh, I feel awful."

Dr. Sturgis stood up, patting B on the back. He looked across at me with a facial contortion I had seen on sickroom visitors trying not to laugh at my appearance.

"Listen, B," he said when he could speak. "Don't feel awful; you're going to feel fine now and it's all over." He walked away, turning back at the door. "And one more thing. This will not be reported to our Board of Health."

When he had gone B raised her head. She was crying less violently. I wiped her face and gave her another Kleenex to blow her nose. The sobs she was checking made her speech ragged but she wanted to talk.

"You took us to the movies in Ardmore and then you came for us. We got out before you came and we were in that driveway along the side entrance and it was dark. I didn't know he was going to but he kissed me"—she paused —"and I kissed back."

"Good for you," I told her.

Her eyes widened and she grinned a little, pleased, surprised. "Well, then." She stopped to swallow, take a breath; the speech was smoother now. "He went home Sunday night. He was only here for the weekend for his skating lessons and that very Sunday night when he got home he came down with the mumps. So he wrote to me and said he thought he ought to tell me because he thought I'd better tell you." Another siren wail interrupted her but she spoke through it. "That's just what I didn't want to do because I'd have had to tell you about the kissing and don't you know when you kiss somebody it's very private? You don't want to go telling it around. That's why on the train I really thought my brace had slipped. Mumps didn't come into my mind at all. It was such ages since, you know, the kissing—I just forgot about the mumps part. I didn't know you had to wait so long. I never prayed so hard in my life as I did in the beginning and sure enough I didn't get it. So then I didn't think about it any more. I guess the reason the praying was no good was

23

it wasn't really right. Then when I did get it and after that when you got so sick I knew it was punishment for not telling."

It was all so logical to a twelve-year-old; certainly twenty-one days one after another makes ages. And if a dreaded event does not happen immediately it is not going to happen at all. Punishment and the form it took was thoroughly logical too.

"Well, if all this was punishment," I told her, "you've had it. Go on upstairs; wash your face."

B jumped up, leaned over, flung her arms around my neck, kissed me.

"Does A have to know?" she asked. "It's the first thing I ever kept from her but my whole life would be ruined if people knew."

"A won't know," I promised, "nor anybody else. Dr. Sturgis won't tell. By the way," I added as she skipped toward the door, "do you mind telling me who the boy was? You don't have to."

"Why, Dickie Button, of course," she said.

The intermission and the commercials in the televised Skating Championship had come and gone. My girls were absorbed again in the program, Dick Button analyzing each coming figure. For me the image on the screen faded to another memory of another doctor detective, to Dr. Cowing and me on the stairs in Grandfather's house on the day he asked if I remembered when my brother had diphtheria. In the years between it had gone into one of the dark closets of my memory, like a single overshoe that gets pushed into a corner by rubbers that match until one day another single appears. The old one is rummaged for, brought out, and they make a pair. Sunday afternoon when I relived the humiliating episode of the mumps, Dr. Cowing's story came out of the dark corner and matched Dr. Sturgis's in persistence and detection.

Dr. Cowing had been our family doctor in Muncie. Physically there was no resemblance between him and Dr. Sturgis. Dr. Sturgis was not tall; he moved and spoke quickly. His voice was decisive and high. His ancestry was Swedish, he had told me; his blue eyes corroborated this, though his hair was light brown. Dr. Cowing was tall; perhaps he only seemed so because I was small when I knew him. His eyes were dark, I think. I know he wore gold spectacles. He moved slowly and spoke slowly too, in a deep voice. Later I could have identified his as the typical Indiana measured speech.

I was eleven when we moved to Chicago, but whenever I came back to Muncie for a visit at my grandparents' I always saw him. He used to drop by to see Grandfather, not professionally, Grandmother said; it was because they both served on several committees and Grandfather was head of the hospital board, so they had lots to talk about whenever the doctor had a few minutes to spare. She would say:

"Charles is in the den, doctor. Go right on back."

To reach the den after he had stopped in the vestibule to take off his hat and coat, putting them on a bench there, he had to walk the length of a wide hall. It was a room in itself with a fireplace, a couch facing it, and comfortable chairs. On the left was the library and on the right the parlor, where the piano was, and alongside it a pianola, that could be attached to the keyboard. The dining room was behind the library, the den across from it with the stairs between. Each opened off the hall. The den was the only room in the house in which Grandmother permitted the men to smoke;

Grandfather spent most of his time there. Halfway up the stairs there was a landing with a balcony that jutted out over the downstairs hall. This was a favorite place of mine for reading. There was enough light for it from the windows at the top of the stairs, and incongruously, on the balcony itself there was a little upholstered settee with cushions across its back. I do not suppose anyone ever sat there, I cannot imagine for what purpose one would have, but I liked it. With some contortion of my legs I could lie on it. Perhaps I imagined I was in a tower, I do not remember; but I do remember the day I called down to Dr. Cowing as he was on his way to the den. I think I was pleased that I startled him but what indented the day and the place in my memory was what he told me. He asked what I was reading and I said Sherlock Holmes.

"Once I was a detective," he said, "at your house when you lived here in Muncie. When I've seen your grandfather, if I have time I'll tell you about it."

When he left the den some time later he did have time. I came down from the balcony, sat on one of the lower steps of the stairs, and he sat down beside me to tell the story. That is probably what has left me with the conviction he was tall because I remember sitting on one step with my feet on the one below, while his legs stretched from beside me down to and across the floor. He began the story by asking if I remembered when my brother had had diphtheria.

Certainly I remembered. Brother was three and I was "going on" nine and I reminded Dr. Cowing I had had diphtheria too. Admitting this, he gave it small importance.

"A very light case," he said.

It had not been a light occurrence in my life; had I known the word at the time, I would have called it a disaster. There was to be an entertainment at our church at night. To be taken to anything in the evening would have been a heady experience but there was more. I was not only to be taken, I was to be in it, conspicuously. I was to wear a dress of my great-grandmother Curry's, who was eighty-eight years old, "lively as a cricket," people said, and not much taller than I was. I was to have my hair put up on top of my head and on that wear one of Grandmother Curry's little flat lace caps. I was to sit beside a make-believe fire and sing a solo, with Mother at the piano offstage. To my knowledge I have not rendered the song since then, but even today I know all the words. The selection was "Just a Song at Twilight" and it began "Just a song at twilight, when the lights are low, And the flickering shadows softly come and go." I did not sing the song, I was not even taken to the entertainment, because I caught diphtheria from my brother. I know to this day, as vividly as I know the words of that song, the fury and despair I could not shout to the housetop and everyone under it because my throat hurt.

"Yes, you caught diphtheria from little Charles but where had he caught it? That's when I turned into a detective. You see, diphtheria was one of the most terrible diseases that could happen in a family. When there was an epidemic many people died. One time in a family of nine children I could only save one." He did not speak for a moment and I tried to imagine such a dreadful time.

"In many churches ministers prayed diphtheria would not strike. The time I'm going to tell you about, it did strike, but only once, and that was your little brother—and you, of course," he added. Only my interest in the story kept me from reminding him sharply of the importance of my case.

"To this day I don't know what made me sure as soon as I

saw him that Charles had diphtheria. They were such early symptoms I could easily have mistaken it for tonsillitis, especially since there had been no case of diphtheria reported."

He had seemed to be talking to himself. He turned back to me. "Anyway I took a culture but I didn't wait for it to develop. I telephoned Chicago for antitoxin. We didn't have any in Muncie because as I told you there was no epidemic, not even one other case reported. They rushed the antitoxin from Chicago on a train in the special care of the conductor. Your father was waiting at the station and brought it straight to me. I heard later mine was the largest amount that had ever been given to a child up to that time but I took the risk, I had to, and we pulled him through.

"It was when he was getting better I turned into a detective."

Dr. Cowing was a good storyteller. He did not make gestures, he did not even raise his voice, but there was something in the slow, thoughtful speech that made my spine shiver. I remember that and almost exactly the very words he used.

"Where could a child of three have been exposed to diphtheria? Over and over I asked myself this question and could not answer it. I asked many people and they could not answer it."

Long after Brother needed his care the doctor had come to the house, he said, to talk to my parents and Zoe, Brother's and my nurse. Mrs. Lothan had gone when Brother was over the worst of the illness. The fact that she had been there at all might have given me realization Brother was very ill had I not been preoccupied with my own resentment. She was Dr. Cowing's standby. Together they had brought into the world a sizable proportion of Muncie's population and she was the one always sent for in any emergency. She had been of no help, however, in tracing where Brother might have been before she was called in. The one who would know that best was Zoe.

Zoe was colored, "like the tassels on ears of corn," I had said. I loved her and I know she loved me, but Brother was her baby and she was fiercely protective of him. She was the one Dr. Cowing talked to longest and, he said, once she realized there was no faintest blame attached to her, but only an urgent need of her help so that other children would not get so ill as her little Charles had been, she went earnestly, fervently, over every detail of his days. Where they went to walk, whom they saw—very few children because he was not yet of kindergarten age. Dr. Cowing would visit every place she mentioned, asking questions there. If it was a store, had any clerks been absent through illness? Had there been illness in their family that had anything to do with a sore throat? He thought, he said, there might have been a case even lighter than mine so it had been diagnosed as tonsillitis when in reality it could have been diphtheria. He could find no such possibility. He asked other doctors to help him. There were not many in the town, but he had their cooperation although it meant a great deal of extra work, and he had a feeling, he said, they thought he was being something of a crank. After all, there had been no other cases reported. Brother's and mine had been isolated so it was all over. I can hear now the tone of his voice when he added:

"They had never seen a diphtheria epidemic. *I* had."

However, the other doctors took on with him the extra load—and every family doctor's was a heavy load—of examining all the schoolchildren and making inquiries about their families.

In the weeks that followed, while Dr. Cowing was digging for clues Brother was getting well. The afternoon of the denouement, the last page of the detective story, Zoe had just brought him in from outdoor play when Dr. Cowing stopped by. She was taking off his outdoor things and as she released him Dr. Cowing held out his arms, Brother dodged them, laughing, and ran toward the back of the house.

"Stop him," Zoe called. Dropping the coat and leggings to the floor, she started after him but Dr. Cowing, reaching out an arm, had already encircled him and questioningly handed him to Zoe.

Over Brother's roars of protest and flailing fists she raised her voice. "He knows his momma don't allow him in the kitchen this time of day."

The temper outburst was soothed by permission to ride his tricycle in the house so long as he did not go to the kitchen. While he circled precariously around and between them—Dr. Cowing remembered he kept having to pull his long legs up out of the way—Zoe told the reason for the rule about the kitchen.

"Every afternoon Frieda, she's the cook, always has coffee and some kind of sweet cake. She's German. She came to us just before the baby took sick. She started a game with him when she first came. She's crazy about children. The baby remembered the game and the minute he was up he wants to play it some more. But his momma don't want him to."

Dr. Cowing, smiling, asked what the game was.

"I thought probably some kind of hide and seek," he explained to me.

"Why, the baby sits up at the table with her and she takes a spoonful of coffee and then she pretends to give him some from her spoon. She don't actually give him coffee, she just lets him lick the spoon, but she does give him some of her cake and his momma don't want him eating between meals. She don't believe in it and especially since we've had such a hard time getting him to eat after him being so sick."

"At that instant—" I remember how he stopped when he said that and I held my breath.

"At that instant," he repeated, "something scratched my mind. It was no more than that but I said, 'Tell me again, Zoe—about the coffee.' "

"Oh, she don't give him real coffee, she knows he shouldn't drink that. It's just pretend. She lets him lick her spoon."

There it was, what Dr. Cowing all the weeks had been looking for. He knew it before he reached the kitchen. He knew when he saw Frieda what he was going to have to do and he felt sick.

Frieda was young, German, pretty, with bright pink cheeks, soft yellow hair that curled around her face, china blue eyes. She was just twenty, and she was a diphtheria carrier. A culture taken from her throat proved it unquestionably. She had to be institutionalized almost as if she were a leper. She could never work as a cook in a family again; she could never even go to any public eating place. She would be under surveillance. Dr. Cowing had solved the mystery.

Dr. Sturgis had traced the source of B's mumps and B said it had ruined her life. She has forgotten she said that. Dr. Cowing discovered the source of Brother's diphtheria and it ruined Frieda's life.

I do not know who won the Ice Skating Championship.

III

Hymn Singing

The day my children's hymn singing and an automobile trip with my grandfather jostled my memory simultaneously, I was on a platform filling a speaking engagement; and I was not talking about my family nor about hymns. I was making a plea to throw out our old methods of teaching foreign languages in this country and teach by ear. The child, by this method, I was saying, would give back exactly what he heard, therefore his accent would be as right as that of the person to whom he was listening. That was the instant when I remembered my children's hymn singing and simultaneously the trip with Grandfather when he and I had sung hymns together. For the strength of my argument of exact reproduction of speech heard, I did not share my memories with my audience. I put them resolutely out of my mind and completed the talk I had been engaged to deliver. Later, alone in my hotel room, I savored them both and now they are linked irrevocably.

At the time I was remembering, my twins were not quite five years old. To many people they looked alike, black curly hair, blue eyes, chubby. Most of the time they were compatible though temperamentally quite unlike; B was the more gregarious. In one activity, however—I cannot diminish its importance by calling it a game—even B eschewed friends. To be accurate, the activity combined two forms of expression; neither was engaged in separately. At nursery school they played singing games and sang marching songs, but the home entertainment was singing and marching. From the volume of sound each produced it would not be possible to determine which took precedence. If any of their friends happened to be present when a need for this expression engrossed their hostesses, the friends were invited to go home because, as A expostulated when a conspicuous lack of hospitality was called to her attention, "they never get the words right but they won't keep still." Quite possibly the words their guests knew were the conventionally "right" ones.

Neither their religious nor their secular repertoire included rare musical items. The exceptional factor was in the rendering of the text, but any attempt to bring their version into line with what the lyricist had intended was rejected with vehemence. At the time I was recapturing, their favorite selections were "Home on the Range," "The Isle of Capri" and, in the category of sacred music, "Onward, Christian Soldiers." These were delivered in a vigorous tempo without modulation of either voice or tramping feet. The playroom was directly above the entrance hall in our house outside Philadelphia. The favorite time for the musical program was late afternoon, just before baths and supper. A guest coming for tea invariably stopped short immediately over the threshold to look with startled apprehension at the ceiling, and the chandelier swinging from it. We were unable, of course, to have any conversation until we had got out of the hall and into the living room.

Sometimes, however, a guest would pause in the hall, in shock perhaps, or possibly to identify with a familiar tune the words. Had I been able to make myself heard I could have explained their marching step that brought the knee not quite to the chin. This gave greater driving power to the downstamp. That the words could be heard clearly above this is an indication of the carrying quality of their voices. I found some comfort, I needed to find some, in their ability to sing in key and on pitch.

In "The Isle of Capri," their only deviation from the text was in the title—"The Vile of Kupree," they enunciated piercingly, and swept into action. They might have developed other interpretations to their liking, given sufficient opportunities for practice; these I had curtailed by a ruling. I had not considered my ruling unfair nor my nervous system unnaturally fragile but at the end of one week of "The Vile of Kupree" I imposed a limit. Each twin could sing it ten times a day, no more. A tells me it was only five times apiece and still feels I was churlish. I maintain either figure was a generous allotment. Heard twenty times in one day, or even ten, any song frays the ear and nervous system.

The treatment of "Home on the Range" included wider variations. These were not developed; they sprang full-panoplied. At the first performance to which I was an invited audience, the announcement of the selection was "Home by the Range." Each syllable thereafter was as clearly articulated as those of the title.

"Oh, there never was heard a scourging word where the deer and the amblions grow."

These words evoked for me a misty, pastoral atmosphere. I did not ask what they conveyed to A and B.

The one interpretation I attempted to modify, tactfully, I

thought, was of "Onward, Christian Soldiers." The anachronism introduced, though startling to hear, was entirely plausible to them. I should have realized this when I heard it since I had been told that at Sunday school, asked if anyone could tell what Jesus did when He grew up, B had said decisively:

"I expect he worked at the typewriter like my mommy."

Therefore, after they had sung "On a Christian soldier, marching to the wars, with a cross of Jesus going on by fours," they moved into, for them, a consistent image. They sang "Christ, the royal master, leans against the phone."

This *dégagé* image of our Lord startled me into spontaneous interference. I repeated the words correctly and explained what they meant. When I had finished B said with lowering severity:

"Jesus likes our way better."

The day Grandfather and I sang in his automobile on the road from Anderson to Muncie, I think we said the words accurately, though the circumstances were unusual. I was the age of the twins at their hymn-singing peak; that may be why the memories returned together in spite of the gap of years between. I was the first grandchild and the only girl in the family. Perhaps it was the novelty of this after three sons that led Grandfather to choose me as a companion at such an early age I do not remember the first excursions.

Grandfather's factory was the Indiana Bridge Company in Muncie, Indiana, and he took me with him to see how constructions were coming along. We never sang on those trips. Grandfather would point out places along the way.

"That's so-and-so's farm," he would say, and tell me a story about it.

When he saw a farmer coming toward us driving a team,

he would stop the automobile at the side of the road so that the horses would not get frightened and bolt. Sometimes he got out and helped the farmer lead them past the machine.

We were not going to a bridge the day we sang. When I stormed that I could not climb around a bridge in a dress, why wasn't I wearing the usual bloomers, Mother said to stop shouting, I was not going to a bridge. I was going to Anderson to see Governor Durbin. Mother's explanation of what a governor was made no sense to me but since he was a friend of Grandfather's I would probably find him acceptable.

Anderson is twenty miles from Muncie and it was a hot day. We must have started at around the hottest part of it because it was after my nap that I stormed about the dress, which would make it around two o'clock. I had lunch, only we called it dinner, at twelve. The month was July, I know, because, passing fields, Grandfather would point and say with great satisfaction, "You see that? Right on schedule. Corn knee-high by the Fourth of July." Another saying I liked the picture of was "When oak leaves are the size of a squirrel's ear it's time to plant the corn."

When he drove the automobile Grandfather wore a long linen coat called a duster, cap and goggles. Grandmother made him wear them to keep the dust out of his clothes and his hair. The pair of goggles was the only part of the costume he said was necessary, but he wore it all. For the same reasons Mother had our seamstress make a coat for me too, and between them they had invented the most uncomfortable head covering I have ever owned, a sort of bonnet with an isinglass front so that I would not breathe in dust and get hay fever. The glass was ambered; everything I looked at was turned yellow. Inside it the sweat ran down my neck and glued my hair to the scalp. Also the sweat tickled, but

to scratch through the bonnet brought no relief, so I squirmed a good deal.

Grandfather was a patient man. Grandmother or Mother would have told me to stop fidgeting but he told me stories about his friend Governor Durbin, who worked very hard most of the year in Indianapolis. We were going to his farm. He could only come there in the summer when he was not so busy, since the legislature was not in session. These were familiar words to me but unpleasant. Grandfather was a state senator. Far too many times, in my opinion, when he had not come to see me or asked for me to be brought to his house I was told he was in Indianapolis, the legislature was in session. He had told me he did not like being in Indianapolis so much either but he had to be a senator because he wanted to get things better for men in prison and the way to do that was to get laws changed. These were phrases I used glibly. I had heard them so often I know now I put them to my own use. When I was disinclined to respond to a summons, I liked to say I could not because I was in session. Opposition to a pronouncement I voiced as "I am changing a law." I have no recollection of either of these pronouncements producing the effect I wanted.

We were talking about Indianapolis when we reached the Governor's farm. Indianapolis was a place I knew because my other grandparents lived there and I sometimes stayed with them.

My impression is of a long driveway from the road to the Governor's house but it could very well not have been. I have learned that distances and heights shrink astonishingly in the years between childhood and maturity. My memory, however, is clear and precise that we had just agreed Craig's candy store in Indianapolis had the best butterscotch drops in the world when Grandfather stopped the automobile and a man in a white suit came out on the porch to meet us. He started down the steps toward us but Grandfather waved him back.

"Wait till I get out of these dust catchers. I don't want to get a speck on that handsome ice cream suit of yours."

The mention of ice cream brought me out and on the driveway in a jiffy, peeling off my coat and my loathsome bonnet. My face and my hair were so wet underneath it, I wiped them with my arm and my hand two or three times. When we came up the steps and Grandfather said, "Emily, this is Governor Durbin," and I shook hands with him, my hand was sopping. He had to take a handkerchief out of the pocket of his coat to wipe off his own hands, but he was saying:

"I'm delighted to meet you, Emily. C.M., it was mighty good of you to drive down here on this hot day. It's a treat to see you."

"Treat" was a nice word, I thought, and hoped it would give the Governor an idea.

"Twenty miles and six-tenths," Grandfather was saying. "Engine ran like a hummingbird, but coming at that speed— we were hitting twenty-five pretty steadily—it does stir up the dust. I would appreciate a drink."

To Grandfather a drink meant exactly what it meant to me, a drink of water. I know now Grandfather had never tasted alcohol, because when he went into the Civil War at seventeen he had promised his father he would never drink so he no more knew the taste of alcohol than I knew it. The Governor said:

"C.M., I apologize for not having it right out here when you arrived. You certainly do want a drink, and here it comes."

The Governor's houseman had come through the screen

door—we never said "butler" in Indiana. He had on a white coat like the one Grandfather's houseman wore, he was colored, smiled warmly and carried a tray. There were two tall glasses on the tray filled with iced tea, I thought, with a fancy touch of sprigs of mint sticking around and above the top of the glass. I knew what mint looked like; we had a mint bed at our house, but we used it for mint sauce with lamb. I'd never seen it raw before with anything to drink, though I liked to eat it from the bed. The Governor said:

"Munroe, Senator Kimbrough has asked for a drink. That's a terrible thing to happen to people like you and me from Kentucky, isn't it?"

Munroe offered the tray to Grandfather. "I'm very sorry sir, but here you are and I'll get something right away for the little girl."

Grandfather took one of the glasses.

"Why, I wasn't expecting anything so special as this," he boomed. Grandfather's deep bass voice always boomed. "I was just looking forward to a glass of cold water after that dusty trip and don't fix anything for Emily. She and I will share this delicious concoction."

I was already reaching for the glass. Grandfather, bending down, put it in my hands.

"Hold it carefully," he said.

To my astonishment, the Governor and Munroe simultaneously jumped at me unmistakably as if they wanted to take the glass away. The Governor even said something like:

"Hold on there, C.M. Let Munroe get her a glass of milk or something. I don't think her mama would want her to have this."

If there was one abominable thing above all others to swallow, in my estimation it was milk. I spun around with my

40

back to the interferers and took a deep gulp from the glass. It choked me a little but I liked the taste. While Grandfather was explaining that Mother let me have iced tea once in a great while, this was a special occasion, I took some more swallows and then out of politeness turned around and gave the glass to Grandfather. He liked it too, said it was the best he'd ever tasted and quite different. The Governor and Munroe did not fuss any more about it. The Governor took the other glass, Munroe left, and Grandfather and I sat down side by side on a wicker settee that had a great many cushions, and hung by chains on either side from the ceiling. It was like one on Grandfather's porch at home and I indicated this was where I would like to be so that we could swing. While Grandfather and the Governor talked I pushed us back and forth—by sitting on the edge I could get one foot to the floor—and Grandfather and I finished the drink between us.

By and by the Governor asked if Grandfather would like another one. He did not say it in the way I was used to, like "Of course you will have," or "I insist," or "Do have another," but Grandfather accepted the offer enthusiastically. So did I, rejecting unequivocably suggestions of sarsaparilla or root beer. I did not take so much of the second one as I had taken of the first. I did not feel so thirsty and the swinging had made me a little dizzy so I stopped that too. The Governor said Munroe would take me to see a new calf and some baby pigs. I went with him but it was hot and I was still a little dizzy from the swing. When I told him Munroe said he wasn't surprised. He expected it was the swing that did it and brought me back to the house.

Grandfather and the Governor had gone indoors and were sitting at a big table in the library. They had a great many papers spread out on top of it and were so busy looking at

them and talking they did not notice me come in. I went over to a big chair in the corner. The chair had a wide enough seat for me to put my feet on and I rested my head on its arm. I do not think I went to sleep because I always resisted a nap, but when I saw Grandfather standing in front of the chair I was in and heard him say, "Why, here she is," I was surprised. He said we must be going, to say good-bye to the Governor. I shook hands with him and remembered to say thank you for a lovely time. He followed us to the top of the steps on the porch. He told me he was glad I had come and didn't like to see us go.

"C.M.," he asked, "are you sure you want to drive the machine back? Why don't you let my man take you and come home on the Interurban?"

Grandfather said he wouldn't hear of such a thing but he did let Munroe crank the automobile.

At the end of the driveway I looked back; that is why I remembered the driveway as long. The Governor and Munroe were still on the top step watching us. The breeze blew my hair all over my head and my face, and I loved it. I was not hot any more or dizzy. I suddenly remembered why I felt so good and so different and said it aloud.

"We didn't put our coats and hats on."

Grandfather took one hand off the wheel and slapped his leg.

"That's it," he said. "That's why I feel so fine. I was just thinking to myself that I don't know when I have felt so fine. I'm never going to wear those contraptions again. I wouldn't have believed they could make such a difference."

He began to sing, and I joined in his favorite hymn:

When He cometh, when He cometh to make up His jewels,
All the jewels, precious jewels, His loved and His own;
Like the stars of the morning, His bright crown adorning,
They shall shine in their beauty, bright gems for His crown.

He will gather, He will gather the gems for His kingdom,
All the pure ones, all the bright ones, His loved and His own.
Like the stars of the morning, His bright crown adorning,
They shall shine in their beauty, bright gems for His crown.

Little children, little children who love their Redeemer,
Are the jewels, precious jewels, His loved and His own.
Like the stars of the morning, His bright crown adorning,
They shall shine in their beauty, bright gems for His crown.

This was better than singing it around the piano on Sunday
night. We sang it loud into the breeze, all the verses, and
when we had finished we went back to the beginning and
sang it all over again at the top of our lungs. Then Grandfather said for some reason or other he felt a little tired. He
wasn't used to driving forty miles in one day. He thought
it might be a good idea to rest a little before we went on. He
pulled the machine to the side of the road, turned off the
engine, and we got out. We had stopped this side of a bank
soft and thick with grass and clover. There was a little brook
on the other side of it and I thought of taking off my socks
and shoes and wading but I was tired too from the driving
and singing. Grandfather took off the jacket of his suit, folding it up to make a pillow for his head, and lay down. I lay
down beside him and looked up at the sky. When I awoke
it was dusk and Grandfather was sitting up beside me.

"By Christopher," he was saying, "I must have dozed off.
We've got to be on our way or they'll be worried about us."

While he was cranking up I noticed I had grass stains on
my dress and knew that would not be well received but I did

not mention this when Grandfather got back into the automobile because I could see he was a little anxious. He climbed out again almost immediately.

"Forgot to light up," he explained. I followed him because I had always wanted to see the lamps lighted and had never been out late enough for it. There was one on each side of a grille. In the middle of this was his monogram that my father and two uncles had given him as a birthday present when he bought the Haines. It was very large and the letters CMK twined into one another. He unhooked and opened the glass front on each of the lamps. When he had lighted and turned them up just right the monogram glittered. I was admiring it and putting my hands across the lights to make shadows but Grandfather told me to hop back in.

"We'll have to skeedaddle" was what he said.

That is the last part of the ride I remember. The singing, the resting on the bank, lighting the lamps are sharp and clear. What happened after that I learned much later from Mother and my father.

They were waiting on the porch when we pulled up to the curb. They had been there a long time except for when they were in the house talking about telephoning Grandmother to find out if she had any news of us, and deciding if she had she would have telephoned them. They would make her anxious if they called her. Grandfather blew three times on the rubber bulb of the big horn that was just outside the door on his side where he could reach it. They hadn't needed that sound to tell them we were coming. They'd been watching up the street and seen the lamps two blocks away—in Indiana we called them squares. They had run down the steps, across the yard, down the other steps and across the sidewalk to the street, saying how glad they were to see us and were we all right. I had not answered. Grandfather told

45

them certainly everything was fine, they'd had a splendid day but that Emily was a little tired after a forty-mile drive and no wonder, so she was asleep. This was their first surprise because they had never known me to welcome sleep and certainly not without eating. The shock came when my father lifted me out and put me over his shoulder. He did not say anything until after they had watched Grandfather drive on to the corner to turn around. He always went to corners for this. I think he liked doing most things with a big sweep and he said himself he disliked reversing. They saw him on his way back up the street to his own house in the next square before they turned round to go into ours. That was when my father said:

"Girl"—this was his special name for Mother—"go around behind me and smell Emily."

Mother, telling me about it, said she hoped never again so long as she lived to have such doubts of my father's sanity and certainly she would never again know such disbelief as when she had done what he had asked.

"Hal," she had told him, and could not get her voice above a cracked whisper, "she smells of whiskey."

Mother said if ever people looked at each other with a wild surmise, she and my father were the most wildly surmising. When the shock abated enough for them to move, my father carried me to my bed while Mother telephoned Dr. Cowing. I was undressed, in bed, a parent on either side of me, when the doctor arrived. The only signs of life I'd given other than my heart beating, Mother told him, were unintelligible murmurs and a snatch of what sounded like a familiar hymn.

Dr. Cowing corroborated their diagnosis but soothed their wild alarm.

46

"Yes," he had said, "Emily is drunk but not dead, and not likely to die. She'll be fit as a fiddle tomorrow morning. Just let her sleep it off. I doubt that she'll even have a headache."

As he left, she said, he called back:

"If you find out where she got it I'd be interested to know. Just in case," he added, "I have other patients with the same complaint." He was going down the steps.

"She's been with her grandfather all afternoon. They drove to Anderson in the Haines," my father told him.

Mother said Dr. Cowing stopped and turned around so abruptly he nearly fell off the bottom step.

"With C.M.? Why, he's never had a drop to drink in his life. I know that for a fact."

As if, Mother always emphasized in the story, this was news to her and Grandfather's son.

"Why, he'd as soon let Emily have rat poison. Where on earth did he take her that she could have got at it?"

"They went to see the Governor," my father told him, and Mother always asserted it was the first time she'd ever seen anybody's eyes actually bulge. If he said anything Mother and my father did not remember it but when Daddy told the story he said the doctor just stood there shaking his head hard like a man with a fly buzzing around it.

They did not go back into the house until the doctor had driven away. They watched him unhook from the horse's bridle the iron weight that hitched her, put it back in the buggy and climb in. They still hoped, Daddy said, he might have some suggestion. He did, just as he was slapping the reins over his horse to start moving.

"Suppose I drop by and talk to C.M.," was his suggestion. Daddy called after him.

"Better not. Leave it alone."

47

Mother said this was typical of Dr. Cowing, a last conversation between the front porch and the buggy. He would call back instructions when he had got all the way down to the corner, leaning way out and cupping a hand to his mouth. His patients always waited on the porch no matter what the weather until he was out of earshot because he always had final instructions after he had started and sometimes they were the most important.

"Beat up an egg in some milk, nutmeg on top; nourishing," he would call back, or "Sweet spirits of nitre; bring down the fever." This time it was "She may need calomel tomorrow; liver."

They went back into the house and Daddy telephoned Grandmother. Mother did not want her alarmed, but Daddy thought he might get some notion of when I might have wandered off by myself where I could have got hold of the whiskey, though he promised Mother he wouldn't mention that. She stood beside him in the back hall where the telephone was, on the wall. When he had hung up and turned back to her, she said he looked as if he had had a shock, and he had.

"My father," he told her, "has gone to bed without any supper and left his clothes in the middle of the floor in his bedroom. Mother says he has never done such a thing before. She says it just goes to show he had no business driving all that way on a hot day. It wore him out."

Mother said she and Daddy stood there in the hall and for the first time since the whole thing began they grinned at each other.

"Your father," Mother told him redundantly, "has had some whiskey."

"Mother says," Daddy added, "the Governor called up to

48

know if Father had got home all right. She thought that was very thoughtful of him but it annoyed her a little. Much as she hates that automobile, she didn't care to have anyone imply Father isn't a skillful driver."

They were still talking it over when they went to bed after another look at me. Mother said I seemed like a cherub until she bent down to kiss me.

The next morning I was evidently fully recovered because I did not have to take calomel. I would have remembered that because of all abominations this was the one I detested most.

Mother did not ask me anything about the visit to Anderson and evidently I had not thought any part of it exceptional because I said only that we'd had a very nice time. Having found out that Grandfather, like me, was in splendid health the next day, my parents did not take up the subject with him. Certainly it was not one about which they wished to speculate among their friends, so the source of my downfall and Grandfather's would have remained a secret, but Grandmother innocently gave it away.

One morning about a week after our excursion she telephoned Mother. They talked or saw each other nearly every day but there was urgency in this call.

"Lottie," she said, "I wish you'd come over. I need your help." Mother said she'd dropped whatever she was doing and had gone immediately.

Grandmother took her straight to the kitchen. Erna, the cook, was stirring something in a pitcher on the sink.

"It's iced tea"—Grandmother fairly spat out the words—"and it's driving us crazy. For a week Charles has been asking every day for iced tea and when we give it to him it isn't the way he wants it."

Mother said Erna poured something into the pitcher and began pounding it as if she were making butter, and she was angry.

"Fifteen years I've been here and he's never fancied iced tea. Now it's all he wants and I can't make it to suit him. Says it's got to have a special mint flavor. I put mint on the outside and now I'm going to put it on the inside and he won't be satisfied."

Then Grandmother took up the complaint and Mother said it was a lightning flash that broke through the clouds.

"The Governor gave it to him that day he went to Anderson," she said. "Charles never fancied iced tea before; and now he says he didn't know how good it could be. It had mint, was all he could tell us, with a special flavor that was the best thing he'd ever tasted. He can't stop talking about it."

It was Erna's turn again.

"I put more sugar in, he says it's too sweet. I put less, it's bitter. Now I've boiled up some mint; I'll try that. He won't like it," she added. When she spoke again her teeth were closed. "So I says, 'Call up Mrs. Hal. She comes from Indianapolis. Maybe they know some kind of fancy tea-making I ain't heard tell of.' "

Grandmother looked appealingly at Mother.

"If you don't know any, Lottie, I'm going to call the Governor and get the recipe direct from him."

Mother said she felt as if the lightning had struck her. She actually leaned against the sink to steady herself, praying for something she could say that would divert that telephone call. Her prayer was answered and she would say, always raising her head at that point with an amused and deliberate arrogance:

"I may not be able to cook but I could have been a diplomat." This is what she told Grandmother:

"You know, I don't believe I would telephone or write to the Governor for that recipe. You see, he comes originally from Kentucky. Southerners have recipes that are handed down from generation to generation and kept in the family. Another Southerner would never ask such a secret to be given away. If you should ask, he'd realize you didn't know this tradition, not being a Southerner, and being a Southern gentleman he would really be distressed. He'd want on one hand to oblige you but on the other hand would be honor bound to keep a family tradition."

Grandmother accepted this and thanked Mother.

"I wouldn't have known that," she said, "and I certainly wouldn't embarrass him. He was showing his Southern hospitality by giving the best he had. Charles will just have to make do with what we offer him."

Erna was still pounding in the pitcher when Mother left.

Grandfather lost his taste for iced tea. By the end of the summer Erna had stopped making it. Every Sunday night after supper at Grandfather's house we all sang "When He Cometh, When He Cometh," but I do not remember singing it another time in the automobile.

IV

Name-Calling

My stepmother, moving this winter from the apartment in
which she has lived since my father's death, asked me to help
her sort out and decide what things could be disposed of.
At the bookshelves, making two piles, one to give to the
hospital, the other to pack, I dropped a volume because of
the shock the words of the title transmitted. The secret companion of my childhood lay dead at my feet. For years she
had been my dearest friend, but sometime in my growing up
she had gone away and I had forgotten about her. I had
created her and now because my reading and I were older, I
had killed her. I know exactly where on the shelves at our
house in Muncie that book and its companion volume had
stood, at just the right height for me to read and to reach;
but I never took either volume from the shelf. Their title,
*Abbeys, Castles and Ancient Halls in England, Scotland and
Wales*, gave me my friend and wide travels.

From the moment I was in bed until sleep took me from
her, I was Abbey's guest at one of her Castles or Ancient
Halls. We arrived together, each on a milk-white steed.

Trumpets blew from the ramparts, pennants were unfurled, a drawbridge was lowered, and we clattered across it into the great banquet hall, to the resounding cheers of the loyal serfs. There we dined, I expect, on creamed chicken, mashed potatoes with gravy, peas, vanilla ice cream with chocolate sauce and angel food cake, the menu for gala occasions with which I was familiar. As a landowner, Abbey made the dukes of England seem property owners in Levittown. We seldom visited twice one of her castles or ancient halls. When our prancing steeds were brought to us, we made a choice, amicably, and on the instant plunged full gallop toward England, Scotland or Wales.

The death of Abbey made me remember how important names have always been to me. I accepted friendship readily, even promoted it with someone whose name I liked. I had never known anyone called Abbie, I doubt that I had heard the word pronounced; but seeing it on the title, I was immediately drawn to a friendship with that girl. I choose to believe incidental the material advantages this friendship offered.

Though I did not know any Josephines, I disliked the name venomously. The Christmas I was six years old, Grandmother Wiles gave me a doll whose clothes had been made by Grandmother's dressmaker in Indianapolis. Every garment from panties to pink-silk-covered-with-net dress was stitched to its body. Each time a visitor came to call on Grandmother, staying with us in Muncie for the holidays, she would ask to see the doll with the exquisite clothes she had heard so much about. I would stand by while they exclaimed over the real lace edging of the petticoats and the fine sewing, "every stitch by hand." Asked what I called this beautiful doll, I would answer, "Josephine."

When I was twelve years old, we lived in Chicago and I went to Miss Faulkner's School. Josephine Root came into our class the middle of the first term and was assigned a seat next to mine. At recess, I told my friends she smelled because that was the worst thing I could think of to say about her. She was bright, gentle and sweet as a rose, and we became friends but not chums. I always felt shy with her. I have never known another Josephine.

"Hector," spoken aloud, marked a day on my calendar to be remembered with joy and a special thank you in my prayers. Whatever their other connotations, Christmas on my calendar was for presents, Valentine's Day, of course, for valentines, Easter, eggs and rabbits, Halloween, dressing up and scaring people, Thanksgiving, turkey and pumpkin pie, and Hector's Day, my first dog. I had begged for one, prayed, made wishes on white horses and the first star, but my father, usually reasonable, had been a man of stone against every pleading argument.

"It always ends in a heartbreak," he had said to Mother, in my hearing. Since my conviction was that my heart would break if I did not own a dog, I could only believe his mind was so addled, my reasonable arguments had not got through to him. The day, glorious day forever marked on my calendar, when his mind cleared, I had heard him say to Mother:

"I haven't heard that since Hector was a pup."

There was my opening and I plunged through it, weeping, pleading, stamping. If my father had had a puppy named Hector, how could he deny me one, how could he let me be the only person in the world who did not have a puppy? If my parents attempted an explanation or a justification, I did not hear it, and suddenly they capitulated. Hector, Saint Hector, had interceded for me.

The line of dogs that came into my possession after that was long but not distinguished. I think only the first one was purchased. After that I gathered them in wherever I found them. Frequently I had to return one with apology to its rightful and distraught owner, but I was philosophical about these transients, confident that I would shortly garner a replacement. I never called one Hector. I think I felt it would be disrespectful to someone I mentioned in my prayers, and the only name I remember until much later years and dogs was the one I gave my first, a cocker spaniel puppy. Actually I gave him two names because they were in stories I had read and I could not decide between them. I added a third because it did not occur to me anyone could be without a last name. I neither used nor permitted an abridgment either when speaking of him or summoning, "Here, White Socks Merry Legs Kimbrough."

Mother's name was Charlotte Emily. She grew up in a family and time of name diminutives. She was the only child of my grandfather's second marriage. Her predecessors by his first wife were called Freddie, Addie and Lulie, and she became Lottie. I do not know for whom she was named. Her mother, my grandmother, was Sarah Jane. Another Sarah might have become Sally but not Grandmother Wiles. I cannot imagine that stately, rigidly corseted figure permitting any trifling with her name at any age. She bore him a child but I never heard her speak of or to her husband except as Mr. Wiles. Mother's figure was slight. Except during pregnancy it never carried more than ninety-eight pounds. She stood, without whalebones, as straight as her mother. All fire and spirit in her enthusiasms and her dislikes, she abominated the name Lottie so much, this disfavor embraced all diminutives. She protested my being named for her and yielded to my father's insistence only if the Charlotte was dropped and no middle name substituted.

"Just Emily," she said. "You can't make an *ie* ending out of that."

It evidently did not occur to her I might have become an Emmy with a *y*, and I did not. I never had a nickname and I always wanted one. Margarets became Peggy, Elizabeths turned into Betty, Patricia was Patty, Frances was Franny, all with a *y*, but I was christened Emily and since, like being a ballet dancer, you have to start young to be nicknamed, I doubt that I will ever be Emmy.

Mother lost out in her insistence on a simple name and avoidance of nicknames when my brother was born. She had wanted to call him Wiles and my father had acquiesced happily, not only to please her but to avoid the continuation of his own. By the same plague that had afflicted Mother, my father had been stamped at his christening with a nickname. The friend honored by the christening was Harold.

"He was always called Hal," was Grandfather's defense of his son's name. "If we had named our boy Harold, which was, of course, our friend's actual name, we would have been temporizing." Grandfather Kimbrough never temporized, so my father was christened Hal.

The day after my brother was born, Grandfather and Grandmother Kimbrough came to our house to congratulate the parents of their first grandson and to meet the new arrival. In my opinion there was a great deal of silly fuss being made over this intruder into my nearly six years of undisputed sovereignty. I was expressing this opinion in the kitchen when I heard Grandfather's arrival. Even had I been sitting on the back fence—a favorite lookout—I would have heard it. Grandfather's voice in timbre was not unlike Chaliapin's; it had a carrying quality. There was a foot's difference of height in Chaliapin's favor but I think Grandfather's head was the more handsome. I had heard my Uncle Frank say that if his father's voice had been a football, Uncle Frank could have carried it from one goalpost to the other for a touchdown above any interference. It brought me on a run from the kitchen. Wherever Grandfather was, was exactly where I most wanted to be. He was in the vestibule. My father was helping him off with his overcoat; anyone would have known they were related, even though my father was slighter and his hair brown and curly; Grandfather's was white. Until I was fourteen or fifteen, I called my father Dada. After that I called him Daddy, because I thought it sounded more grown-up and stylish. Dada told me to help Grandfather take off his overshoes while he removed Grandmother's carriage boots. It was the twenty-second of December.

They sat side by side on a bench that was part of our hat-rack, with hooks on either side and a mirror behind them. The bench was really the lid of a holdall. Dada called it the junkyard. He would say:

"If you can find a ball in the junkyard, I'll play catch with you."

Dada was untying the ribbons that fastened Grandmother's carriage boots and I was pulling at Grandfather's overshoes when Grandfather said:

"Young Charles is a buster, I hear; ten pounds."

Dada stopped untying and looked up at Grandfather. I was surprised too. Grandmother turned toward him as much as she could on the narrow bench. She was just over five feet tall, with lively brown eyes, soft brown hair. (When she died at eighty-four, her hair was still brown.) Her displacement was modest. Grandfather was an expansive man. She spoke sharply.

"Lottie is calling the baby Wiles. I told you that, Charles."

59

Dada echoed:

"That's right, Father."

Grandfather beamed at them both, and down at me.

"Of course she's going to call him Wiles and so are all of you, but he's going to be Charles to me, Young Charles."

Dada and Grandmother exchanged a look; Dada went back to untying her carriage boots and I pulled off Grandfather's overshoes. We pried my grandparents off the bench and Dada took them to Mother and the baby's room. Mrs. Lothan came into our living room to meet them. She was the nurse who came where there was a new baby. When I went to a friend's house and Mrs. Lothan was there, I knew a baby was too.

Grandmother and Grandfather told her they were so glad to see her, and Grandfather added how much happier than the last one this time was. Grandmother said quickly:

"Hush, Charles, don't talk about that."

Grandfather went ahead with Mrs. Lothan. I heard Grandmother say to Dada, and she was shaking her head:

"I can't do a thing with your father, Hal."

And Dada laughed.

Years later when I was old enough to know what she meant, I remembered how often she would say to Mother:

"I've spent most of my married life, it seems to me, jerking at Charles' coat sleeve, and it hasn't done one mite of good."

She may have said it that morning, but what I remember is Dada smiling and asking her:

"Would you like to lay a bet that by the time we come back here, the baby will be named Charles?"

When she told him that mustn't happen, Dada told her he would be delighted if it did. They went out of the living room, not asking me if I wanted to go with them. Those days of my brother's arrival no one seemed to care whether I came or went, or noticed me at all. I was not supposed to be there anyway. Mother had told me I was going to visit Grandmother and Grandfather Wiles in Indianapolis. They would come over as usual for Christmas and I would go back with them. I was looking forward to that, but I had an ominous feeling this business of a baby's arriving had upset the schedule and was going to play havoc with my visit.

Grandmother and Grandfather Wiles, I'd heard, were coming over right away, three days ahead of Christmas, to see this baby, I supposed, and were going to stay at the big house with Grandmother and Grandfather Kimbrough instead of with us. No one had said whether I would go back with them or not go at all. It was my bitter contention, frequently and loudly expressed, that adults never stopped to explain anything fully. They were always going somewhere, dropping off bits and pieces of information as they hurried by.

It would be unrewarding, I decided, to resume the conversation in the kitchen the arrival of my grandparents had interrupted.

Even before the interruption, the conversation had not been to my liking. Conversations I enjoyed followed one of two patterns: a concentrated attention on what I was saying or full and explicit answers to questions I submitted. When other people did not live up to my standards, and this occurred frequently, I talked to myself. I enjoyed listening to my stories, but I was not always satisfied with the answers I gave to the questions I asked. Deciding to talk to myself, I sat on the floor in front of the fire, introducing a Socratic dialogue with:

"Why is no one paying any attention to me?"

Answer: "Because Christmas is coming in three days."

Question: "Is that why Lena does not want me in the kitchen?"

Answer: "Yes. She is cooking surprises."

Question: "Zoe is *my* nurse. Why does she tell Lena she can't wait to get her hands on that baby?"

Answer: "She was telling Lena what I am going to get for Christmas and changed the subject the way people do."

Question: "Why is Mother in bed?"

Answer: "Overtired. That's what everybody has been saying to her: 'Lottie, you mustn't get overtired.' Only, Dada calls her Girl."

Question: "Why does Dada call her Girl?"

Answer: "That is a silly question, because I've already asked Dada that and he told me. He said, 'Because she's my girl.'"

Question: "Why are Grandmother and Grandfather here to see this baby and not me?"

Answer: "Because it's new. They came to see our piano the day it was delivered."

Question: "Are people going to go on paying attention to this baby?"

Answer: "I don't know."

Question: "People say, 'Isn't it wonderful to have a brother?' Is it?"

Answer: "I don't know."

Question: "If they name him Wiles or Charles, what will you call him?"

Answer: "Brother."

The others were coming back. I heard them laughing. When they walked into the room, I saw Grandmother was shaking her head and she was not laughing; her mouth was tight. That meant she was not pleased, but Grandfather was in high old feather, as I'd heard said.

"Why, I never expected the baby to be named for me," he said. "I just told Lottie he would be Charles to *me*. It didn't take her a second to tell me that's what he would be for everybody, Charles Wiles."

"She took time to ask you why you hadn't named any of your own sons after you," Grandmother suggested. Grandfather spoke to Dada:

"I had no idea it would mean so much to me. I was a lot younger then, but, Hal," he added, "I don't want to overstep."

Dada patted his father's sleeve. "Listen, Father, Girl would do just about anything you asked, and we're keeping the Wiles, so Charles Wiles makes everybody happy. Emily, honey, aren't you forgetting something? Stand up for the grownups."

I stayed where I was and looked back in the fire. Dada was probably going to make me get up, but I heard Grandmother say, "No, Hal, leave her alone. It's a hard time for her, with her nose out of joint."

This was an appalling suggestion on top of everything else that had happened, but I would not give them the satisfaction of seeing me feel my nose for the damage.

They went past me into the vestibule. I think Dada was going to call me to help with the overshoes again because Grandmother said:

"No, Hal, I beg you, leave her alone."

Dada asked Mrs. Lothan to tell Lena he was going to the big house for dinner, he would be back early in the afternoon. While he was helping Grandfather put overshoes on, Grandmother came back into the living room to Mrs. Lothan. She wanted to be sure, she said, everything was all right. Was Dr. Cowing satisfied? Mrs. Lothan told her everything was just beautiful. Grandmother said:

"Two weeks early, and after the other terrible time we've been sick with worry. I'll call Mrs. Wiles again. She's nearly crazy with the trains not running on account of the snow, not even the Interurban; but they say the tracks will all be cleared by tomorrow."

Grandfather called and she hurried off.

Mrs. Lothan sat down on a chair, close to me by the fire, leaning past my shoulder to warm her hands.

"Emily," she told me, "don't be upset about what's going on around here. It will all settle down pretty soon, and you're going to love your brother and learn to help Zoe take care of him, but don't worry Mother and Dada. They're so happy."

This was the first time since she had come in the night, two days before, she had spoken to me more than a word or two. Her voice stirred a memory. I looked up at her.

"You've been here before, haven't you?"

She nodded. "I didn't think you'd remember. You were only four."

A picture was shaping.

"You brought another baby."

She nodded again. "Yes, I did." She shook her head, biting her lips. "That was a bad time."

The picture was growing clearer.

"I sat in the chair you're in. You put that baby on my lap. You let me hold it. You said it was only going to visit us for a little while."

She looked frightened and asked in only a whisper:

"You remember that?"

"You told me to hold out my arms. You put the baby there. You stood in front of me. You were just going to take it back. Something happened. Dada called you. You left it with me. You went away. You were running."

Bit by bit, I was piecing it together.

65

"I held the baby a long, long time. You came back. My arms were asleep but I held on. You said I was a fine nurse. Then you took the baby away. I never saw it any more. What happened to it?"

Mrs. Lothan got up from her chair.

"She went away. I wanted you to hold her before she went. I didn't mean it to be so long. Your mother needed me. I had to go."

She smiled down at me. "I have to go now. That fat brother of yours wants to be fed. I can hear him. But everything's just fine."

Her stiff skirt made a pleasant noise when she hurried. That and her voice were what had brought back the other time. Something made me sure that if I stayed exactly where I was, keeping as still as "Still Pond, No More Moving," but remembering hard, the whole of that other time would come to me. It did come and it is as clear today as on that December morning in front of the fire. My mother and father never knew I had sat there with a baby, never knew what I had heard.

Mother had called out in a high voice:

"Was there no one to speak for her? All strangers."

Dada's voice was rusty like someone with a cold:

"Girl, Girl, listen to me. I would have lost *you*." And Mother's voice over his:

"A stranger, a stranger. And no one to speak for her. She is Ruth, Ruth, Ruth." Over and over and over she said it:

"She is Ruth, Ruth the stranger, Ruth, Ruth."

That day I was taken away to Grandmother and Grandfather Wiles' in Indianapolis. When I came back after quite a long visit, Mother and Dada had been on a trip. Everyone was happy at being home together again. If I asked where

66

that baby was I had seen for a few minutes, I do not remember.

The headstone in the family plot at Muncie reads:
Ruth Kimbrough.

V

Improbabilities

One day this summer during lunch, we exchanged anecdotes about improbable personal happenings. There were four at the table—Cornelia, Sophy, Alice and I. My friendship with Cornelia and Sophy began during our schooldays. No one of us wishes to be more specific than that about the length of time this has covered. The last few summers we have rented a house together in Rhode Island. Alice was our guest. Her physical proportions are diminutive, her spirit and convictions of Herculean proportions. She exercises these as a distinguished member of an international organization. The improbable occurrence she told us about had come upon her in Teheran, where she had gone for a meeting of this organization. Arriving, she had learned, to her discomfiture, she was to stay at a hotel located on the outskirts of the city, chosen because it provided a more pleasant environment than the congested midtown area. Certainly the happiest choice, she assured us, had she been there for pleasure, but since all the sessions were held midtown and the social occasions immediately following were also in the heart of the city, it was hard to accommodate to the schedule the distance to be traveled for changes of clothes.

"It really doesn't take a long time for me to dress," she interpolated apologetically and unnecessarily, because we know the tempo she follows makes her always the first among us to be ready for any occasion. Over the eighty-odd years of her life her pace seems to have accelerated.

On the day in Teheran this preposterous thing happened, she said, there had been very little time in the schedule between the closing of the afternoon session and a state dinner. Even for those lodging in the city it was tight planning but for her on the outskirts it was more nearly a marathon test. She had come out of the meeting at a trot, and with luck found a taxi immediately, given the name of her hotel and indicated in pantomime the driver must hurry. There was no common language to share; she had tried every one she knew. The driver had set off at the usual man-, child- and animal-slaughtering pace customary in that area. She had learned a request by any method to drive more carefully was incomprehensible, so she had closed her eyes.

"I opened them suddenly, dreading what might be under the wheel because the car had stopped, though I'd felt no bump. The driver was getting out, and I indicated my anxiety. He understood, shook his head and smiled reassuringly. Then he patted his stomach and pointed to a café on the other side of the road. I watched him cross over, select a table, seat himself at it and pick up a menu. I called out to him in fury; he waved a reassuring hand. A waiter came and took his order, returned after some little time with enough dishes to provide a full meal and, at a request, came a second time with a small bottle of wine. The food was eaten, the wine drunk with the leisure of enjoyment. The check was called for, paid and after a last tipping of the wine bottle to make sure no drops remained, my chauffeur rose from the table, selected a toothpick from the container there, and employing it, sauntered back across the road. Reaching his car he flung the toothpick away, leapt into his seat, turned to smile at me and resumed his pursuit of whatever game could be run down."

Savoring every aspect of the episode—Alice's fury and helplessness, the driver's bland indifference, the incredibility of such a performance—Cornelia said ruefully, "Isn't it maddening you could never put that in a story?"

Alice was obviously surprised. "But it *is* a story," she countered. "I don't know what you mean."

Explaining, we talked over one another.

"If you were writing a story that involved your being late to the dinner and gave this as a reason, no reader would believe it. You'd have to invent something more prosaic, much less colorful. Every writer dreads the accusation of an incident being 'contrived.' Even if you're doing a straight chronicle of, say, a trip, you have to understate things that have happened in order to *make* them credible. You're always discarding something you really want to put into a story because it's too much, it won't go over."

Alice broke through the babel. She was nodding her head.

"Well, that explains something I've never really understood. Years ago I was on a ship with Katharine Cornell and Guthrie McClintic and I happened to be standing beside them when we came into the Bay of Naples. It was sunset. There were boats with red sails reflected in the water. I was nearly speechless over the beauty of it, but I did say to Mr. McClintic, 'What a setting in a play that would make,' and do you know what he said?"

Cornelia, wise in the theater, smiled. "I can guess."

"He said," Alice continued, " 'No, you could never use it. It's too much.' So that's what he meant."

"It's like the well-known long arm of coincidence," I said. "It happens to everybody, but you can't make it believable in writing." Over a chorus of agreement, and Alice's look of puzzlement, I developed my assertion. Here's an example, a story my stepmother tells: The summer she was eighteen, she and her cousin Pauline, the same age, went with their respective mothers to Venice. When she was born, Pauline's father had begun a string of pearls to be given her on her eighteenth birthday. The pearls were graduated in size to a large center one. She was wearing the necklace on a morning when the two girls went to the American Express office that is on Saint Mark's Square. As they were crossing the square on their way back to the hotel, Pauline stopped abruptly, cupping her hand over her chest. She was trembling, my stepmother said, and so frightened she could scarcely speak, except in a kind of croaking: "My pearls." Evidently, in those days pearls were not strung with knots between, so they had scattered. Pauline was sure it had happened at that moment so they were careful not to move from the spot as they gathered up, they hoped, all of them. They were still only a few yards from the American Express office so they turned back, put the pearls on a table there and counted them. They found all but the center one, the biggest. Pauline tied the others into a handkerchief, put it in her bag and they started again for the hotel, Pauline in tears now, saying over and over she could never tell her father, all those years he had spent collecting the pearls, especially the big one, what could she do?

Every tourist to Venice knows the thousands of pigeons that meet in Saint Mark's Square and the vendors of little paper cornucopias that hold a kind of white bean pigeons seem to like. Tourists buy the beans, pigeons perch on the head, the shoulders, the hands of the feeder and the enterprising bean vendor, with a camera handy, makes postcard snapshots the tourist happily distributes to his family, friends and memory book. Fighting among themselves, the pigeons frequently drop the bean and swoop down to retrieve it from the pavement. A pigeon swooped down for one at my stepmother's feet. She will never know what made her say "Shoo" to that bird among the thousands and pick up the bean it dropped. The bean was that pearl, the biggest of all. "Just try putting that in a story," I ended.

"Cornelia and Sophy can verify most of this one," I told Alice. Overriding their suggestions that I had told enough, I gave her another improbability.

Cornelia and I were bridesmaids in Sophy's wedding, in Devon, Pennsylvania. Cornelia and her family had recently moved from Bryn Mawr to New York and I was to stay with them there after the wedding. Mrs. Skinner had come over for the wedding and was staying on a few days with friends. Cornelia was making her Broadway debut in *Blood and Sand,* in which her father, Otis Skinner, was the star. Sophy had moved the day of her wedding from Saturday to Friday so that Cornelia could be a bridesmaid, since certainly the actress could not miss a performance. Nevertheless she had to leave early and as she got up from the bridal table, I realized I did not know the New York address. She called it back to me and the usher sitting at my right wrote it down on my place card and I tucked it into my bag. Some hours later, arriving in New York, I went by taxi to the address the usher had written. I had expected to tell a doorman which apartment I was visiting, but a maid came across the sidewalk as I was paying the driver. She said:

"We're expecting you, miss, but you'll have to come round by the back way for they're painting the front. I'll show you."

She took my bags and I followed her up a back stairway. She led me into a bedroom, put one bag on a luggage rack and opened it. Those were the days when bags included monogrammed fittings in the lid. It must have been the sight of these and the initials on them that caused her to start suddenly, turn on the overhead light and look at me closely.

"Oh, miss," she said. Her voice quavered and she looked agitated. "Are you coming here?"

This, I thought, was an odd question, and I answered it with some indignation:

"Of course I'm coming here."

Then I felt in my stomach bewildered misgivings.

"Isn't this Mr. Otis Skinner's apartment?" I asked.

"Oh, no, miss, this is Mr. Morgan's *house*."

Perhaps I waited a second for this information to penetrate my confusion. My recollection is that I jumped past her, slammed down the lid of the bag, snatched it up, ran from the room down the stairs and out into the street again. If she said anything or followed me, I did not know it in my panic to get out, and I did not stop running until I was on the sidewalk, facing a policeman.

"Anything the matter, miss?" he asked.

"This is the wrong house," I told him. "I'm looking for Mr. Otis Skinner's. I must have got the number wrong," and I thought balefully of that usher. Excitement and maybe champagne had obviously addled him and I hoped he would end in a drunkard's grave.

"Well," the policeman said, "I don't believe you're so far off. There's a Mr. Skinner on my beat, just around the corner. Give me your bag and we'll go round there."

73

He rang the doorbell of the house he knew and after a long time and a second ring, it was opened by what I then considered an old gentleman (he was probably fifty or a little under), wearing over pajamas a handsome brocade dressing gown. One look at him and I knew panic.

"Oh," I wailed, "you're not the right Mr. Skinner," and was on the run again. Perhaps the policeman stayed to apologize. He had not caught up with me when I reached the corner simultaneously with a cruising taxi I hailed and flung myself into. The driver asked me where I wanted to go; I realized I did not know. It would not have occurred to me to go by myself to a hotel and I could not think of friends I could telephone at that hour, waking their families as I had wakened the wrong Mr. Skinner. I did not know where to find a telephone, so I told the whole story to the taxi driver. Telling it, I had a brilliant solution. He could take me back to the Pennsylvania Station, I told him. I would get the midnight train to Philadelphia. I had done that many a time before when a group of us from college had come over to see a play. Then I would get a train back to New York. A train was the safest place and I would ride back and forth until it was not too early in the morning to telephone someone in Philadelphia or New York, whichever place I happened to be.

"Well, before you do that," the driver suggested, "I've got an idea that just come to me. I know a stagehand at the theater where your Mr. Skinner is at. Maybe he hasn't quit work yet and maybe he'll know where that Mr. Skinner lives or know how to find out."

Thankfully, I agreed.

The front of the theater was dark, of course, but as the driver was telling me he would hunt around for an alley to

the back, the door to the street opened and Mr. Skinner came out. Mr. Skinner later said he was thankful no enterprising press agent was in the vicinity to see a girl rush at him from a taxi, fling her arms around his neck and burst into sobs, saying over and over:

"Oh, thank God, I've found you at last."

It was the one night in the whole run of the play, he also said later, he had stayed after its closing because a friend catching a late train had come to his dressing room for a chat and there was no time to go elsewhere.

By the time we reached home (the right address had one difference in numerals that spanned some thirty-odd blocks), I was serene again, thoroughly enjoying myself. We found Cornelia giving an excellent performance of every tragedy queen, pacing the floor wringing her hands. She had come home from the play, worried a little, and after an hour spread her alarm. She had telephoned her mother in Philadelphia; her mother had telephoned Sophy's poor family, asleep at last after the long wedding day and the departure of the last guest. No, I had not stayed the night with them. They had seen me off, but certainly they would start making inquiries, poor souls. We called them immediately the reassuring news that I had arrived. Their voices when I spoke to them had not the warmth I had always known. I was even cut off in the middle of telling everything that had happened to me.

Some months later Mrs. Skinner wrote me a letter:

"I must tell you something that happened to me yesterday at a tea party. A very distinguished-looking gentleman came up and asked if I was Mrs. Otis Skinner. He said he had had a disheartening experience a few months before when in the middle of the night his doorbell had rung and he had opened the door to a policeman and a young girl in obvious distress. At the sight of him her distress had become greater. She had said, 'Oh, you're not the right Mr. Skinner,' and run away. Very disturbing and unflattering. The policeman who had brought her to me told me she was looking for Mr. Otis Skinner and I realized what an inferior brand mine is, as I am, alas, only a satin Skinner—you know, Emily, the Skinner satins?"

Several years later, at a party one night, someone asked me to tell the story of that night in New York. When I had finished, one of the guests was looking at me round-eyed and with more breathless interest than it seemed to me the story warranted. She barely let me finish the coincidence of the Mr. Satin Skinner. She was calling to her hostess across the room from us:

"You remember when Miss Kimbrough came in tonight, I thought she was Mary Smith?" (I don't remember the actual name.) She turned back to me.

"Mary Smith is an old friend of mine and I know another side of your story that really ties it up. It used to be a favorite dinner-table conversation piece in her family, everybody giving his solution of the mystery."

She included the group in her explanation. "Mary is a cousin of the Morgans. She lives on Long Island. She had been abroad with her family for the summer but had come back ahead of them to look for a job in New York. She had graduated from college in June—" "Just like me," I interjected, stressing the likeness between us because I was so fascinated with this story. The guest nodded and continued:

"The house in town had not been opened. The family was still in the country and some painting and redecorating was being done. But there was a maid there, a comparatively new one, at least she had never seen Mary. The maid, Irish and excitable, was told to expect the arrival of a family relative, have a room ready for her. She did what she was told but when she opened the suitcase of the visitor she saw initials that did not match the name she was expecting and had carefully memorized. When she asked the young lady if there was some mistake, she had been frightened out of her life by the young lady's actions, jumping past her, slamming down the lid of the suitcase, grabbing up her coat and running like someone possessed all the way down and out into the street before a body could stop her, 'Like she was a burglar, surprised in her wicked work'—I can quote verbatim, I've heard it so many times. There was no trace of the intruder, though the maid had opened the front door and peeked out, so maybe she was in the house, hiding somewhere. The maid, scared to death every step of the way, had found the night watchman down in the basement, and together they'd searched the house. Not a trace could they find. Together they decided the family ought to be warned about this and had telephoned to Long Island. The family did take it seriously enough to notify the police, ask them to keep a special watch on the house. The favorite theory was that the girl visitor was the tool of a gang of burglars. They'd used her likeness to my friend— her picture was pretty frequently in stylish magazines—to get her into the house, knowing it was closed and the family away. Once there, she was to case the joint and bring back to the gang the layout of the upper floors." She turned back to me. "I want to bring you and Mary together so you can see for yourself. What a table conversation piece this is going to make when I tell her family!"

Mary and I have never met and I have not been in Mr. Morgan's house again.

The day after these table conversation pieces, Ellen Garrison came to spend the night with us. Though any time with Ellen is unmitigated delight, over the telephone I had urged her not to come because the day before, a hurricane had roared through their countryside and ours and I had been hearing on the radio about the roads that were blocked by fallen trees, and flooding. Ellen said in their immediate area the storm had been a tornado; she and Lloyd, her husband, standing at the window, had watched it come, a whirling black mass that went over them in less than a minute and left over a hundred trees on their own place uprooted, a heartbreaking thing to see, and their road impassable. But the county team had worked all night, the road was cleared, and certainly she was coming. Since Ellen has been a very dear friend since our classmate days at college, I have reason and precedent to know she carries out whatever plans she has set down; her scant hundred pounds are welded by her determination into a dynamo of energy.

She arrived jubilant with triumph that though she'd had to go thirty miles out of her way, she had made up the time by driving at 80 and had fortified herself by eating, as she drove, a sandwich she'd brought with her.

We waited to ask her about the storm and the roads until we had eaten dinner and were relaxed around a fire. Though we had been swimming in the morning, the evening had turned chilly. The storm, she repeated, had been a tornado but not a twister. She had this information from the weather bureau. Ellen likes accuracy and detail and tends to emphasize both. The tornado had come and gone so fast it allowed no time, watching it, to be frightened. It would take weeks to clear the place of the fallen trees. She was glad to get away for a little while from the sight of those uprooted,

79

dying live things. Once she'd detoured from that immediate area the drive over to us had been by the way she'd always come; the highways were clear. When I reminded her she said she'd gone thirty miles out of her way, she admitted with some embarrassment that had been her fault, not the storm's; she'd missed the turnoff. "I think I was looking for my sandwich. But when I found what I had done," she added, and grinned sheepishly, "I was so desperate that I'd be late, I very nearly offered a propitiation, only a piece of sandwich did not seem quite appropriate."

For all her insistence on the specific, Ellen can be obscure. Catching the looks exchanged among the others of us that indicated lack of enlightenment, "I didn't tell you about that time on the dreadful road in Greece. Well, I'd better tell you so you'll know what I meant," and she began her story.

"It was, of course, just coincidence but so extraordinary you would never have believed it if you had read it in a book."

She interrupted herself to ask why I looked so startled and had made a funny noise. "I haven't even told you yet what happened." I urged her for heaven's sake to go on with the story; I would tell her later. Watching me a little doubtfully, she did continue.

"It happened during a cruise we took in Greece on the Stephen Curriers' boat, a lovely congenial group of ten, five couples. We had put into Leonidion, a little harbor on the coast of the Peloponnesus, south of Nauplia, and we had to be in Nauplia in two days because one couple, the Woffords, had to leave us there to get back to Athens for their flight home. However, we had a day between, and Stephen suggested that instead of spending it in Nauplia, a place we knew quite well, we might get a car and drive to Sparta, which we'd never seen. Stephen and Lloyd worked it out on the map and it looked very easy. The Woffords decided not to come because they had packing to do and letters to write. So eight of us left the boat; we would be back in plenty of time for a farewell dinner on board.

"In Leonidion the men scattered to round up two cars and drivers. We'd done the same kind of day trip several times on the cruise and never had any trouble getting cars and drivers. There was always someone right on the dock who would tell us where to go, or lead us, or had a car himself and a relative who also had one. Here there didn't seem to be any cars or relatives. Finally the men rounded up two ancient vehicles with drivers; Lloyd and Stephen showed them Sparta on the map, and the spot where we were. Could they take us there? Was it a good road?

"With a great deal of talk, of which we understood one or two words, and swaggering pantomime, they gave us an assurance that no one in all Greece knew so well the way to Sparta, and the way was beautiful. So we got into the two cars, the women in one, the men in the lead. I don't know why we divided up that way, but that's how we started off.

"After a very short distance it was evident to all of us in the second car that neither driver had the faintest idea how to get to Sparta. The road was certainly not a highway; it looked and felt as if it were used only for goats to travel. Whenever we came to a farmhouse, and this was not very often, or saw a shepherd in a field, both drivers would leave the cars and have a long talk, come back nodding to us and to each other that certainly they were right and we were on the road they knew so well. Then they would stop again at the next person they saw. Our impression was the people they talked to had never heard of Sparta. The so-called road climbed and climbed up a mountain we later found out was Mount Hagios Elias, and the higher we went, the deeper the ruts. We came out on a great wide plateau and there we got totally lost. We even lost the road, such as it was. Then the rains came, and we crawled, slithering and jouncing. A little brook crossed the plain, and that's where we stuck when we tried to cross it."

Ellen stopped, looking at each of us speculatively.

We responded like a Greek chorus.

"Go on, for heaven's sake."

"Well," she said, "to tell this part makes me a little fidgety.

"The men got out, took off their shoes and socks, rolled up their pants and pushed. Nothing happened. Then they tore out parts of hedges that marked off the fields and wedged them as much as they could under the back wheels. Lloyd didn't get the stickers out of his arms and legs for days.

"Claire Simon was the one who suggested we stop work, squeeze into our car and eat the lunch we'd brought. Everyone thought lunch was a good idea. We squeezed to make room for the men but we were all jammed together so tight the women were getting almost as wet from the men's clothes as the men already were. The two drivers were in the men's car ahead, the one that was stuck. We were munching our cheese and bread soddenly, not talking, when Claire made another suggestion. Lloyd was opening a bottle of wine. I remember every detail of what happened at this moment and afterwards. Claire laughed a little, but it was self-consciously, and she said:

" 'You remember last night on the boat, when we were having dinner and it was all so beautiful, Stephen proposed a libation to Poseidon as a kind of thank you and tribute for making his sea so beautiful and calm for us and we all thought that was a fine idea and everybody poured a little of his wine over the side of the boat?' Of course we remembered. 'Well, we didn't make any offering to Zeus, and the gods, you know, are supposed to be very jealous.'

"We got the idea at once and each of us handed his glass over to the ones on the outside, so a little wine was poured into the rain from every glass."

Ellen stopped again and we prodded her impatiently.

"Well." She was a little defiant. "You probably think this was all very silly but we were so wet and cold and discouraged we were glad of any distraction to take our minds off our own misery and the endless talk, while we were huddled in our car and the men were plowing back and forth with brambles, of how we were ever going to get out of this slough of despond. That's what Stephen had named it, you know, from *Pilgrim's Progress,* and he had said earlier if we ever did get out he was going to leave behind a marker of some kind like staking out the North Pole. Anyway this is what actually happened, and it couldn't have been more than a minute after the last libation had gone over the side of the car. There were two shattering claps of thunder, one immediately after the other, following two zigzags of lightning over the mountaintops ahead of us. Until that moment there had not been one sound of thunder nor even a distant flicker of lightning. I don't remember that anybody said a word, and I'm sure everyone knew as surely as I knew that something was going to happen, so we just sat staring and waiting. We didn't wait long, maybe two minutes.

"The two drivers in the car ahead began yelling, jumped out of the car waving their arms, jumping up and down, turning back to us and pointing ahead, and we saw two tractors coming. Their drivers blew their horns to let us know they saw and heard us and turned in our direction. They couldn't have been nicer or more friendly and efficient. They hitched our cars to theirs, took us down the mountain they had just climbed, and there was Sparta.

"One thing I forgot to say," Ellen added. "Lloyd was the first one out of our car. When he stood on the ground he stopped, looked around and put out his hand with the palm up the way you do, and as he started toward the drivers of the tractor he called to us, 'The rain has stopped.' "

There was nothing supernatural about the birth of my twins but the circumstances around it were as improbable as those around Ellen's story, though the connection between the two is of the utmost remoteness. At some time during that evening around the fire Sophy urged me to tell it, and the fact that Ellen had dared our incredulity gave me the courage to challenge theirs. I cannot remember a time when I was not fascinated by personal incidents of the unlikely coincidence. I realize this almost morbid interest is because for years I have been chafed by accusations, about anything I have told, of overstatement. When my twins happened to be born on Labor Day, I had a telegram from a dear friend that read, "You always did exaggerate." Once more I affirm I do not exaggerate one detail of the happenings of their birth on September 2, in a year of grace.

Some weeks before that date my obstetrician had told me this was to be a Caesarean birth, and included several instructions, severely and emphatically given, that at the first faint indication of labor I was to notify him at once and come immediately to the hospital. This was some forty minutes' drive into town from the suburb of Philadelphia in which we lived. A friend of more years and means than ours, learning this requirement and urgency, insisted that simultaneously with the call to the obstetrician she must be informed; she would have her car and chauffeur on call for that moment. They would reach me far more quickly than John, my husband, could come from his job at the far side of the city.

About a week before this plan was put into operation, a friend of John's telephoned he was in America. Like John he was British and they had been at Cambridge together. John immediately asked him to stay with us. When I was told this I asked who the friend was.

"Old Bunjie, one of the best. You'll like him, I'm sure, though I doubt he's ever met an American."

This left in the air what response I might kindle in Bunjie at any time, but particularly when I would not be putting my best foot forward; even more specifically in the present circumstances, my foot could scarcely be seen at all.

Bunjie arrived, a silent but pleasant man. I remember his tweed jackets with pockets that always sagged from the tobacco and pipes he carried in them. I have no recollection of his face; most of it was hidden a great deal of the time by his pipe. In the daytime he walked, taking with him our two dogs, a Great Dane and a Sealyham. The Great Dane was named Multash and I do not know from what source John had derived it. The Sealyham, I explained to Bunjie, was named Cherry because our colored cook had said the first time she saw him he made her think of "Swing Low, Sweet Chariot." When I told him this there was a silence while Bunjie, ruminating, filled his pipe. When it was lighted and giving him satisfaction, he inquired:

"Now tell me, how did you happen to think of the name Cherry? Odd name for a dog, what?" He did not inquire about the origin of Multash. This must have seemed to him sensible and appropriate.

In the evenings the two men reminisced happily about Brains, Rolly, Toodle and other friends, whose exploits and pithy sayings in my unvoiced opinion were not sensational. I knitted tiny garments until the evening ended for them with a small whiskey—I never heard John say Scotch because for him there was only one whiskey—a splash of soda, certainly no ice, then we went up to bed.

One morning about a week after Bunjie's arrival I felt a twinge. Only the doctor's emphasis made me take notice of it. However, I opened the program set down for me with a telephone call to the doctor and another to Nancy, for the car and James. I caught Bunjie as he was starting his morning walk with the dogs, called him back to the house, and apologizing for delaying him, gave the telephone numbers of the hospital and John's office. Would he notify the hospital that I was on my way and tell John to meet me there? I had a few last-minute things to put into my bag and must check once more with the household the routine to be followed in my absence.

When I came out to the car I was astonished to find Bunjie waiting there. I remonstrated that this was not included in the entertainment of a guest even in America. He told me to get into the car and stop nattering, he was not going to let old John down. After telling me John had been out of the office when he had called but the message had been left to meet us at the hospital, my companion put his pipe in his mouth, though he did not light it, and there was no more conversation the rest of the way into town. I had a number of things to think about but I would have welcomed a distraction from them.

John, arriving at his office, had felt a disquietude that would not let him settle down to work. He thought, he told me later, of telephoning back to the house to make sure I was all right but had not wanted to communicate any apprehension. He

86

decided instead to come home, making up on the way some excuse for his return—like paper work that needed solitude —something that would justify his staying close by. The instant he had made this decision, he explained later, and resentfully, instead of feeling reassured he had felt even more unhappy, so that by the time he had got out the car and started for home he was jumpy with nerves. As he put it, "quite irrational."

Total dementia is in my opinion an inadequate diagnosis of his reaction to the sight of Bunjie and me coming toward him in a strange car. He thought we were eloping. The likelihood of a man running away with a woman who momentarily expected a baby and looked it is difficult to conjecture, but to John at the moment, this was the only possible explanation of our being on the road.

By the time he'd become a rational man again, reason, prevailing at last, telling him Bunjie and I were on the way to the hospital, the realization so flooded him with increased anxiety he first stalled the car and then very nearly stripped the gears. Endeavoring to turn around, he backed into another car. By the time he had exchanged imprecations and insurance cards with the other driver and finally gotten under way again, we were long out of sight.

A nurse was waiting just inside the door when Bunjie and I reached the hospital. My doctor had told her, she explained, to take us straight to my room; we need not stop at the desk to fill in the forms that are required and take considerable time. Bunjie, realizing he was being included, shied visibly and tried to bolt.

"Oh, no, Mr. Wrench." The nurse patted his arm. "You don't have to leave her yet. She'll want to have you around, I know, until she has to leave."

My intention was to explain the situation and release Bunjie but a full-bodied pain caught me and I clamped my jaws together.

"Bring her suitcase and take her other arm, Mr. Wrench," the nurse ordered. "We've got to keep going."

Bunjie was in shock, apparently. His mouth was open but there was no sound from him, though I could hear him beside me breathing noisily.

Another nurse and a doctor were waiting in the room I was to occupy. At the doorway Bunjie dropped my suitcase, wheeling around for a takeoff, but our usherette caught him with an iron grip on his arm.

"I'll take you to the room where fathers wait." She led him off, his mouth still open.

Very shortly my activities were curtailed by anesthesia. What happened to the bystander, Bunjie, the most innocent of them all, I learned from John some days later.

John had arrived at the hospital wild-eyed, he admitted, and demanding at the desk my whereabouts, was told he was not permitted above the first floor; only an immediate relative was allowed to accompany the patient. John's bellowed announcement of his relationship was received with frowning disapproval as an attempt at jocularity thoroughly out of place. The more John protested that the man who had gone upstairs with me was an impostor, not intentionally, actually a friend who happened to be staying at the house, the more violently inarticulate he became. His incoherence was aggravated by the icy disbelief of the receptionist. When he pounded on the desk, she spoke and he heard her. It was the voice of authority to a child who was having a tantrum. He would either take a seat in the general waiting room downstairs or he must leave the hospital. John felt no doubt, he said, that she would see either program enforced. Momentarily silenced, he was wildly formulating some other plan —perhaps a telephone call from a booth outside that would bypass her for a sympathetic ear—when my father walked into the hospital and joined him at the desk.

My father had given us no word of his intention to come on from Chicago for the accouchement, but knowing it was imminent and egged on by my stepmother, had taken the train the night before, telephoned the house from the station, learned my whereabouts and come straight there. Without difficulty he established his own identity and, not so easily, John's. A nurse's aide was summoned to bring them to my room but when they reached it I had already been wheeled away. The sight of the empty room brought John to the very brink of total collapse. My father had to take his arm to steer him in the wake of the nurse's aide. There was only one occupant of the waiting room for parents when they reached it, unhappy Bunjie. He and John wrung hands silently. Father surmised the two men knew each other but no introduction was made to him. He said the stranger opened his mouth to let a few guttural sounds escape and John answered them with:

"I know, I know, old fellow. Just stand by, won't you?"

Bunjie obeyed this request literally but Father sat down on a chair by a table, took from it a magazine and endeavored to read. There was no further talk, unless the guttural sounds from the unknown were interpreted as speech.

Father did not remember how long they waited; several days, he thought, admitting this was unlikely. At a noise of furniture moving he looked up from his magazine to see John not merely pacing, but pacing off the room with industry and concentration. He was taking in his stride its dimensions.

As Father watched with interest, John took from his inner pocket a notebook and pencil and wrote down the estimated length, width of the room and the diagonal distance from corner to corner. To be fair and accurate, he had moved toward the center the furniture that had prevented his start with heel to one baseboard and ending with toe pressing the opposite one.

A nurse interruped his work. Father did not know she was the one who had brought Bunjie and me to my room. He saw she carried a small medicine glass and smelled ammonia as she passed him on her way straight to Bunjie. Reaching him, without a word she pushed him down into a chair in front of which he happened to be standing. With one hand she seized his forelock and tilted back his head, with the other poured ammonia into his mouth, which he opened involuntarily, unless, as Father said, it might have been open all the time.

"Mr. Wrench," she said, "you have beautiful twin daughters and Mrs. Wrench is just fine." When I interrupted at this point Father's account of the story: "Didn't you explain to the nurse? Where was John?" Father defended himself.

"I was astonished at the news of twins and thankful you were all right—and John wasn't there. I just stood staring at that man trying to get his breath and the nurse grabbing his head—it could have been attached to a rubber hose from the look of it. Then the nurse shook my hand but, thank God, she'd used up all the ammonia she'd brought and she left the room. Because I was dazed, I suppose, because I thought it was so important to straighten out the paternity, I called after her, 'You made a mistake about—'

"She wheeled round and stood in the doorway.

" 'Oh, no I haven't. It's twins, and they're beautiful.' She was gone.

" 'Why in the name of God didn't *you* tell her?' I said to John, and he wasn't there. I said, 'Where's John?' but I might as well have been talking to myself. That man I was with in prime condition was no talker, and now all he did was wave a flabby hand in a kind of circular motion and shake his head, whatever that meant. I didn't know how John could have got out of that room. He had certainly been in it when the nurse arrived, and it was not a room you could get lost in. I felt a need to sit down and went over to the couch. It was well away from the wall, where John had pulled it to get to the baseboard for his measuring. Automatically I tried to push it back into place but I could scarcely move it an inch. I looked over the back to see what it had caught on. It was John stretched full length, just coming to. He had been in the act of measuring when the nurse had come in, and hearing the news had fainted quietly on the spot."

Some days later I asked John about Bunjie. I'd had flowers from him. John said when he and Father had got home that night of the double-header day, Bunjie was gone. The report of the household was that he'd come in a taxi, kept it waiting, gone up and packed his bag and left. Two or three weeks later John showed me a letter thanking us for our hospitality and saying he'd gone straight back to England. He was going to raise Sealyhams. I wonder what he named them. Come to think of it, I never knew Bunjie's name either.

92

VI

Family Codes

One day recently at a cocktail party I was talking to a friend who is a particular joy to see not only for herself but because she is so well tailored; hairline, hemline never drooping. We saw at the same moment her husband come in with a small group of late arrivals and she waved to him. When he had joined us she said:

"Emily, please forgive us, I'll explain another time, but, Harry, my shoes are worn out."

"O.K.," was her husband's answer, "let's go." They made their way to the door.

She telephoned the next day to ask if I would lunch with her. Across our eggs Benedict she apologized for their abrupt departure the day before. I interrupted.

"I knew something had happened that made you want to get away quickly, but I recognize a family code when I hear it. What was the message, if it isn't a secret?"

Kay admitted it was a code but not secret. Then she told me.

"Years ago when my cousin Fred was a little boy he went

to spend the night with a friend. It was the first night he'd ever been away from home.

"All afternoon they played together, having a good time, but when it got dark Fred suddenly realized he didn't want to spend the night. He went in the house to the little boy's mother, and told her he was very sorry but he had to go home immediately. The poor woman was evidently surprised by this unexpectedness and I'm sure very inconvenienced about getting the child back. She asked him why he thought he must go. Evidently it hadn't occurred to Fred he would have to explain this sudden decision, but he met the crisis.

" 'Because,' he said, 'my shoes are worn out.' Certainly she took him home.

"The little boy's mother told Fred's, and his irrefutable explanation became family vocabulary. When you heard me use it at the cocktail party I had just seen another man coming in at the same time as Harry. That man invariably tries to bait me and make snide jokes about my 'causes.' He always says the word in capital letters. I just didn't feel up to coping with him so I told Harry."

If I were offered a wager that somewhere there exists a family that does not use among its members a word or phrase of special meaning I would accept that wager on the spot and double the bet. I declare categorically and challenge denial that wherever there is a group closely associated, incidents are shared, and remembered. Gradually, reference to any of them becomes abbreviated and applied to other situations. Given time, these references become a code intimately understood. I repeat, for insistence, every family has one.

Sometimes when a piece of family lore is shared with an outsider it is prefaced by a credit line: "My grandmother used to say," or "An uncle of mine . . ." I like very much an opinion originally voiced by Anne Page, John's Great-Aunt Mary.

"When the good Lord calls me," she had said, "I hope to be ready but I'm in no hurry." Anne says her children and her grandchildren use part of it for something unhappily anticipated: "I'm in no hurry."

My granddaughter Eliza was riding in a horse show this fall when her wretched pony relieved itself spectacularly in the ring. Another grandchild, Alis, sitting beside me, exploded into one squeal of laughter and immediately clapped a hand over her mouth. Though her eyes brimmed with tears of joy, I heard her mutter fiercely to herself a phrase I recognized. Startled, I said evidently she knew that story, and she nodded. "Mommie told me." "Mommie" and her twin sister had been four years old when they created this story; now it had become family language.

We lived outside Philadelphia and on Sunday afternoons, as a family we went to the house of friends a few miles away. Their house was on a considerable acreage and to take advantage of this they had instituted one of the happiest programs I have ever known. In the spring and the fall their friends were asked to come every Sunday afternoon with their children for outdoor games in a meadow. All ages were accommodated to the games or the games to them. Parents, even grandparents puffed up and down the field; when they dropped out from want of breath, they joined other panting rooters on the sidelines.

A lofty teen-ager would share his base with a six-year-old. Only the smallest fry were fenced in a separate play yard supervised by the family nanny. When parents threatened to lie down on the field, the games were called off. Then the

group separated, the teen-agers to a playroom for more noise and for refreshments, the old weaklings to the library for tea or stronger, the little ones to the nursery for milk and cookies.

To my twins these Sunday afternoons were weekly excursions to paradise, the days between of interminable dullness. Shortly after their initiation into this happy throng, however, they entered an exasperating behavior phase. I have no idea what began it. Anna, their nurse, and I were without prudery; but suddenly one day anything connected with the bathroom became a reason for giggling. The word "bathroom" whispered between them would induce paroxysms of joyful hoots; anything associated with that room from fixtures to functions was even funnier. I was bewildered, dismayed and mortified by this sudden display of lewdness. Reluctantly, and only because I had reached a point of desperation, I confided to two friends of longer and wider parental experience than mine this depravity my little cherubs were enjoying. To my astonishment each assured me this was a phase common to all children, and each gave the same advice.

"Ignore it," one said. "Make the act a flop," said the other. "It's just a bid for attention. They want an audience and if they don't get it they'll try something else."

Following my principle—either do what the doctor tells you or don't bother to go to a doctor—I told Anna we would both follow the prescription offered. We followed. We ignored, ignored, ignored. Nothing changed; still the giggling and the unrestrained happy laughter.

One day I knew I had reached the bottom of the bottle and could not take another dose. I made up my own prescription. I took them into my bedroom, closed the door, set them side by side on a couch and myself on a chair in front and I talked to them. I told them Anna and I had noticed they liked to laugh about bathroom things. (To say we had noticed was a Mount Everest of understatement.) This was of no interest to us—the hell it wasn't, was my inner thought—but it did show what babies they were. I had thought they were growing up to be people, but I must have been mistaken because they were still little babies. Grownups didn't think those things were funny because everybody had a potty just the way everybody had a bed or a chair and that wasn't funny. I had their attention; I felt I had reached the moment for a crafty suggestion, seasoned with a little bribery. I was not lowering my standards in this. I had practiced consistently, according to circumstances, either the application of the palm of my hand to the buttocks of the offenders, or a tempting bit of cajolery. The manual technique in this instance seemed to me thoroughly inappropriate. I was ready for the other and prayed they were. I reminded them of the Sunday afternoons at the Geyelins'; but—I think I paused dramatically at that —babies were not allowed.

"Now," I said, "I'm afraid I'm going to have to telephone Mrs. Geyelin you aren't so grown up as she thought; you are still babies."

They were people, they assured me. Very grown-up big people. They had stopped being babies that very minute. They would never laugh again at the silly things babies laugh at. Never. They would show me.

The warning in those words passed me by; I was exulting in my handling of the situation with an inward *yah, yah* to my experienced friends and advisers.

The following Sunday afternoon we went to the Geyelins'. When the games were finished and the groups separated, fresh arrivals from the neighboring countryside came in for tea. One of these said to me:

"I hear your twins are here. I'm dying to see them." Turning to the hostess, "Couldn't they come down for just a minute?" Over my protests she agreed politely, and sent word for the children to come downstairs.

They stood in the doorway holding hands, pink-cheeked, wide-eyed. I called in the idiot voice only mothers use:

"Come in, darlings, and say how do you do." They went round the circle of some twenty people and each one of them as she shook hands said gravely, to the speechless astonishment of the recipient:

"How do you do. Everybody has a potty, everybody has a toilut"—Anna's deplorable word—"and it is *not* funny."

At the horse show, Alis, my granddaughter, had checked her laughter with "Everybody has a potty. It's *not* funny."

When one of my daughters says, "Why, Bishop Wright," she knows the source of that phrase. I am not sure my grandchildren do but they all use it to another member of the family as a terse, derisive comment on some addlepated banality another member has uttered. We owe the origin of the phrase to my grandmother and the happy chance that my grandfather overheard her use it. In Indianapolis, my grandmother followed one of the social customs of those days, an "at home." During the season of these events, particular days were specified on the invitations that went out in the early fall. These "at homes" were tea parties, though I have been told hot chocolate, bountifully topped with whipped cream, was the preferred refreshment. My grandmother received her guests at a wide entrance arch to the parlor, and frequently Grandfather Wiles joined her because, he pointed out, gentlemen often dropped in to these "affairs." Grandmother's wry comment was that he enjoyed the company of ladies and paid no attention to the gentlemen.

Since her particular enjoyment was in the company of gentlemen, this was an arrangement agreeable to both.

One Monday, or whatever day of the week was allotted to these titillating occasions, Grandmother was in her bedroom completing her toilette when a maid brought her the distressing news Bishop Wright had arrived and was waiting in the parlor. Shocked by the impropriety of her tardiness and understandably flustered, she hurried from her room to the stairs. This was a steep flight terminating in a broad entrance hall, polka-dotted with small Oriental carpets known as prayer rugs or scatter rugs. Beneath them the floor was waxed to duplicate the surface of an ice skating rink. Grandfather Wiles said they were called scatter rugs because that was the way you were likely to find bones and brains of people walking on them. In her agitated rush Grandmother, a dignified but always an impulsive woman, who seldom moved slowly, tripped on the top step. Had she gone headfirst she might well have justified Grandfather's description of the rugs as a depository, but she landed instead sitting down and in this position descended the flight buckety-buckety and, ending up at the bottom on one of the rugs, rode on this carpet across the hall into the parlor and to the feet of the Bishop. At the sound of this staccato descent that gentleman had risen to his feet and watched, with what emotion I can only guess, his hostess' approach. As he bent down, assisting her to stand —and Grandfather, coming in the front door at that moment, joyfully heard her—she said:

"Why, Bishop Wright, I never come downstairs that way."

Savoring this in repetition, Grandfather maintained it was a pity to create and shatter simultaneously a picture of Grandmother habitually using this form of rapid progress.

One night my father, my stepmother, Achsah, my daughter

B and I were playing a card game called, I think, Oklahoma. I have not played it since and I have no recollection of how it was played then, but that evening we had been taught the game. The only thing I do remember is the phrase it brought into family use. My stepmother was wearing a delectable robe, called then a tea gown, of pale green velvet with a cascade of lace down the front and a train. At a point in the game when evidently my father thought he was about to make a coup, my stepmother outmaneuvered him. He put down his remaining cards, looked across the table at her with affectionate but rueful exasperation and suggested:

"Why don't you go down to the firehouse, dear, and talk to the boys?"

B and Achsah looked at each other in bewilderment at the suggestion, and at my joyous laughter. Neither of them had lived in a small town. They could not savor the full flavor of my father's proposal. In Muncie, Indiana, where my father was born and I was too, the men in the fire department, when not in action on pleasant days, sat on straight chairs tilted back against the front of the firehouse on Main Street. They watched the world go by. No lady would ever have dreamed of stopping to talk to them but there was little that escaped their notice and comments. Therefore, a waggish comment on a particularly fruity tidbit of gossip was invariably, "You must have got that from the boys at the firehouse."

When her children are provoking her, B says, "Why don't you go down to the firehouse?" It is a signal to clear out and they obey it.

Achsah has brought into the family, by way of a bishop other than my grandmother's, a phrase we have all adopted. Its source, and it may be apocryphal, is a story of a benign, kindly gentleman, a Bishop Anderson, who lived in Saint

Paul, where Achsah's family has its roots. Walking along a residential street one wintry day, the saintly man saw a little boy on the porch of a house he was passing. The little boy, too short to reach it, was trying to press the doorbell by jumps that were ineffectual. He had taken off his mittens in order to reach the bell more accurately but was having to stop intermittently to blow on his hands. The Bishop promptly changed his direction, went up the steps onto the porch and, one arm protectively around the boy's shoulders, with his free hand pushed the bell vigorously. This done, he smiled down at the poor little waif shut out, because he was so small and helpless, from the warmth of home.

The little waif, looking up at him, said:

"Now we run like hell." As he followed his own counsel, the front door was opened to the Bishop. Somewhat distorted, it has become a family slogan of advice in a touchy situation: "Run like Bishop Anderson."

When a friend, trying to assemble from the directions I was reading aloud to her a kitchen device she had ordered, muttered, red-faced with fury, "Yah—the men will know," I knew this was family language. After her anger had been diminished by putting all the pieces back in the box and the box in the trashcan, I had the temerity to ask the source of "the men's" knowledge. She managed to laugh a little and told me. Her husband, whom I knew as a distinguished writer, had a mechanical knowledge, she said, barely sufficient for the replacing of a burned-out electric light bulb. Among their friends another couple lived under the same imbalance. The husband, a scholar and recognized authority in his field, had never been able to remember, for instance, which way to turn a valve to bring heat into a radiator or shut it off. The two men one summer had decided to buy together a small boat with outboard motor in which to take their sons fishing. It seemed expedient to the two wives to accompany their husbands when the purchase was made. The salesman, a dapper young man of massive self-assurance and amiability, had devoted his attention exclusively to the two husbands. Each wife, recognizing on her husband's face a well-known expression of vacant incomprehension, had ventured to interrupt the young man's torrential salesmanship with a few pertinent questions about operation and repair. The orator had not paid the slightest attention. Finally annoyed, my friend had asked sharply for an answer to her question and the young man with pitying condescension had answered:

"Dear lady, the *men* will know."

Their unspoken reply, mouthed to each other, was "*What* men?"

Mother's family was of the Society of Friends, and although after her marriage she went to the Presbyterian church with Father, she always used Quaker speech to her relatives and other Friends and maintained some Quaker customs. One of these was silent grace at meals. A cousin on Mother's side of the family, Alida Marsh, came to spend the night with us when she was about five years old and I was the same age. Alida was one of five children. Mother said afterward, probably by the time she came along her parents had stopped explaining why they did certain things, and she had simply fallen unquestioningly into the pattern. My memory of the evening she was with us is only that we had supper with my mother and father. That was unusual, but certainly I know the incident because it was transplanted into family language. Evidently Alida had felt uneasy as a visitor but lifting her head after silent grace, with a deep sigh of contentment she had said:

"This is just like home. We smell our plates too."

I knew Alida's words had come into family language when, some thirty years later, I heard my daughter A consoling B, B wishing aloud she'd never accepted an invitation to a weekend house party; she had never been there before, she probably wouldn't know anybody.

"You'll have a good time; you won't feel strange. They probably smell their plates too," A told her.

When a group of friends shares an experience, a phrase from it sometimes becomes a coin of their realm and it is used from then on among them. In 1956 or thereabouts, five good companions, and I was one of them, traveled canals in England and Wales on a boat we chartered. Howard Lindsay and his wife, Dorothy Stickney, were members of our nautical party. Howard plunged with such enthusiasm into the life of water men, he bought and wore a yachting cap, and one day with a man-of-the-sea nonchalance told the captain he believed he would take a turn at running the boat. Hearing this and the captain's acquiescence, the rest of us moved involuntarily into his immediate vicinity, not to be back-seat drivers, only to watch with interest—and some apprehension. We all saw a boat bearing down on us from the right—we thought it affected of us to say starboard—but Sophy, the only genuine sailor, knew, as she explained later, a fundamental rule afloat: the vessel on your starboard has the right of way. The knowledge broke her silence.

"Howard"—her voice was sharp with authority—"there's a boat to starboard."

Howard nodded complacently. "*He* sees me," he said.

There was no collision, only a few angry words from the skipper as his craft swerved from ours. Dorothy explained later:

"That's the way Howard drives a car. When I tell him we're going to be hit, he always says, '*He* sees me.' It's hard on the nerves—mine—but," she added ruminatively, "we never have been hit."

Since that day, any one of us, wishing to shrug away personal responsibility, is likely to say, "*He* sees me."

Each one of us, too, in that happy band has appropriated another phrase from the Lindsays. Howard said its origin was an old vaudeville joke. An actor stranded in a small town was eating dinner in its one hotel. The waiter asked him:

"How is your soup, sir?"

The actor told him:

"I'm sorry I stirred it."

Of a situation in which unintentionally I have found myself involved, and deeply regret it, I say, with thanks to the Lindsays:

"I'm sorry I stirred it."

Lacking code phrases, communication within the family is without flavor is my assertion, and to share, outside the family, a code phrase is a stronger bond of friendship than a fraternity grip. To hear a family code used by a stranger, however, is a Popocatepetl of surprise. The code I heard at Bergdorf Goodman's in New York was not a phrase; it was a language.

When I was a child in Muncie, Indiana, Betty Ball was my closest friend. Our parents were friends and sometimes when they talked within our hearing about things they did not wish to share with us, they used a language that was, to our fury, incomprehensible. Suddenly, gleefully, we discovered the key. We never by look or smile let them know we had found a Rosetta stone—that was a pledge between us—and it was a long time before we admitted to each other what we were now able to translate was boring. Our own use of the language was more exciting. Well out of our parents' hearing we baffled and infuriated our contemporaries.

As in "The Hunting of the Snark," I skip forty years.

Something happened recently so astonishing I still doubt its credibility. I must reassure myself it did occur. Otherwise, I would never have broken our pledge of secrecy, and I hope Betty will forgive me. The key to the language is this: You must insert the letter *g* in every syllable of each word—a hard *g*. For example, "you must do this if the word has only one syllable" becomes: y-g-ou m-g-ust d-g-o th-g-is i-g-if th-g-e w-g-ord h-g-as, and so on.

One day a few weeks ago, I went into Bergdorf Goodman's late in the afternoon, so near to closing time I was the only customer in the department. Three or four of the salespeople were sitting together facing the stockroom, evidently waiting to make a quick departure when the closing bell rang. As I passed the group, one of the women, making no effort to lower her voice, spoke to her friends.

"I-g-i th-g-ink th-g-at i-g-is a-g-an a-g-actre-g-ess b-g-ut I-g-i d-g-on't kn-g-ow wh-g-o sh-g-e i-g-is."

A man with a gun directly pointed could not have stopped me more decisively. The years rolled back as fast as a movie film rewound. I was in Muncie again talking to Betty and the words came as trippingly from my tongue as if I really were.

"No, I am not an actress," I said in the language, "but I thank you very much."

The saleswoman who had spoken, screamed, jumped to her feet, clapped her hand over her mouth and bolted into the stockroom. Her friends, wide-eyed with apprehension, moved involuntarily more closely together. A woman coming from the stockroom intercepted me as I reached it.

"I'm extremely sorry, madam," she told me, "for any discourtesy. I'm sure it was not intentional. Miss Crandall"—I think that was the name—"is very upset."

The loyal friends, breaking their huddle, surrounded us, protesting, explaining no harm was meant, and I, trying to talk above them, said over and over what a happy moment this had been for me and could I please say so to Miss Crandall.

When Miss Crandall was finally persuaded to come back and, reassured, to talk to me, I learned this had been a language her parents and the parents of her best friend had used. She and her friend had one day discovered the secret of it and from then on had made it their own. Over the years she had forgotten about it until late one afternoon like today, she said, waiting to go home, and only one or two customers there, she had taught the language to her group. After that they had fun making comments about people around them "because," close to tears, she added, "I promised them there wasn't another living soul that understood the language. My parents and even my friend are dead and I never dreamed there was anybody else in the world who knew it." That, I told her, was just what I had thought.

So you see, Betty, it is not really our secret any more. That's why I have taught it to my grandchildren.

VII

Midsummer Nights

2090 Horatio Road
Cleveland, Ohio
March 15, 1971

Dear Miss Kimbrough:

Miss Dorothy Stickney suggested that I write you because she thought you would have information that would be of use on a study of Miss Margaret Anglin.

I have spent a year doing research on the career of Margaret Anglin in preparation for a doctoral dissertation at Chase Western Research University in Cleveland, Ohio. My dissertation will center on Miss Anglin's Greek productions which she produced between 1910 and 1930. . . . According to the program of the 1915 production you were in the chorus of *Medea* and also *Electra*. I thought you might perhaps feel like sending me some comments or thoughts on your experiences with Miss Anglin. . . .

I thank you for whatever help you may be able to give.

Sincerely,
Arnold Johnson

P.S. Miss Stickney did not know anything about Howard Lindsay's contribution to the 1915 production. Would you be able to tell me exactly what he did in the production? He is listed in the program as the assistant director.

Miss Stickney would not know anything about Howard Lindsay's contribution, I wrote in my answer to Mr. Johnson, because she was not married to him then; she had not met him in 1915. I met him then and I could tell Mr. Johnson more details of that summer than of last summer or the one before because the summer of 1915 was what I would have called the most thrilling time in my life. Thinking about it today, when my evaluations are more moderately voiced, I will not modify that description. I was fifteen years old that summer and I was on the stage in the company of Margaret Anglin. Mercifully for Mr. Johnson and his dissertation, I have not included in my letter to him the circumstances of my being there and, to him, other irrelevant details but in my own chronicle almost every detail is relevant to the miracle of the whole and this is how it began:

A cousin of my mother's, Dr. Richard Boone—I called him cousin Richard too—was a professor of philosophy at the University of California at Berkeley. He wrote Mother and her half sister Louisa—Aunt Lulie to me—urging them to come out for the summer to see the San Francisco Exposition; another professor, a friend, was going abroad with his family for the summer and his house would be available for us to rent. Aunt Lulie, a widow, and her son Charles—their last name was Robbins—lived in New York, where she taught at Columbia; we lived in Chicago.

There evidently was a spate of agitated correspondence between the sisters when this invitation came. I remember my father at breakfast suggesting there might be less confusion if one waited for an answer before writing a follow-up letter to the one preceding. I do not know that Mother followed this suggestion; I do know we went to California. Daddy went with us, stayed a week, and came back for our last week there.

We traveled both ways on the Santa Fe, train No. 3, the California Limited. We left Chicago at 8 P.M. the first Sunday in June and arrived in Oakland at 8:10 A.M. on Thursday.

The California Limited, its souvenir pamphlet said, "runs on rock-ballasted and oil-sprinkled tracks, safeguarded by block signals . . . equipped with compartment and compartment–drawing room sleepers . . . the entire train is ventilated by the Garland process. It is electric lighted throughout . . . electric fans are also provided."

I shared a compartment with my brother Charles, who was nine. Mother and Daddy had the adjoining one and there was a door between which could be opened. Brother and I had grimy hands and faces most of the time because we liked to sit facing each other, each one at a window so that we could look out, and we liked the windows open. Screens kept out rocks and pebbles the speed of the train kicked up, but let in dust, soot and small cinders. I always sat in the seat facing forward because riding backward made me carsick, overriding Brother's protest of this arrangement by telling him in great detail what would happen if we changed places. This was the reason he said he preferred to sit in the observation car at the end of the train. I know the reason was that he liked meeting and talking to people and I told him so, because everybody on the observation platform rode backward. When I was sent to bring him to bed one night I heard him say to his neighbor:

"I see that you have a great many more stars out here than we have at home."

When I told Mother I could not make him believe this wasn't true, she said she was only thankful to hear he had been talking about the stars. Each time she had gone to fetch him she had heard him sharing with all the occupants of the observation car minute details of our family life.

Hilda and Gertrude were in the car next to ours and Hilda was supposed to look after Brother. She did come in once in a while to scrub him down. She was our cook; Gertrude was her friend and had asked to come too in order to see the San Francisco fair. At Berkeley she shared a room with Hilda and was our waitress. When we got home to Chicago she went back to her other place, and we only saw her when she came to visit Hilda in our kitchen. At our house they were very quiet but on the train there happened to be a number of other Swedish people, with whom they made friends and had a gay time. They had all brought baskets of food; when I could not find Brother on the observation platform I knew he was in their car getting things to eat.

The day we arrived in Oakland Brother was not allowed to visit either of his favorite places. After he was washed he put on a blue linen suit of short pants and a sailor blouse with white braid around the collar. I remember hearing Mother tell Hilda, who had left her friends to come in and help us pack:

"I brought six suits and that's the last clean one."

He and I sat facing each other by the window but the windows were closed to keep us clean. It was so hot, sweat was trickling down our backs. My hair was long, pinned at the neck by a large barrette. The barrette marked the boundary I had reached after a stormy spring's battle for permission to put my hair "up." At least it wasn't hanging loose like a ten-year-old's but I told Brother bitterly if I had been allowed to put it up I wouldn't be so hot. He wasn't listening; he was an inventive boy. As I was complaining about my hair, holding its thick tail in the air away from my back, he slid off the seat facing me, went to the john in the corner, lifted its green velour lid, knelt down and put his face into it, pushing with his hand the pedal that released the aperture at the bottom. When he was dredged up by an exasperated parent as we were pulling into the station, his face was blacker than it had been on the observation car; he explained he had just been getting some fresh air to cool off. Mother was still making him spit into her handkerchief and wiping his face in the vestibule when the train stopped, the porter opened the door, and we came down the steps to the platform.

The Boones were waiting for us—cousin Richard, his wife and their grown-up son, Richard, Jr. With them was Aunt Lulie, short, plump, trim, quick—she fitted her name Robbins —with her sixteen-year-old son, Charles, tall, thin, slow, laconic. I heard him ask Brother if his face was striped like that from a disease; Charles had a scientist's detached curiosity. Brother explained his air-cooling invention and Charles approved it. "Good idea," he said. I doubt that the others noticed Brother's face, there was so much talking going on among them and so much to do: Hilda, Gertrude and their bags collected with ours, enough redcaps gathered to take care of it all, trunk checks turned in at the baggage counter and arrangements made for delivery in Berkeley. Finally we were on the ferry, everyone pointing out things for us to look at, no one interested in our telling them we had seen from the train real oranges on trees, and palms. Brother was interested in the ferry ride across the bay, but I was lofty about the experience, explaining I had been on a boat, from Hoboken to New York.

The first sight of the house routed the indifference I was trying hard to assume as my pattern for the summer. I had seen roses before in gardens and on trellises but I had never walked through a gate, up a gravel path to an entire facade, except for the doorway, so overlaid with pink roses it was impossible to see what the house itself was made of.

Inside the house I was taken aback by the library. I had never before seen or heard of one on a second floor, and it seemed to me a not very respectable place for it. We did not have a library in our apartment in Chicago, only bookshelves in the living room and the bedrooms, but at my grandfather's and any other house I knew, a library was on the first floor, always dark, and you had to wash your hands first if you were going to look at any of the books there. This one went all the way across the front of the house, with shelves to the ceiling between windows, a little movable ladder in front of them. Standing in the doorway, blinking in the sunlight, I shaded my eyes to see the room better. There were comfortable chairs and a big long table down the center with books, magazines on it. You could even come here in your nightgown, though I had certainly never heard of doing such a thing.

The rest of the house suited my idea of what was proper. Charles Robbins and my brother Charles had to share a room but I had one of my own, and since that was the only important requirement I was not interested in arrangements for the others. Aunt Lulie and her Charles had been there nearly a week so they knew where everything was and Aunt Lulie was impatient to show Mother the garden. Hilda and Ger-

trude were unpacking and said I was in the way, so I went too. The garden was the third surprise. It was big but not neat, there was lawn in the center, very green. The beds all the way around it were too wide to jump across—Brother tried—with the flowers jumbled in colors and kinds. Along the back there were trees. Orange and lemon and a kind I learned was avocado, and that was the summer I learned to eat avocado except that we called it alligator pear. Years later I heard the word "avocado" without an idea of what it meant.

The details of our trip and our arrival at the house are sharp in my memory, but there is a blur over the sequence of days that immediately followed. The red-letter one was so dazzling it put all others into shadow, brightened only by such moments as on the day Charles with Brother went on a hike into the hills: they took their lunch with them and brought back a bagful of snakes they emptied into the garden. I remember vaguely Charles' indignant explanation of the opportunity for study given by the proximity and the number of these harmless specimens, but what illuminated that day for me was the sight of Hilda taking a bag of garbage through the garden. Her purpose was to empty it into a large bin in a fenced-in small area at the far end. She did not empty it there nor in any one place. She had happened to choose for this daily excursion a time almost immediately after the moment when Charles had emptied his sack and gone with Brother into the house to invite their mothers to come and see the wonderful trophies of their hunt. Hilda was the first to see them and by heaven-sent timing I happened to be standing at my bedroom window that looked on the garden. Hilda saw one snake, dropped a few orange peels and announced her discovery with a bellow powerful

enough to be an echo of a Viking ancestor sighting the coast of Ireland. It brought Gertrude on a gallop from the kitchen. Hilda was on the gallop too, heading back for the house. Their collision knocked each runner on her back and spilled considerably more of the garbage. Whatever the Swedish word is for snakes, Hilda was using it in a rising crescendo and pointing. By the time the family reached them the daughters of Vikings were up on their feet again, both yelling. I stayed at the window, of course; it was the best seat in or out of the house. Even from the second floor I counted six snakes. Hilda and Gertrude agreed there were two hundred. Charles stated categorically and sulkily there were twenty; that was as many as he had been able to find. I am sure Charles was right, but they scattered so widely, their number could have seemed greater. It was a joyous sight to watch but not one to talk about; the topic was forbidden. Mother and Aunt Lulie cooked our supper; Hilda and Gertrude were given the evening off. The rest of the summer Charles and Brother alternated emptying the garbage. The snakes went back to the hills, to Charles' disgust and Hilda's disbelief.

We went to the fair several times, I remember. It was beautiful. My legs ached and I had to go find Charles and Brother when it was time to go home. I remember too trying to impress my cousin Richard Boone because I had a crush on him and had been told he was a great scholar, so I took long walks every morning before breakfast in the direction I thought he would go. I carried *The Autocrat of the Breakfast Table* because of all the books in the rented house, this seemed to me the most intellectual. I sat down at a place I thought my cousin would pass and read the book, not much of it because I found it dull. My cousin did not once pass that way; I have not read it since.

If coming events do cast shadows before, the first of these was a tea party given by the Boones to which Mother and Aunt Lulie were invited, and I was not. This selection was agreeable to me. I had been included in one party that in my opinion turned out to be very flat. The guest of honor had been David Starr Jordan, and I was told he had been president of Leland Stanford University and was an ichthyologist. I recognized the Greek sound of this because I had been reading Greek from an early age, thanks to an idea of Mother's she wanted to try out. At the Girls' Classical School in Indianapolis, her alma mater, Greek and Latin had been part of the curriculum in the primary grades. Because of her delight in them, and wanting me to share it, she reasoned that since to a child all letters looked strange and were difficult to copy and remember, Greek would be no more baffling than English; so she taught me to read Greek before I went to school. At Miss Faulkner's School in Chicago I had continued Greek, but not brilliantly. When I heard the word "ichthyologist" I associated it with *ichor*, which I happened to know was the word for the blood of the gods, so I went to the party for David Starr Jordan with high hopes of stories with lots of blood in them. When I asked Dr. Jordan if he would tell some bloody stories he looked surprised. When I reminded him tartly I thought that was his specialty, he told me apologetically it was fish, and not much blood to be got out of them. Between my mortification and my disappointment, the party sank into interminable tedium. Possibly I showed my glum disapproval of it because I was not invited to another.

Came the day and the party. Mother was calling me as she came home, up the path to the house. We met on the stairs.

"Come into my room," she said, "while I take off my things. I've something to tell you."

Mother had an exasperating habit of drawing out any piece of good news; bad news she always told quickly and directly. She pulled off her white kid gloves, one finger at a time, blew into them and put them in her glove case on the dressing table. She took off her hat and put it carefully into a hatbox, talking half to herself.

"I don't think I have ever made such an idiotic, fatuous remark in my life and I devoutly pray I'll never make another one of such inanity. Now sit down, not on the bed." (This was never permitted.) "I'm sure you've heard Aunt Lulie and me talking about going to the plays in the Greek Theater this summer?" I nodded. "Well, you'll never guess for whom the Boones' party was given today. They hadn't put it on the invitation because they weren't sure she could come. It was Margaret Anglin."

Certainly I knew who Margaret Anglin was—no ichthyologist. Whenever my allowance permitted, I always bought a copy of *Theatre* magazine, cut out of it and kept in a scrapbook the photographs of actresses and actors I had seen, had a crush on or hoped to see. I had pictures of Margaret Anglin, though I had never seen her. I knew she was one of the greatest, and I could have recited her biography and a list of plays in which she had been a star.

"You didn't actually meet her?" Mother nodded, and visibly blushed.

"I was so taken aback, I told her I had been delighted to learn she was giving three Greek plays out here this summer because—my daughter was studying Greek and this would be such an incentive to her. As if this was why Margaret Anglin had come to California."

"Oh, Mother." I was blushing for her.

"I know, I know. Blithering idiocy but let's not dwell on it. Now this is what she said, that great woman: perhaps

since you were so interested in Greek"—Mother shuddered
—"you—would—like—to watch—the—rehearsals."

If, before fainting, the room you are in spins around and
you feel violently sick at your stomach, then I was close to
it. Mother must have sensed something like this might happen, because she had answered Miss Anglin, with far more
than her usual kind of remark, that if I recovered from the
swoon into which such an invitation would undoubtedly send
me, she was sure I would indeed like to watch the rehearsals.
"They begin tomorrow," she added.

Perhaps I slept that night; I doubt it. I was dressed and
ready to go at half past six. Mother came out of her room
as I was tiptoeing down the stairs.

"You will have to wait until eight o'clock—all right, all
right, half past seven then," as I had started to protest. And
looking at my face, added, "You needn't eat breakfast." She
knew I would lose it. One of the reasons I was trying to get
out of the house was my anxiety that Mother would go with
me, as if I were a little girl being taken to the first day of
school. My relief that this was not suggested was so great, I
accepted the later departure without protest. I have no recollection of how I filled that interminable hour.

The theater was within easy walking distance of our house.
I ran most of the way. My cousin Richard had taken me to
see it when he was showing us the university. There had
been no performance or rehearsal going on so he had sent us
to the top row and when we reached it had stood on the
stage and said, scarcely above a whisper, the "Friends, Ro-
mans, countrymen" speech. We had heard every word as
clearly as if we had stood beside him. That morning as I ran
up a hill and through a woods to reach it, I knew for the first
time the pungent smell of eucalyptus. In 1943, on the morn-

ing of my first day of work in Hollywood, I had breakfast on a little balcony outside my apartment. As I came on the balcony in the early morning, I took a deep breath and was on the instant running up a hill in Berkeley, California, in 1915, and knew simultaneously the reason for my flight in time. The trees fringing my balcony were eucalyptus. In 1955 I was climbing a hill to reach the great theater at Epidaurus. I stopped suddenly because I was on another hill running through eucalyptus trees and these at Epidaurus were eucalyptus.

When I came into it, the theater was as empty as it had been on the day of our sightseeing tour with cousin Richard. I learned later rehearsals began at ten. It was not quite eight o'clock when I stopped running and in order not to be noticed sidled through the nearer of the two wide entrances that flanked the bowl. They would be used by the audience and sometimes during the performances were entrances and exits for the players. On our sightseeing visit I had thought the theater big, like a football stadium, where I had once seen a game. A football stadium filled with people is a bandbox compared to my impression of the Greek Theater when I stood alone in it. I knew I had never seen so big a place so exposed. If I climbed to the top row where I had heard cousin Richard speak I would be as easily spotted as if I stood in the middle of the stage. I very nearly followed the course of the French king who marched up a hill and then marched down again, yet I said to myself as I climbed up the outside edge to a halfway bench, "I was invited to come," but I was not surprised to realize I was walking on tiptoe. When I stopped tiptoeing and actually sat down, I knew on the instant here I was at last and here I would stay. During the two hours I was alone, I was as exposed to the sun as to anyone who might come, and the sun was hot. I stuck to the seat with as much sweat as determination.

Then they were all there. I heard them less than a minute before they came through the entrance I had used. They made a large group, everyone talking, calling to one another. These were real actors and actresses and it surprised me a little that they were talking and laughing like ordinary people. One of them, nodding his head toward the other side of the theater, said something and they all stopped talking. A woman was coming down the opposite ramp, a man on either side of her. I had no idea who the two men were but I knew two things simultaneously: the woman was Margaret Anglin, and having your heart turn over could actually happen. I could not see Miss Anglin's face nor the color of her hair because she wore a white hat with a broad drooping brim. She said, "Good morning, good morning," laughed and added, "Like every other one here, it's a lovely day." That was my true and lasting recognition of Miss Anglin. I would not need to see her features nor the color of her hair. I have never heard a voice so rich and full, though soft, with a curious little break, like a grace note in it; and this was not the rapture of a fifteen-year-old. To this day I have not heard a voice of that special quality. I am sure of this because the sound of it is as recognizable in my ear today as the tune of "The Star-Spangled Banner."

The two groups met at the foot of the ramp below the center of the stage. There was some discussion between them I could not hear. Then they scattered. Some moved up the steps onto the stage, others sat down along the front- and second-row benches. Perhaps there were thirty or forty people all told; I did not count. Miss Anglin sat down in the center of the front row, the same men who had come with her on either side. She spread open on her lap a large book in a black cover. The script of the play, I suppose, though I did not know then the word "script."

"Does anyone know if Mr. Platt is here?" As she spoke she looked around the theater and unmistakably caught sight of me. I saw her turn to the men on either side of her and nod in my direction. They looked where she indicated and like any crowd following something noticed by one or two people, so did most of the company turn my way. I was leaning forward, half standing in my excitement to get a better view of them. At that moment I wished I was flat on the ground, underneath the bench. I knew what I must do, but I was not sure my knees were steady enough to carry me. I reached Miss Anglin by saying to myself I *had* to do it. When I spoke, my own mother would not have recognized my wavering treble.

"I am Emily Kimbrough," I said. "Mother met you yesterday and you told her I might watch rehearsals."

Miss Anglin smiled immediately and put out her hand. She was a woman of iron control, because she did not wince when I put my hand in hers and it must have been like taking from a bed a hot water bottle that had been put there the night before.

"Of course," she said, and to the two men, "Emily is studying Greek, her mother told me, so I have invited her to watch our rehearsals."

Though I wanted to say how mortified Mother was over what she had said, and that my study of Greek had not taught me the difference between blood and fish, I was tongue-tied and muscle-bound. I had intended to say, "Thank you for letting me come," and then go back to where I had been sitting. I was unable to do either; the two men smiled at me abstractedly and there I stood. I think Miss Anglin understood that I did not know how to go away. She said, "Here comes Mr. Platt; I must talk to him about the *Iphigenia* costumes." It was a kind way of releasing and dismissing me. That night at dinner I told my family I had a delightful talk with Margaret Anglin, Livingstone Platt, the set and costume designer (I had overheard a member of the company tell another who he was) and two other gentlemen.

The next morning by nine o'clock I was back in the seat I had appropriated: I did not want to risk missing anything; the day before I had had nothing to eat until dinnertime. The second morning I brought lunch with me. That day I learned the play they were doing was Euripides' *Iphigenia in Aulis* and, from hearing their names called, I began to sort out some of the people involved. The two men whose base was on either side of Miss Anglin were Henry Hull, her husband—and I wondered how he had ever had the courage to aspire to such an honor—and Walter Damrosch, who, I found out later, had composed the incidental music for the plays. Carolyn Darling was Miss Anglin's secretary and also a member of the chorus. I thought her name exactly right because she came over, introduced herself and talked to me while I was having lunch. She said the man who told them what to do and where to stand, speaking in a heavy accent, was Gustav von Seyffertitz, an Austrian, and his title was director.

It was on the fourth or fifth day of my vigil that all of the Fourth of Julys in my life rolled into one simultaneously exploding pinwheel, Roman candle and skyrocket. Actually the day had not begun well. Mother had caught me as I was leaving the house. She had forgotten the night before, she said, to tell me they were all going across to the fair, spending the day. She knew I would not want to miss that. I think she was shaken by my boisterous outrage that anyone could think I wanted to do a childish thing like traipsing around a fair, when by special invitation I could be in a theater watching a play. She yielded; but I think she may have felt her authority slipping a little, because she made me go back to my room and write a letter to my father and one to my grandparents. So instead of being the first one at the theater I bolted in as red, hot and breathless as I had been on the first morning, and the company was already assembled. They were not on the stage, however; Miss Anglin was in her usual place and most of the others were standing near her, not talking. She saw me, unmistakably beckoned me to come to her, and I wished I were dead or had gone to the fair with my family. She had not spoken to or even noticed me since that first morning. Now she was going to tell me they did not want outsiders any more, or perhaps she had heard the noise of my coming and found it disturbing. I went to her thinking this was the last time I would see this wonderful place and these magic people until I came like everybody else to the performance.

"Emily," she said, when I had reached her, "we've had an accident this morning. One of our girls in the chorus fell and has sprained her ankle badly. I know you have been watching every day. Would you like to take her place in the chorus?"

That is the moment when inside me all the pinwheels, Roman candles and skyrockets exploded. Miss Anglin said later, considering to what lengths stagestruck young people would go in an effort to set foot in the theater, mine was an extraordinary invitation to appear on the stage, and mine was an unusual response.

"Oh, Miss Anglin," I told her, "if my family will let me." I did not know why everyone within hearing laughed.

"We will hope," Miss Anglin said gravely to the company, "they can be persuaded." Then briskly, "In the meantime, perhaps you would stand in. Carolyn, would you show her the place she's to take?"

As I followed Carolyn up the steps I remembered thinking if the family did not consent I would die but I would die at the summit of my life: I had stood on the stage in Margaret Anglin's company.

Permission did come but not easily and not without an aftertaste of bitterness. For nearly a week I did not tell Mother what I was doing because I thought a surprise announcement on the very day of the performance would be glorious, and also because I was afraid to ask; but on the morning it was announced that on the following Monday we would carry over to night rehearsals on through to the performance, I knew there was no postponing the surprise.

The moments of gratifying excitement at my news were brief; second thoughts followed immediately and they were dour. I was young, I would be in a group of older, far more sophisticated people, in a world apart. When I shouted I was neither young nor unsophisticated, I was told to keep quiet and let Mother think. The result of her thinking, after conferences with Aunt Lulie and the Boones, was a telegram to my father in Chicago, the first of a series of exchanges between them. When I was not at the theater I either cried or prayed. I did not dare say to anyone in the company I might not be allowed to stay. They had teased me in the beginning about my answer to Miss Anglin's invitation, but they thought I had said it out of embarrassment. By the end of the first day's work I had realized that for these people on their own, making a career, earning a living, any uncertainty about being allowed to do it was grotesque. Mother was sympathetic to this and when I told her to put herself in my place and try to see what it would be if I had to go to Miss Anglin and tell her, after days of training, I would have to drop out and they would have to start over again with someone new, she wrung her hands.

"I know, I know all that, Emily, don't think I don't understand but *you* don't understand." I know now that I didn't understand because to be fifteen in 1915 was to be very young, and to a family that had never touched its outer fringes, the theater was a glittering and dangerous world. For a girl who on school nights had supper at six and was in bed at eight-thirty, half past nine on Fridays and Saturdays, even physically this was a trial of strength.

The deciding telegram from my father came while I was at the theater. Mother was watching for me and came running down the path waving it above her head.

ALL THINGS CONSIDERED, it said, LET HER DO IT. TRUST YOUR JUDGMENT. GREAT EXPERIENCE FOR HER. ALL LOVE HAL.

"I think my last telegram did it," Mother told me with obvious satisfaction, after I had stopped yelling and waltzing her around. "I said since the plays were outdoors it would be very healthy for you."

There was the galling aftertaste that is with me today. A deciding factor in my going on the stage was not a great talent it would be wicked to deny, but that I would be in the fresh air. No one in Miss Anglin's company ever knew how brief my stay might have been and why it was not.

When the company was dismissed in the late afternoon of the day we were to have our first night rehearsal, Miss Anglin sent for me. She had not spoken to me except to include me in her good morning to everyone since the day of her invitation. She wanted to know where I was going to have supper. I told her Mother was coming and would bring it.

"That's all right then," she said. "But in the meantime"—she indicated a steamer rug on the chair beside her—"I want you to go up to the top of the theater away from everybody, wrap this around you and go to sleep. You can, you know, if you try. Anyone in the theater learns to go to sleep whenever there is a chance for it. Then you'll be fresh for the rehearsal tonight. It's very important in the theater, too, to take care of yourself; that's another thing you must learn."

I doubt I would have experienced in any other company such thoughtfulness from its star.

When I woke it was dusk. Mother was sitting not far from me and someone was singing. "Who is that?" I demanded, louder than I realized because I was startled and not yet awake.

"Hush," Mother told me. "It's Schubert." I had meant the singer, of course, and wide awake knew it was Merle Alcock. I had heard her lovely voice in solo passages of Mr. Damrosch's music. When I asked what part she played, I had been told she was not in the acting cast but would be on the program as a first soloist. Once she had spoken to me. With this superiority of acquaintanceship I unrolled quickly from my blanket and went over to introduce her to Mother. To my exasperated discomfiture, as I reached them Mother was saying, "And I will always remember your beautiful performance in *The Yellow Jacket*." Since I had also seen *The Yellow Jacket,* I might have said that too, instead of just simpering when she had spoken to me, except that it had never occurred to me this pretty woman could have been that Chinese mother.

There were no other soloists in the chorus so I do not

know why Merle Alcock was called the first one. As a group we would be moved on cue with specific gestures. Some of the members had speaking parts; the leader, Gertrude Wagner, had a long one. Once, generously, I was given a line but when "Death is the lot of all" was heard in my piping soprano, Miss Anglin said she had never heard a happier canary, and the line was quickly allotted to another maiden.

Mute, I was inconspicuously adequate in the chorus, or there was no one else available. At any rate, I was not asked to return to the benches and at the end of the first week I was paid. I still have the envelope with my name on it. I was not quite so levelheaded as to think everyone in the company was there for the pleasure of it, but I truly thought mine was an invitation generously given to an outsider. Actors' Equity was a new organization and its rulings were not recognized then. Certainly I had not heard of it and since the eighteen dollars in my pay envelope was larger by sixteen dollars and fifty cents than my weekly allowance, I would have considered daft anyone who wanted to improve working conditions in the theater. We rehearsed from ten in the morning until around midnight with pause for lunch and for dinner. I considered this an ideal schedule. I might have come out of my euphoric mist if I had heard around me any expressions of dissatisfaction. On the stage I was dumb because I could not speak a line convincingly, but I was not mentally backward nor was my hearing defective. In the intervals when we were not on the stage the members of the chorus talked and I listened. I learned about their families, their lodgings, their previous engagements, matters of love, but I never heard a protest about work and pay in the theater.

The work in the chorus consisted of specific movements on cues. Since from the first grade our school curriculum had included "aesthetic dancing" and eurythmics, I could follow directions without anxiety, though Mr. von Seyffertitz gave them in highly individual phrasing. One of his instructions is a favorite in my family to this day:

"I want you should move, young ladies, oh so leetle, almost hardly." He was punctiliously formal when he addressed the players but since he could not remember their names he would say:

"Mrs. Clytemnestra, may I ask you please to come on the stage and, Mr. Agamemnon, if you will stand here just so." However, I never heard him address Miss Anglin as Miss Iphigenia.

On the second of the night rehearsals Mother sent Hilda and Gertrude up the hill with supper for me. She thought they would enjoy watching a rehearsal. She also thought between them they could bring something more than sandwiches, milk and fruit for me since she had noticed, she said, how skimpily the people around her had been eating the night before. I do not remember what they brought that night in the basket they carried between them, but after that nothing could keep them from their nightly visit nor the feasts they provided. It was not love of the theater nor certainly of me that prompted this devotion. It was because Pedro de Cordoba, tall, dark, handsome, would station himself at the entrance to the theater and peering down through the eucalyptus trees begin his nightly call. That with some variations was:

"Do I hear the two most beautiful women in my life coming up the hill? How I love them, how I wait for the evening to be with them. Are they carrying between them a basket of beautiful things? Surely they will not let their own Pedro go hungry tonight."

Simpering, giggling, the two Scandinavians would come

in sight, panting and breathless under the weight of the basket that grew heavier each evening in direct proportion to the increase in Mr. de Cordoba's protestations of fervor and devotion. My own allotments from the provisions remained the same. Sometimes Mr. de Cordoba and his chosen group, among the more exalted members of the company, sent over to me and my humble associates a few tidbits.

Livingstone Platt's stage decorations were simple, classic and beautiful. High double gates in the center upstage marked the entrance to the palace of Agamemnon in the plays *Iphigenia* and *Electra,* and to the palace of Medea in that play; the costumes had far wider variety. The material was of a soft cotton crepe. This was dyed and, when the dye had set, was dampened and wrung as one would wring out a towel, then allowed to dry in tight folds. Released, it was like accordion pleating, soft and clinging. The colors were as soft as the texture, purple, lavender, magenta, rose, greens and orange. The costume was in two pieces: a basic straight shift from shoulder to heel; over this another layer of the material in a color contrasting to the shift was draped and it was not pleated. No two members of the chorus had the same arrangement of draping. Mr. Platt himself did each one individually. In our shifts and carrying our extra material we waited our turn, watching him create on the ones ahead of us an arrangement that would not be repeated. Sometimes an end trailed almost to the ground; on another girl it became a cowl with soft folds under the chin. Madam Fralick, the wardrobe mistress, stood beside him, holding a tray heavily loaded with safety pins of all sizes and strips of elastic of different lengths and widths, the kind of elastic—attached to a hat—from which I had recently and with vehemence been emancipated. The ones on Madam's tray were not to go under

the chin; these were put on like belts when Mr. Platt wanted to make a peplum or confine the whole draping in folds below the waist.

On the night of the *Iphigenia,* I was standing in line moving up to Mr. Platt when Carolyn Darling found me, with a message that Miss Anglin wanted to see me in her dressing room. Until that instant I had not felt the slightest nervous tremor. I am embarrassed to remember that; I must have been a clod or numb. I know that during the day, since there was no rehearsal, I had done unimportant things with the family, but there had been no talk of the play other than discussion of what time they should all start and a telephone call to the Boones to set a place for meeting. I have no recollection of saying to myself, "This is the greatest night of my life," nor having any anxiety about being at the proper place and with proper movements on cue.

When I left for the theater Mother had said, "With your shield or on it." She always said that on the day of examinations at school.

If my friends were not so casual and easygoing as usual when I joined them at the theater, I did not notice it. Someone told me to put on my shift, bring my drapery and wait in line for Mr. Platt. It had been more exciting the first time at the dress rehearsal the night before, but when Carolyn Darling told me Miss Anglin wanted to see me I knew panic. What had I done that was so awful Miss Anglin was going to dismiss me? Did she think I was so incompetent it was better for the performance to have nobody? Carolyn turned away from me to talk to the other girls, wishing them luck. She knew how nervous they were but they were going to be fine. Several of them said they had not been able to eat all day. One of them said she had thrown up three times and hoped the fourth wouldn't be on stage. This was why I was being dismissed, I decided. I had eaten at the usual time and the usual amount and had not in the least felt like throwing up. I had no temperament. I was sick now, not because I was going on the stage, but with the humiliation of leaving it, and the thought of my family coming to see me—and, of course, Miss Anglin and the play—and not finding me. I would certainly not wait for them after the play as Mother had planned. No skulking around for me, trying to keep out of sight; I would go home now or somewhere; perhaps I would never go home.

Carolyn said, "Coming, Emily?" I wanted to say good-bye to the others, thank them for being so nice to me, but I could not make sounds. I looked back at the door; no one had noticed my going.

Miss Anglin was at her dressing table.

"Come over here, Emily," she said, "and stoop down. No, I think it would be better if you got on your knees here in front of me." Flat on the floor was where I wanted to be. "That will be an easier height for me."

She turned away from her dressing table and reached for a tube that was on it.

"It suddenly came to me you wouldn't know the first thing about making up, so I thought I'd better do it. Now then, put your chin up a little so the light is better."

No one noticed when I came back to the chorus dressing room. Mr. Platt was draping the last girl. I took her place when he had finished. The world was beautiful; I was beautiful. I wondered did anyone recognize this ravishing creature I had just seen in Miss Anglin's mirror? I could not speak about the terrible thing that had almost happened to me and the wonderful thing that had happened, but I needed to talk.

"Oh, Mr. Platt," I said, and shivered extravagantly, "it's going to be cold out there tonight. Just listen to that wind."

Mr. Platt sat back on his heels and took a safety pin from his mouth.

"Child," he said, "that's the most beautiful sound in the theater; and for people in the theater," he added, "the most beautiful sound in the world. That's not wind, it's people, fourteen thousand of them, come to see you."

Then it broke over me, as if I had been knocked down by a giant wave; strangling, I gasped for breath. This was not the gymnasium of Miss Faulkner's School for Girls in Chicago, filled on an evening with parents and friends brought by duty and loyalty. Of the fourteen thousand people out there whose rustling movements came to us like a high wind, mine was probably the only parent of all of us who in a few moments would be on that stage. It was Theater that brought them. For two hours they would be lifted, carried up from their own world; they would be surprised and a little bewildered when they first returned to it. Long afterward they would say, "On such and such a night I saw Margaret Anglin in her production of *Iphigenia* and I will never forget it."

Certainly in that moment of strangulation I was not shaping this realization coherently, but I was whispering, and I remember it, "This is the theater and I'm in it." I also remember with equal clarity, the realization scared me witless. Compared with it my despair over Miss Anglin's summons was a shrug.

Mr. Platt finished draping me, called cheerily to all of us he knew we would do him proud. Mr. von Seyffertitz shook hands with him in the doorway telling him how stunning the set looked and called to us good luck and a laughing admonition to remember all the "leetle things." The door closed behind them on a silent room where we waited. No one was talking about being sick, or being sick. Gertrude Wagner, the leader of the chorus, crossed the room from the makeup table at which she had been sitting with her head in her hands, opened the door a crack. At the same moment the callboy said through it, "Overture." I had learned only a few minutes before, the title "callboy" and his purpose.

On that instant the wind outside dropped to scarcely a breath. Walter Damrosch was on the podium; his music began. We heard the passage for flute, piercingly sweet. We tiptoed out of our room to watch Merle Alcock pass us in the wings and move with exactly timed grace. As the lights came up slowly she sang the prologue to the play. No amplifiers distorted the beauty of her voice; its pure clarity rose without effort to the highest row in the theater. Mr. von Seyffertitz's direction had forestalled any interruption by applause. His Mr. Agamemnon, on the program identified as A. Fuller Mellish, and Paul Harvey, as Aegisthos, came through the gateway from Agamemnon's palace on the second the song ended. An involuntary spasm of applause was stopped immediately. For us in the wings the most important moment in the play was coming closer. We moved silently into position. Gertrude Wagner looked quietly back to see if we were all in place, gave a nod and led us from our hiding place backstage outside, around the rim of the theater nearest us and the stage, but not yet onstage. Her timing was so exact, at the moment we reached our starting point the orchestra gave us our cue, and the twenty maidens of Calchis flowed down the ramp and up the center stairs onto the stage. For me, at that moment, the play began.

The San Francisco *Chronicle*'s report of the performance said: "Flourish of trumpets preceded the cry 'Iphigenia is coming!' The music denoted the approach of Queen Clytemnestra and her daughter; the trumpeting and the shouting came nearer and the effect was carried on magnificent crescendo until through the southern gate the cavalcade appeared. Slaves marched down the ramp to the front of the amphitheater's broad stage, archers followed, then the soldiers bearing lances. Wedding gifts and bright arrayment were carried by a score of attendants. When the thrill of the spectacle was at its height, a chariot drawn by four horses abreast brought Clytemnestra and Iphigenia upon the scene. It was an entry full of life and spirit, splendidly dramatic in the climax." (I had thought this entrance anticlimactic to ours.) The paper also said: "There was not a seat nor even standing room available. It was the largest audience in the history of the Greek Theater."

I had heard the sound of it.

Medea was the next play. When I was told what hour to report for the first rehearsal my heart felt several pounds lighter and I was less disagreeable at home. I was no longer a substitute but actually a member of the company. There was a difference too in the others, a difference, that is, toward me. I had been a sort of kid sister treated with affectionate tolerance, though I doubt that any one of them was more than five years older than I. In 1915 the width between the ages of fifteen and twenty was a generation gap and from a nonprofessional family the distance to the country of the theater was as far as Spain from the beach of Atlantic City. To the featured players I was identified without a name as a good provider at suppertime. After night rehearsals or a performance, I knew they all gathered somewhere before they went home, and that many of them lived in the same boardinghouse. I loved to hear them talk about it. I went home with Hilda and Gertrude or Mother.

Everything changed when the *Medea* began. People called

me by my own name, Emily; it took me a long time to have the courage to say theirs. Mr. Platt asked me—I never called *him* Livingston—to help paint Medea's chariot; he would leave a dab of the proper color on each part of it, and give me the tins of paint. I doubt that Hebe bearing a cup for the first time felt more exalted. I had read the *Medea* so many times I knew it almost word for word, including the directions, and among those were: "Medea appears above the house in a chariot drawn by dragons. She has the dead bodies of the children with her." Medea, Margaret Anglin, would stand in a chariot painted by Emily Kimbrough. I was discomfited to find the masterpiece was not to be entirely my own artistry. But when the person Mr. Platt said would paint with me turned out to be a man, an "older man" who played one of the two messengers in the *Iphigenia*, I was reconciled to a degree of simpering pleasure. The term "older man" must not be confused with an "old man." To a fifteen-year-old, an older man was over eighteen and under thirty; beyond that he was old. This older man and I talked as we painted. One day when I told him, since there was no rehearsal called, I was going that evening with Mother to see the Exposition at night, he asked if he might come too.

We met by agreement at the ferry and I introduced him to Mother. He talked more to her than to me. It did not occur to me he might have found her the more interesting. I thought it was because I stayed apart from them; I was mortified because he did not wear a hat. When I asked if he had forgotten it, he looked surprised at my concern and told me he didn't own a hat. I pondered this as he and Mother talked and I reached two decisions: that if you were in the theater you were not like other people and you showed it, and until I found a way of my own I would copy my friends and not wear a hat again to the Exposition so that everyone there would know I was an actress.

A few days after this trip and my decision, Howard Lindsay, the assistant director, came to the theater with a hat he said he had gone to San Francisco to find. He was jubilant with success; I was dumbfounded. I had never seen a hat like it nor even a picture of one. I reasoned he wanted to look "different" too, but since he was not an actor, he could not be without one; perhaps to wear this would identify him as a director. When he saw my bewilderment he told me the hat was called a topee and was made for explorers and other people who were not natives in tropical climates, to protect them from the sun. He must have sensed I was looking at him with awe and I was, thinking I had never dreamed I would ever be talking to one person who was both a theater man and an explorer. He said quickly he was not going on any exploration. He and I were going to do a special job for Miss Anglin. The pith helmet was part of the equipment he had bought for it. Miss Anglin would tell me; would I please go to see her about it?

"I want literal translations of some of the passages in the play," she told me. "Just for my own study. I'm sure you can do this. I remember what your mother told me." She smiled and I, immersed in a beet-red blush, thought about matricide.

"Howard Lindsay can translate Greek too, so I would appreciate it very much if you would work together. I have shown him the passages I want."

We worked at the top of the theater away from everyone. Mr. Lindsay had bought two copies of the *Medea* in Greek, a dictionary, a trot, a long yellow writing pad, pencils and the topee. Since there was no place for us backstage where we could work in the shade undisturbed and without bothering other people, we would have to work in the open theater, on the top row to be by ourselves. He was taking precautions, because he was very sensitive to the sun.

The selection of topees could not have been wide because the one he had bought was several sizes larger than his head. In addition to my copy of the text open on my lap, I kept beside me a dictionary and the trot. Mr. Lindsay with the text had the long yellow writing pad. He kept the book open on his knees, the writing pad and pencil on the seat beside him. His right hand was free but he used the forefinger of his left to hold up the topee. He was a friendly, warm, charming but impatient man. He cleared away immediately most of my shyness, told me to forget he was a director and for heaven's sake call him Howard. A minute later, while I was looking up a word, he shouted a plea to God to explain why it took me so long; surely I must know the alphabet. His further objurgations were muffled because, reaching across to take the dictionary from my hands, he released the prop of his index finger and the pith helmet fell over his face. Its fall was swifter than its replacement; getting it back over the promontories of ears and nose was accomplished with tender care, and the descent always snuffed out his irascibility. When the contemplative pose—forefinger to the brow—was resumed his affability was restored. I can say this "always" occurred because the first time it happened evidently gave him no suggestion of how to avoid a recurrence. He neither removed the helmet nor took over the dictionary nor exercised patience; but we made and delivered to Miss Anglin the translations. I do not know how much they benefited her. They did not benefit me. Four years later at college, an examination set by my Greek professor included some of those passages. I failed the examination.

Recognition of Howard Lindsay as one of the most dis-
tingushed playwrights and actors of our time did not come
to him by way of translations. Nevertheless, when I saw him
and his wife, Dorothy Stickney, in the immortal *Life with
Father,* I recognized nostalgically the irascibility that gave
authority to his interpretation of the role of Father. As in
"The Hunting of the Snark," "I skip forty years"; actually,
perhaps half that number. Howard Lindsay had moved up
steadily and brilliantly in the world of the theater. I had
been in the obscurity of education and jobs unrelated to the
theater. Our paths came together again on a book I had written. The difference in age had been closed as always happens
by the stitches of time; he and Dorothy became my dear
friends. Talking one day of Howard's portrayal of Father,
Dorothy explained, "He's not a *bad*-tempered man, he's *quick*-
tempered." And that, I thought, was exactly the right translation of Howard. "I skip forty years" or half that number back
to the summer of 1915.

One morning a week before the performance of *Medea* I
came into a nearly silent theater. Always before reaching the
top of the hill I had heard sounds of activity that made me
run the last part of the way lest I be missing something. That
morning I had run because there were no sounds. No car-
penters sawing and banging bits of scenery or whatever
required carpentry, no electricians calling out their technical
jargon to one another, no bellowing summons for Livingstone Platt or Mr. von Seyffertitz or Howard Lindsay, nor
the buzz of actors passing the time of day until the call of
"Places, please" would silence everyone. I knew I was not
late enough for that call to have been given. I wondered if
there was to be no rehearsal that day and I had not been told.
I was running when I came through the entrance and stopped

because everyone seemed to be there and no one seemed to be talking. There were three groups of people: Miss Anglin, surrounded by the important ones, the lesser members of the cast with the chorus, and at a little distance from both, the working staff. I was even more bewildered to see Madam Fralick, the wardrobe mistress, and the only woman among the mechanics; I had never before seen her out front, even at a dress rehearsal. What made it become frightening to me was that there was no audible sound coming from any of these people. I could see Miss Anglin speaking and the people around her answering and talking among themselves with an occasional gesture. Their voices were so low no sound of them reached me. I went, probably on tiptoe, to my own group; I know I whispered to the girl I reached first.

"What's the matter? Has something happened?"

"Has something happened?" she echoed. "Only that the Messenger fell on the ramp this morning. He's been taken to the hospital; we're waiting to hear how badly he's hurt." We had all fallen into Mr. von Seyffertitz's habit of calling the actors by their play names. I suppose to make sure this appalling news was true and we were talking about the same person, I said, "You mean Pedro de Cordoba?" They were all listening; several of them nodded, one of them added:

"He came early, to work on his entrance in the big scene running down the ramp, saying his opening lines."

"He told me"—another one spoke up—"he told me yesterday he wasn't satisfied with the timing of the running and the speaking. He wanted to speed it up. He said it had to come all in a rush."

"I don't understand why he fell," someone else said.

"Probably had on rubber shoes like Margie." This was Lucille Evans speaking and she turned to me. "She's the girl who had your place and got hurt on the ramp."

A man came out on the stage from somewhere in the back. I had thought no one was left there. He spoke as he walked forward.

"It's the hospital calling Miss Anglin."

Miss Anglin jumped from her chair but Howard Lindsay put his hand on her arm. "I'll take it, Miss Anglin," he said. She did not persist. She sat down again immediately. "If you would, Howard, thank you."

One of the girls behind me said, "She hasn't the strength to go. She's so afraid of what they may tell her." I am sure no one spoke in the next few minutes; I know there was complete silence when Howard came from the back and walked across the stage, down the steps and to Miss Anglin. He made no effort to lower his voice.

"It's bad," he said. We all heard him. "Compound fracture."

Someone gave a long, low whistle; there was no other audible sound. Everyone was certainly, like me, counting over in his mind the implications and ramifications of this announcement—pain, hospitalizing and weeks of inactivity for Pedro de Cordoba; disaster for the play. In 1915 a replacement could not be flown out from New York. Geographically Hollywood was nearer than New York but it was just a place then. Miss Anglin interrupted the silence with a laugh that was forced, and not gay.

"Now if this were only happening in a play," she said, "someone of you would rise up at this point and say, 'I know the part, let me play it,' but—"

A young man from our group stood up; my friend, the one who did not own a hat. He shuffled his feet, coughed, made a few *eh* sounds and finally said in a rush of words, "I do happen to know the part, that is, most of it. I don't know if you'd consider letting me—" What he said was like a fresh

143

wind blowing; we were out of the doldrums. Miss Anglin jumped to her feet and everyone followed.

"Take your places, please." She reached the center steps and stopped. "No, I'll watch. Carolyn, take over for me." She went back to her seat. Mr. Damrosch must have joined her. I did not notice then.

My friend went up the ramp, the chorus on the stage divided into the grouping for that scene. Carolyn Darling, in Miss Anglin's place, came through the great doors, stood on the first of the steps leading down from the palace. Miss Anglin called, "Now."

Down the ramp the Messenger came in wild panic flight, like an animal stampeding from death, but over the noise of his feet a voice of horror reached us. We had not heard the like of it.

"Get thee away, Medea, get thee away. Fly." Then he was up the steps to the stage, spilling out to her the dreadful recital of the death of the princess, Jason's bride, from the poisoned robe Medea had sent as a wedding gift, brought to her by Medea's and Jason's two children; and the death of the king, father of the princess, when he had knelt, "and groaning low, folded her in his arms and kissed her," and been himself enmeshed in the robe. "And there they sleep at last, the old proud father and the bride."

In that scene, we in the chorus knew exactly what we must do, each move to make, each word in the Messenger's speech that was our cue. From the moment the hair-raising yell of "Get thee away, Medea" had reached us, not one of us stirred. We were frozen in our places.

When the scene ended and we realized we were breathing again, with a quick glance from one to another we knew what we had failed to do; but on the instant we were all

144

of us turning to look down at Miss Anglin. She was staring at the Messenger, smiling tremulously, shaking her head as if in wonder.

"The part is yours, of course," she said, "but you've brought a moment in the theater I think not one of us will ever forget."

Mr. Damrosch stood up. He had been sitting beside her. He walked over across the ramp, stood below the stage to one side of the steps. He reached up his hand.

"Young man," he said, "tell me your name. I want to thank you for a great experience, and I have known a few."

The young man came to the lip of the stage, squatted awkwardly on his haunches, stretched his hand down. I thought how big it was and saw his face and neck were fiery red. He reached Mr. Damrosch's hand with his own.

"Why, thank you very much, sir. My name is Alfred Lunt."

Postscript: That autumn I was sent to boarding school, to Miss Wright's School in Bryn Mawr, Pennsylvania. During the winter Alfred Lunt came to Philadelphia in *The Country Cousin,* by Booth Tarkington, starring Alexandra Carlisle. I had not been reticent about my stage experience and my friends in "the profession," but when Miss Wright told me I was to be sent in to a matinee as a special treat, so that I might see my friend, I wished God would punish me for boasting, by striking me dead. When Alfred Lunt was the Messenger, I had been a member of the chorus. When I went to see Alfred Lunt in *The Country Cousin,* I was in the school uniform of a blue serge sailor suit, called a Peter Thompson, and I was accompanied by a chaperon, Miss Janney, my English teacher. Prodded by her, I had to send backstage my name and a request to see him after the performance. We went back, I hoping at each step I could run away, but I did not; I only stood mute, wet-handed, unable to answer his polite inquiries about my present activities, because I was afraid I would vomit. Miss Janney filled a ghastly silence.

"Mr. Lunt," she said, "I have brought an invitation from Miss Wright, and this is a surprise to Emily, a treat for her and for all of us. Miss Wright would be happy to have you as a guest of the school on Sunday afternoon at our Evensong."

For one beautiful instant, there was a flash of understanding in a look he gave me across Miss Janney, and I answered it. He regretted that because of another engagement he must forgo the pleasure of such an occasion. I have seen him very infrequently since that day. I am sure he forgot it years ago. I will never forget it and I never forgave Miss Wright and Miss Janney.

VIII

Homecoming

The evening of the day the mail had brought Mr. Johnson's letter about Margaret Anglin, I had dinner with Katharine Cornell at her house. She has been a cherished friend for more years than we can remember. I told her about the letter.

"All day I've been reliving that summer. I dug up from my storeroom in the basement an album of photographs taken then. The back of the album was off. I'm going to have it rebound."

Kit urged me to tell her about the summer, not the album, but I would not be persuaded.

"Too long for telling now, but I'm going to write it and," I added, "the story of your opening night in Buffalo in *A Bill of Divorcement.*"

This obviously startled her. She began sentences and interrupted herself. "What on earth made you think of—Why would you—?"

"Because," I cut in, "I always seem to think, at least to remember, in pairs. When I thought about the night of *Iphigenia*, I almost immediately remembered the night of the *Bill of Divorcement* opening. They were great experiences in the theater—separate but equal—so I connected them."

Kit shook her head ruefully and laughed. "I didn't know you were there."

Her laughter surprised me as much as evidently I had surprised her. "In the whole evening," I said, "there was nothing to laugh at, though Lord knows it was joyous."

"You tell me how it was for you," Kit suggested, snuggling into the cushions of her chair like a child waiting for a bedtime story, "and then I'll tell you why I laughed."

To set the stage a little, I told her about my family's moving from Chicago to Buffalo because of a postwar reorganization in my father's factory at North Tonawanda that we both know is under an hour's distance from Buffalo. The stay was to be temporary, but in my dour anticipation a week was too long a duration, so I had spent as little time there as possible, going for holidays from college, except at Christmas, on visits. When college was finished and some family coercion had been applied, I came to Buffalo, where I did not know anyone and was positive I never would. I could not have been more mistaken. "I did make friends, have gay times, and I never met anywhere a more attractive group."

Kit nodded. "Buffalo people are like that, when you know them."

"You and I can never remember where we met and through whom, but I can't imagine why, until now, we've never talked about that night." My friend urged me to stop speculating and get on with it. I obliged.

"Well, I did make friends. I even collected a few beaus and one of them, Jack Sprague, invited me to go with him to the opening night of *A Bill of Divorcement.*

"The moment it was announced the play was coming to

Buffalo, I began hearing about you. Everywhere I went people talked about Kit coming and who Kit was and how she was tops in sports, tops evidently in everything, until I began to be a little bit irked about the one and only Kit. I wasn't irked, but I was surprised, when Jack told me everyone would wear evening clothes to your opening. I'd been to the theater in Buffalo and I'd never seen an audience there in evening clothes. I knew your father owned the theater; there were few things I hadn't been told in the incessant conversations about you. You had recently married but in Canada, and everyone was looking forward to meeting this Guthrie McClintic. So I thought this was the reason for our dressing; there was probably going to be a party, a belated wedding reception after the play.

"Jack was right about wearing evening clothes, but they were not evening clothes, I discovered, for a minor party. As the audience settled in, taking off coats, I saw many of the men were in white tie and tails; the women, dressed for a ball, were pulling up and smoothing long white gloves. Another thing that surprised me was the comparative silence of the audience. Usually people waved across the house or talked back and forth with friends in the row in front or in back. I had learned that, unlike Chicago or New York, Buffalo was a community in which you were bound to see friends in almost any audience and if it was a special event, as this one certainly was, practically everyone but me would know everyone else and be talking and calling across the floor, even up to the balcony.

"The curtain went up and I forgot about everything but the play. At the moment of your entrance, Jack whispered to me, 'There's Kit,' as if I didn't know, and from the silence around he must have been the only one in the audience who said anything. I had expected a crash of applause, stamping feet; I had even picked up my bag and program in my lap for a standing ovation. There was nothing, absolutely no recognition. I was so confounded I whispered back to Jack:

" 'You said Kit, didn't you?'

" 'Hush,' he said, or it may have been 'Shut up.' I know I was cowed by it.

"No one else came onstage who could possibly have been you and certainly I had looked at the program. I knew Janet Beecher was playing the part of your mother, Margaret Fairfield, and I had seen her before so I recognized her immediately. Allan Pollock was playing your father, Hillary Fairfield, but he had not come on as yet and anyway there would be small likelihood of my confusing you with *him*. I had not seen before the actress playing the part of Miss Hester Fairfield but I could not have mistaken that vinegared, tight-lipped, elderly spinster for you, and finally there you were on the program, Sydney Fairfield, Katharine Cornell. To clinch the whole thing your mother, Mrs. Fairfield, had gone to the foot of the stairs calling, 'Sydney darling, shall I bring up your coffee?' I remember the line to this day, and your voice answering. And then your appearance and dead silence from the audience.

"Well, the play went on and I was absorbed in it, paying no more attention to the apathy around me.

"When the curtain went down on the first act, Jack and I moved out with almost everyone else in the audience to the foyer. We joined a group of people we both knew. I was impatient with the usual round of hellos and how are yous and interrupted, 'Isn't she wonderful? Katharine Cornell, I mean, of course! What a voice, and how beautifully she moves.' There was a dead silence that was almost physical, as if I'd been slapped in the face. Someone broke it by saying Elizabeth and George Field were back in town, had anyone seen them? I was so embarrassed I moved off to another group. The same thing happened there. At the mention of your name, I was snubbed as if I had laughed aloud in the middle of a funeral, and the general atmosphere wasn't unlike one. People were talking in subdued tones and I didn't hear your name mentioned except by me; after my second attempt I was even more subdued than the rest of them seemed to be. I didn't speak to Jack again when we were back in our seats, and he showed no inclination to talk to me.

"We didn't go out in the intermission after the second act; I think very few people did; stragglers, nothing like the crush in the aisle we had worked our way through the time before, but I was so immersed in what had gone on on the stage I wanted only to think about it and Jack seemed disinclined again to talk, so I was not particularly aware of other people; but my impression is nearly everyone stayed. I did come out of my absorption enough to realize how still the house was all through the intermission, as it is usually only at the moment when the curtain goes up.

"The play moved into that inevitable heartbreaking end. As long as I live I will not forget your scene of renunciation of the boy you loved when you'd discovered there was insanity in your family; deliberately provoking him to quarrel, flouting him, accusing him of being in love with another girl and then when you sent him off bewildered, furious, calling after him impishly, 'You'll give her my love?' and when the door had slammed behind him, I'll never forget the change in your voice and that line of despair, 'You'll give her *my love.*' I don't cry easily and almost never in the theater, but that moment and the rest of the play undid me. I was wiping my eyes with a sodden wad of handkerchief when the curtain went down.

"When it went up again it was to something I've never seen the like of in the theater before nor since: sheer, glorious pandemonium from the audience. Every member of it was on his feet, certainly it was a standing ovation; it was a cheering, laughing, shouting paean-of-joy-and-pride demonstration. Old ladies around me were waving handkerchiefs and calling, 'Kit, dear, dear Kit.' Men were shouting. In the overall noise I couldn't hear what any of them were calling out except Carl Sprague, Jack's older brother, who was in the row ahead of us. He turned round to us, his back to the stage. 'Did you see the way she jumped over that couch?' he said, 'just the way she's always jumped into a canoe; never saw such balance in my life.' Tears were running down his face; he knew it and didn't care.

"Then *I* knew why all these people had been so strangely quiet between the acts, so remote during the intermission, abstracted as if they were thinking of something else, and why they had snubbed me when I mentioned your name. It was because you belonged to them, all of them. You were not an unknown little girl from the other side of the tracks. This was your circle, a closed one around you, and I was an outsider. This was your family, eager and apprehensive, dressed to do you honor, holding its breath until you should prove yourself and then pouring out its love and praise. You had come through with all they'd hoped for and they told you so. You remember when Allan Pollock came out to take a bow he brought you with him? I can see him now as he stood smiling understandingly at the tumultuous crowd and then with a little bow to you and a lovely wave of the arm

circling the audience and you, as if he were saying, though certainly he couldn't have been heard had he tried to say it, 'She belongs to you; I have no place here,' and he left the stage and you alone on it. I doubt that the audience saw any part of that; it was talking directly to you.

"I know I didn't meet you that night but I was longing to tell you some of these things I as an outsider realized. Jack and I went to a party. Nobody there talked of anything but the play and you but you weren't there. When I realized you were not coming, I decided that because I was a newcomer and outsider we had not been included in *the* party."

Kit shook her head. Her eyes were unnaturally bright at the moment. I think she was close to tears, remembering. She shook her head.

"I wasn't at that party," she said. "I wasn't at any party. I'll tell you the ending of that night and why I laughed." She smiled again. "Guthrie and I had not been in Buffalo since we were married and Guthrie had never been, so this was a double homecoming and double nervous excitement for me, I might add. Professionally and personally any opening is such anguish as to make you wish to God you'd never walked through a stage door. To give a performance to an audience with friends and family in it is double death.

"On top of that, if anything could top it, I was nervous about introducing Guthrie. I wanted everybody to feel a little the way I felt about him. I made an idiotic start in that direction. Guthrie was doing a play and could only get away for two days and only this by the insistence and double work of the company. Instead of being very touched and grateful, I was horrified to find he hadn't brought evening clothes. Poor darling, there was nothing in the world he hated more, and certainly it hadn't occurred to him to wear them to the theater. What with one thing and another, I was evidently hysterical in my insistence. It scared him so, he told me later, he promised he would get them, and wear them. You can imagine the telephoning: asking someone to dig them out and find a way to send them; this was the day before the opening. The solution was to put them on the night train in the care of the porter of the Buffalo car. The train got in around seven in the morning and he met it. You can imagine what that itself was to an actor. All I knew was that he had them and would wear them. So I could concentrate my hysteria on the play. You know this was my first big part; the only things I'd done before in Buffalo were bits in the Jessie Bonstelle repertoire company there and since my father owned the Majestic Theater, in which it played, I was just Dr. Cornell's little girl. This was my first chance to prove I was perhaps a little more than that. So you can imagine what this added to the inevitable opening night fever. Well, you were there, you know how it went off and of course the response at the end of the play was certainly something I'll never forget.

"When I finally got back to my dressing room, Guthrie was waiting there, so handsome in his evening clothes and so understanding of how overwhelmed I was. He was too, for that matter. I think I probably cried a little on his shoulder. I know I rushed then to get into my very best clothes that I'd brought down to the theater so that I could match him. I sent word that I was ready and Guthrie and I stood by the door like a receiving line.

"After a while we moved back into my room and sat down. We talked about moments of the play and made other conversation. I suppose it was perhaps an hour or so later, when we'd run out of talk anyway, that Guthrie said apologetically he was awfully sorry but he was afraid he would have to leave or he'd miss his night train back to New York.

"We got hold of a taxi somehow; there was no one around the theater when we came out. We went straight to the station; he had brought his bag down to the theater with him. I saw him to the train; I'd kept the taxi waiting and when he had left I drove home. No one was up. The maids had gone to bed and Father was at a party with his contemporaries. He'd taken it for granted, he said later, we were going somewhere with our own friends. I let myself in—I still had a key to the house—turned on the lights as I went through to the kitchen. I got a bottle of milk out of the icebox and found some crackers on the shelf. I sat down at the kitchen table and had the only food I had eaten that day. Then I went up to bed, read for a while and turned off the light.

"The next morning the telephone began ringing before eight o'clock and from then on it didn't stop. Every conversation began with something like, 'Darling, I knew you would be too tired after the performance to have to talk to people so, of course, we didn't go backstage, but I want to tell you . . .' Bless their hearts, they knew so little about the ways of the theater, it never occurred to them you're so keyed up after a performance it takes hours to unwind and that of all the nights in my life this was the one when I wanted my old friends around me and Guthrie." Kit laughed again reminiscently. "That's how the big night ended," she said.

IX

Of Relative Importance

One day last summer when we had finished the marketing list, Bessie said she must speak to me about something else. Bessie is my cook, housekeeper, friend, counselor, and I listen to her.

"It's about Eliza," she said. "She's got me worried. I think she needs straightening out. You'd better speak to her mother."

Eliza's mother is my daughter, with whom I enjoy speaking about a great many things, in which the bringing up of her children is not included. One reason for this abstention on my part is that I find her children delightful, congenial individuals, possessing too another quality that is perhaps old-fashioned of me to appreciate—good manners. Therefore it ill behooves me to make suggestions, let alone criticisms. A parent with any sense at all knows that after her child is married almost any suggestion unsolicited is ill behooving. Therefore I temporized with Bessie about Eliza. Eliza and a friend, Bitsy, each of them twelve years old, were spending two weeks with me at the seashore in Rhode Island. They were so self-sufficient, with so many projects, I had seen very little of them except at shared games in the evening. I wondered uneasily if I had exercised sufficient supervision.

"If they've been bothering you," I suggested, "I'll tell them to stay out of the kitchen." Bessie protested this.

"They don't bother me. I like having them there. You wouldn't find nicer little girls, but Eliza needs talking to. This morning I was fixing the breakfast trays. They were helping me. Bitsy seemed to know exactly what to do, but Eliza had to be told everything, so I said to her, 'Eliza, you look at Bitsy how she knows her way around the kitchen. She's going to be a wonderful wife one of these days but you better watch out and learn a few things or you'll never get a husband.' And do you know what she said to me? She said, 'Bessie, you don't have to worry about that at all. I don't have to know about these things, because I'm going to marry a horse.'"

When I had left Bessie in the kitchen, reassured that the possibility of such miscegenation was not immediate, I allowed myself a modest cavorting in the back hall. As recently as the day she had brought Eliza and Bitsy, my daughter had made reference to the shocking ignorance of sex among the youth of my generation, contrasting it with the perhaps too easy familiarity of the present.

"Eliza and our two boys," she had said, "have known everything since they were five years old. What her approach to it will be at the age of, say, sixteen or seventeen, I just don't know."

More immediately than at sixteen a few vital statistics would have to be inserted into Eliza's range of knowledge. The happy prospect of telling my daughter this had prompted the previous moment's skittishness. Sobriety returning, I knew my daughter's thoroughness. Eliza undoubtedly at some point had stopped listening, retaining only what at the time had seemed interesting. I remembered then a plaintive admission Stephen Benét had made to me when his children and mine were small. Rosemary, their mother, had decided the time had come for imparting this knowledge and insisted Stephen should bestow it. When Rosemary Benét was Rosemary Carr and I was eleven years old, we had become friends. I knew her gentleness, sweetness, warmth—and strength of purpose.

"So one evening," Stephen had told me, "after I'd rehearsed for a week what I was going to say, sweating over it as much as over anything I've ever written, I told them the 'facts,' and do you know what's happened?" When Stephen expressed astonishment, his eyes behind his glasses seemed literally to grow half again their usual size. "It's turned out to be their favorite bedtime story. So now I have to tell it over and over. They make me skip some parts. We've cut out the bees and flowers completely."

When my daughter A, Eliza's mother, was ten years old, she delivered our miniature poodle, Sarah, of four puppies. In my program of education in the "facts," this event had not been intended as an object lesson. It was to have taken place some days later at the vet's. Confident of the date, I had gone to New York. A's twin sister, B, after a siege of illness, was at school for the winter in Arizona. Other than A, Sarah and her approaching family, the only other occupants of the house were Bertha, the cook, and Mary, the waitress, who was timid.

Over the telephone in about the middle of the night, I had the first news of the accouchement from A, who burst into tears during her joyous recital. When I had persuaded her to relinquish the telephone to Bertha, I gave instructions of bed with a hot water bottle, aspirin, sleeping late, no school, and I caught an early-morning train home. A was in good health and spirits, Sarah and the puppies were in splendid condition.

Bertha seemed a bit haggard. She filled in parts of the story A's tears had blurred. She had been asleep when A had run down the back hall and pounded on her door, telling her to get up quickly and help her, Sarah was having puppies. Mary had heard her too and, according to her own story, at the news had got out of bed, bolted the door and gone back with the covers over her head.

Bertha had flung on a robe, met A in the hall. "That child knew what she was doing, so I just minded what she said. She was the general. She told me to go down to the kitchen and boil a kettle of water, so that's what I did."

A's story, more coherently told than on the night before, was that she had been wakened in her room next to mine by "funny noises" in my room. She had promptly and typically investigated. In her life, A has never locked a door and gone back to bed with the covers over her head. She had found Sarah on my bed and, watching her, was alarmed. Using the telephone on my night table, she had immediately called Dr. Ivens, the vet. Holding the telephone, she said, in one hand and patting Sarah with the other, while she described the dog's symptoms, she had burst out, the doctor said later, like a popgun the minute the telephone was answered. He had interrupted her.

"Now listen to me, A," he had said. "This is Dr. Ivens, Sr. Bill's out on a case and you know I can't come to you." She knew Dr. Ivens, Sr., had given up practice after a heart attack.

"Now I'll tell you exactly what's the matter with Sarah and what you're going to do. Sarah is going to have puppies, and you're going to help her."

She had repeated his instructions back to him before she

hung up the telephone and had immediately called Bertha.

"He told me," was A's recital, "to sterilize a pair of scissors in boiling water, so I told Bertha to make some. He said get a box of some kind. There wasn't any in your bedroom and I didn't want to leave her, so I dumped your hats out and took that one. I filled the hot water bottle only a little bit, the way Dr. Ivens told me, put it on the bottom of the hatbox and folded a bath towel on top of it. I yelled to Bertha to bring me up some newspapers and I lifted Sarah up and put them underneath her. She didn't want to get off the bed and I didn't know where else to put her anyway."

To my bewilderment, A seemed not so impressed by the arrival of the puppies as by the importance of the things she herself must do.

"He said the puppy would come in a little sac and mostly the mother would know to bite it open and tear it off, but maybe Sarah wouldn't because this was her first litter, she might be nervous. If she didn't, I should crook my first finger, hook it in enough to break the sac but not too deep and then peel it off myself, and I did. He said there would be a long cord attached from the puppy's stomach to Sarah's. If she didn't bite it off, I was to cut it, not too long and not too short—that's what the scissors were for! He told me how to measure it against my own finger. And that's what I did. Then I gave the puppy to Sarah. She licked it and licked it and pushed it from one side to the other, but I wasn't scared because Dr. Ivens said that was what she would do until the little puppy began to squeal. Then I took it away and put it on the bath towel in the hatbox. I wanted to see if it was a boy or a girl but I guess I was so excited I couldn't really tell. Of course I knew where to find out. Bertha said it was a boy. I took off the sacs and cut the cords for each of them;

162

Sarah seemed to want me to do it. When Bertha and I were sure there weren't going to be any more, we took the puppies out of the box and gave them to Sarah. She knew exactly what to do then and the puppies did too. It was just wonderful. After that I called up Dr. Ivens and told him all about it. Dr. Ivens, Jr., had just come in, so he came on the telephone and I told him too and he said he didn't believe he needed to come over at all; I had done everything. I don't think I got quite enough newspapers on your bed. I'm sorry about that."

When I had given wholehearted praise of her competence and steadiness, I told her a very special part of the experience had been that she had actually seen what I had told her and B about the way *they* were born.

A looked at me severely. "Well," she said, "I hope *you* had sense enough to take off the sac and bite the cord; after all, it was your first litter."

B's response to my explanation of how mothers nurse their babies I have not forgotten either. B's questions were always practical and pertinent.

"Is there cream on top?" she asked.

Stephen Benét's assertion of selection I can corroborate. My children selected to remember only the parts that interested them and frequently rejected an explanation given, preferring one of their devising. Sensing an unexpressed preference, I sometimes answered with wild inaccuracy; I carry no sense of guilt about it. One night when the twins had been put to bed and I was dressing to go out to dinner B had called me time and again to her room, telling and asking me trivia in a desperate effort, I knew, to push off the bleak isolation of waiting for sleep. When with finality I called back there must be no more summonses, she begged urgently for just one more question and certainly I yielded. Looking up at me as I stood beside her bed, fastening my dress, she asked:

"Mommy, when you and I were born together in a hospital, did the sheep and the cows move over to make room for us?"

"Yes," I said, "that's just exactly how it was. Now go to sleep."

When I looked in five minutes later on my way to the party, she was in sweet untroubled slumber. She had selected a way in which she wanted to be born and had only wanted corroboration. It had not been an appropriate moment for enlightenment.

Selectivity, undoubtedly, was responsible for my deplorable ignorance, when I entered college, of the basics in sex. Since Mother, who died when she was only forty-eight years old, is not here to defend herself, I cannot dishonor her by an assertion that "she never told me." Disliking with contempt any sentimentality, she would not have swaddled the facts of life into cotton-batting obscurity. Undoubtedly I chose to remember what interested me. My absorption was in birth, not what preceded it. A seed was planted and from then on interesting things happened.

The only even vague speculation I remember occurred one day in eighth-grade Latin class when I asked Miss Faulkner what a bastard was. She told me to look it up. I said I had looked it up and the definition was "illegal." That, I knew, meant against the law; I did not see the connection. Miss Faulkner, obviously hedging, said she did not want to take up the time of the class in explanation. Would I ask my mother to tell me?

Mother said a bastard was a baby whose parents were not married to each other and that was against the law. She added a law of her own making. When I came upon a word like that I was not to introduce it in class; I was either to wait until I got home and ask her or at least to wait until the class was dismissed and ask the teacher. There were things that were better discussed privately. At some time after that, in ancient history class, I had felt a need to know more about a word used in the textbook. The sound of it suggested to me kinship with "bastard." Observing Mother's law, I asked Miss Boyce if I could speak to her after class. When the room was empty—Miss Boyce reminded me of it many years later —I had stood on tiptoe, whispered into her ear, "What is a roisterer?" She had told me a roisterer was a bully, someone who was a troublemaker.

I formed my own kinship between the two: bastards were produced by roisterers. Whatever the means was of no consequence.

Science was not a college entrance requirement. I took advantage of this in my determination to avoid biology, the one science course offered at school. I wanted no part in cutting up frogs. Even had I taken it, I might not have been enlightened about basic structure, because my contemporaries have told me the vital parts were omitted in textbooks then.

In my freshman year at college a lecture was given, extracurricular but compulsory, under the title "Hygiene." The lecturer was a maiden lady of frightening convictions. She told us nothing anatomical, but she thundered to our astonishment an awful responsibility we must recognize and carry. A youth's unsullied progress to manhood was jeopardized whenever he danced with a girl who was wearing a dress of georgette or chiffon. Many a man whose life ended in the gutter could thank for the beginning of his downfall a dancing partner in a chiffon dress. After a foxtrot or one-step

with a Bryn Mawr, Smith or Vassar houri, the distraught young man went from the ballroom straight to hell.

This appalling revelation scared most of us out of sanity. For months, the weekend following that lecture had been marked jubilantly on the calendars of the favored ones who had bids to the Princeton prom.

After the lecture, contrary to custom, my group of friends did not meet in what we called "soul scrapes" to make our decisions. Each of us struggled privately with her conscience and the future of young manhood, because each of us had a chiffon or georgette dress. The result was a spate of telegrams like a snowfall, each carrying a message in one form or another that due to unforeseen circumstances she could not come to the prom. When the young men telephoned irascibly to demand the reason for their being "stood up," we could not of course tell them it was for their own good. Meeting one another dismally on our own campus that weekend, we tried to find comfort in our nobility and our martyrdom. Only one was absent from the melancholy scene, a girl named Frances Jones, and called Jonesy. Jonesy, we learned, had been saddled by her parents with a taffeta dress. Following the lecture she had gone straight in to Philadelphia, purchased at Wanamaker's a flame-colored chiffon and headed for Princeton on Friday afternoon.

Jonesy had beaus. We all wanted them; not Jonesy's, just ours. In Freshman Show we sang a song that began, "I want to have a beau of my own, Before all beaus are gone." With some variations, it was like making a stamp collection, only we called them "scalps." No village postmistress knew better the correspondence in her community than we in a dormitory, scanning the mail table, knew that the morning a letter postmarked New Haven came to the girl who up to then was including Cambridge, Princeton, Amherst and Williamstown in a week's allotment of mail, that girl had acquired another scalp. In theater vocabulary a heavy is the villain; in ours a heavy was a suitor who was serious.

Jonesy's mail was fat and widespread. She admitted her success and attributed it to her line. A girl who did not have a line was a flop, a prune. She could have a soft line or a sweet one; some even had a speedy line. Without one or another of these she might better stay at college and be a greasy grind.

In the pursuit of beaus, the current saying was, "A Bryn Mawr girl says, 'How much does he know?'; a Vassar girl says, 'How much has he got?'; a Wellesley girl says, 'Who is he?'; and a Smith girl says, 'Where is he?' "

Smarting under this classification, girls from Bryn Mawr exacted a promise from the beau who had asked her to a prom never to say Bryn Mawr, but to tell his friends his girl was at a school outside Philadelphia.

Jonesy, in the winter of our freshman year, with business acumen, capitalized on her recognized success by giving lessons in a line. On her door she tacked a long sheet of yellow-lined paper from a writing pad, marking the hours when she would be available and leaving spaces between for applicants. I doubt that any signature appeared more frequently than mine. She charged twenty-five cents a lesson, and to squeeze that much out of my allowance for several lessons a week meant forgoing all fudge sundaes and mocha cake in the village. My teacher reclined on a window seat in her room, an open box of candy beside her, and on a table within easy reach a Victrola. The candy was, of course, from one of her scalps. Between directions and watching her pupil she nibbled a bonbon held in a pair of silver tongs. I wore my hockey uniform because I always came immediately after athletics period. The component parts of the uniform were a white middy blouse, blue serge bloomers, black-ribbed heavy cotton tights and black gym shoes. The hockey stick I held in front of me was my dancing partner.

After telling me what I should say and how to say it, Jonesy would start the Victrola and I with my hockey stick would move into a foxtrot or whatever the music required. Dancing was easy. I loved it, but that was not enough and I knew it. At the count of one, Jonesy taught me, I lowered my head, saying simultaneously, "No," in a tone of astonishment; held my head down, for the count two, three, four;

raised it; opened my eyes wide, and said, "Really?" on an up inflection of amazement. She wanted me to open my mouth a little when I looked up. I practiced it over and over but she made me cut that part.

"You open it too wide," she said. "It's supposed to be alluring. You look moronic."

Round and round the room. "No," two, three, four, "Really?," two, three, four. Then I could go on dancing with the assurance that my partner, responding to my breathless interest, would tell me more. When there were indications of his running down, I was to revive him quickly with "No," two, three, four, "Really?," two, three, four. There were variations on this but the clincher was a repartee Jonesy guaranteed to be surefire. She would have to charge a dollar to reveal and teach it. I bought it by washing another girl's hair for a dollar. The dollar revelation was, "You're so big and strong," and you were to say it as if you could hardly get your breath for admiration. He would answer—they always did—with something like, "But I'm really awfully sweet and shy."

When I asked what I should answer to that, Jonesy said I needn't bother, everything would take care of itself.

The investment was not a sound one for me. I tried it on a boy with whom I had been dancing for a very long time and no help in sight; it was a moment when surefire was needed. There was one disturbing factor I hoped would not deflect my aim. My partner was shorter than I by nearly two inches. Nevertheless, crouching a little, I murmured down at him, with well-rehearsed breathless pauses, "You're—so —big and—*strong*." He, throwing back his head, like a startled fawn, looked up at me wide-eyed.

"You're awfully strong too," he said.

170

For all our pursuit of trophies, we were as chaste in the hunt as Diana. I venture to assert this in spite of Scott Fitzgerald's chronicles. We were of his era, but not his set. Say I was backward, and I was, but from talking to my contemporaries I know that if a school for backward girls had been established, there were enough of us to fill it. By day we studied English and French literature, philosophy, economics, politics, history of art; intellectually we were reasonably competent. At night, in our bathrobes, while we drank cocoa with marshmallow whip on top, a concoction known locally as "muggle," we discussed religion, careers, marriage and children. Religion was the only factor in our lives that we questioned and into which we probed. We were serenely confident of our success in the others. Sex in itself did not enter into the qualifications we listed for a good marriage. The nearest we came to it was a night I remember at a muggle session when we decided closing your eyes when a boy kissed you was more passionate than looking off into space. "Passionate" was a word frequently used in our conversations.

One spring evening the year of the hygiene lecture, a beau calling on me suggested a walk on the campus. Halfway down an avenue of trees that bordered Senior Row—and I was uneasy about setting foot there because it was a forbidden promenade to all but seniors—my beau suddenly backed me against one of the trees and kissed me "passionately" on the mouth.

On the instant the earth came back under my feet and the sky was overhead again, I was shaken by a convulsion of horror. In that one moment of folly, I had ruined my life and disgraced my family, who had trusted such high hopes to me. I would have to leave college, but I could never go

home. I would run away to live in sordid obscurity. I did run up Senior Row establishing, I am sure, my all-time record of speed. My beau, left behind at the tree trunk, came after me calling, but I outdistanced him. In my room, I applied with great pain the only antidote I could lay hands on. When I was sure there was nothing more I could do, I went downstairs again, uplifted by a sense of noblesse oblige. My betrayer was standing at the foot of the stairs looking up with obviously bewildered anxiety.

"Are you all right?" he called as I reached the landing. I came down the rest of the way and took his hand.

"I hope so," I told him. "I've done everything I could. But no matter what happens," I assured him, "I will never hold you entirely to blame."

Because I could not trust myself to say anything more, I bolted back upstairs but I was sobbing before I reached my door, and I think I did not stop until sometime in the early morning, when I fell asleep.

In the days and nights that followed I prayed fervently, sometimes in snatches, sometimes at length, and one glorious day—I was thoroughly knowledgeable on the distaff side— I knew I was delivered from shame and disgrace. During the interminable time of apprehension and prayer, I had not confided my guilty secret even to my closest friends, but now, jubilant over my successful action, I let it be known that if any girls got into trouble I could help them.

Within a week of my generous and selfless offer exposing my own frailty, I was summoned to the Dean's office. I did not know why I had been sent for but since I had broken no college rules, I went with a light heart. The Dean, with no preliminaries, told me my presence at college was no longer desirable. Chicken Little was afraid the sky would fall on her head; I knew it had fallen. I had breath only for a whispered "Why?" The Dean was astonished, she said, that I should ask, as if my own appalling degradation was not enough to warrant my expulsion. My efforts toward commercializing this unspeakable activity had dragged down the name of the college, subjecting it to a kind of notoriety that could close its doors. What she said was so bewildering, I felt as if I were listening to a language I had never heard before.

"Notoriety?" I echoed, though I still had very little voice. "Why, I've done nothing to bring notoriety—"

She scarcely let me finish the word. "Are you telling me that spreading information about abortion is nothing?"

"Abortion" was a word I was not sure of, but "spreading information" was enlightening. My shameful incident had been discovered and I burst into sobbing incoherence. It had all been so unexpected. Certainly I hadn't meant to do anything that would disgrace the college; I would never let such a thing happen again, but I had thought, perhaps, other girls might have been overtaken as I had been and threatened with a terrible consequence. I wanted to help them by telling them what I had done, because it had worked.

"I want the name of the unspeakable person you have recommended," was her answer. "We shall, of course, report it to the police."

I was on my feet trying to see my way to the door.

"I didn't send them to anyone." I found it hard to shape the words while I was crying. "I just told them what to do."

The Dean suddenly got to her feet, knocking her chair over. I thought she was going to spring at me. Blurred as the image was, I could see she was trembling. Her mouth was open and her eyes looked wild.

Backing away from her, I said, "I would have told them to gargle with peroxide full strength. It burns your mouth terribly but that's what I did."

I had been reaching for the doorknob and could not find it. She put her hand to her forehead and drew it down over her face. When she had taken it away, I saw her whole expression had changed. She looked sad, not wild any more.

"Come back," she said, "and sit down."

I was still uneasy but not so frightened. I went to her desk again, picked up her chair for her. She fairly dropped into it; she seemed weak. She leaned forward, put her elbows on her desk and rested her head between her hands. I had not sat down. I wanted to ensure a quick getaway if she went into a rage again. When she raised her head, to my amazement she was smiling, but sadly; perhaps she felt a little sorry about expelling me and I did not want pity.

"There has been a misunderstanding," she said. "I must give this some further thought. Meantime I will ask you on your honor not to make known our conversation this morning and above all not to make any further offers of assistance to your friends."

I had stopped crying. I could speak but my voice was harsh. "When must I leave college?" I asked.

"You are not going to leave college. As I told you, this was a misunderstanding."

When I had reached the door, she stopped me once more.

"Miss Kimbrough," she asked, "have you never talked with your mother about childbirth and procreation?"

"Oh, yes indeed," I told her. "Lots of times."

The widely read syndicated column "Dear Abby," in the *New York Post* of Monday, March 20, 1972, included these communications:

DEAR ABBY: I hope you won't think this is too dumb to answer. Can a girl get pregnant from kissing?

GLORIA

DEAR GLORIA: No. But it's a good beginning.

In the same column:

Confidential to "FROM THE OLD SCHOOL": Welcome to the club. Very few of us who had "old world" parents were told "the facts of life" by our mothers. All my mother told me, God bless her, was never to put bananas in the refrigerator.

Plus ça change, plus c'est la même chose. They just don't listen.

72 73 10 9 8 7 6 5 4 3 2 1